East End Jews

East End Jews

Sketches from the London Yiddish Press

Translated by Vivi Lachs and Barry Smerin,
with Introductions by Vivi Lachs

WAYNE STATE UNIVERSITY PRESS
DETROIT

© 2025 by Vivi Lachs. All rights reserved. No part of this book may be reproduced without formal permission.

ISBN 9780814351345 (paperback)
ISBN 9780814351352 (hardcover)
ISBN 9780814351369 (ebook)

Library of Congress Control Number: 2024939543

On cover: *Watney Street Market*, lithograph by Pearl Binder, 1932. Courtesy of Pearl Binder Family Collection. Cover design by Will Brown.

Publication of this book was made possible through the generosity of the Bertha M. and Hyman Herman Endowed Memorial Fund.

Research for this book was supported by the Arts and Humanities Research Council Grant number AH/V001345/1.

Although most of the descendants of the writers in this volume are known or out of copyright, some writers cannot be traced far enough to find living relatives. Significant attempts have been made to find the families of Judah Beach, L. Beyneshzon, Moshe Domb, Y. Finkelstein, A. M. Kaizer, Avrom Margolin, Rachel Mirsky, Mosheh Oved, and Ella Zilberg. If there are relatives of these families, please contact the publisher.

Wayne State University Press rests on Waawiyaataanong, also referred to as Detroit, the ancestral and contemporary homeland of the Three Fires Confederacy. These sovereign lands were granted by the Ojibwe, Odawa, Potawatomi, and Wyandot Nations, in 1807, through the Treaty of Detroit. Wayne State University Press affirms Indigenous sovereignty and honors all tribes with a connection to Detroit. With our Native neighbors, the press works to advance educational equity and promote a better future for the earth and all people.

Wayne State University Press
Leonard N. Simons Building
4809 Woodward Avenue
Detroit, Michigan 48201-1309

Visit us online at wsupress.wayne.edu.

This book is dedicated to Zach, Annie, William, Tami, Osian, Sonia, Tamara, Izzy, Blime, Rakhmiel, Aleph, Matt, Rachel, and other young British and UK-based activists who are working hard to stimulate and maintain an interest in Yiddish language and literature.

CONTENTS

Acknowledgments	xi
Introduction: Urban Sketches in the London Yiddish Press, 1884–1954	1
1. The Golden Years of London Yiddish: 1884–1914	13
ISAAC STONE	17
Busy and Slack in London	17
MORRIS WINCHEVSKY	21
How Do You Become a Poet?	22
Reformed Noses	24
Money	27
YOSEF HAIM BRENNER	30
A Tale of Reincarnation	31
LEON KUSSMAN	35
The Whitechapel Politician	36
Y. FINKELSTEIN	43
In the Grocery Shop	44
The Nationalist	46
An "Honest" Servant	48
Antisemitism on the Tram	49
Flower Day	50

viii   Contents

2. Yiddish through the First World War: 1914–19   53

YANKELE   55
An Evil Decree against Flower Sellers   55
The Tramway Strike   56
The Whitechapel War Office   58
Wartime Livelihoods   60

LEON CREDITOR   62
In Woolwich Arsenal   63
An Air Minister   65
I Settled the Coal Strike   67

AVROM MARGOLIN   69
A Monologue of a Whitechapel Recruit   70
At the Ball   72

YANKEV YITZKHOK CAPITANCHIK   75
That Unforgettable Thursday   75

BEN-A SOCHACHEWSKY   78
The Last Resort   79

3. Interwar Yiddish Culture: 1920–39   83

KATIE BROWN   85
In the Women's Kingdom   86
The Cantor's a Presser!   93

BAL REKIDE   96
A Torah Scroll Procession in Whitechapel   96

ASHER BEILIN   99
My Neighbor   99
A Jew Takes a Pleasure Trip   102
Fun at the Theatre   105

ESTHER KREITMAN   113
The Question   113
The Dowry   116

YEHUDA ITAMAR LISKY   120
A London Girl's Secret   120
Mendl and the Torah Scroll   122

Contents ix

ARYE MYER KAIZER 127
A Free Hand! 127
The Hanukkah Miracle on London Bridge 130

MOSHEH OVED 135
Ben-Eli 136

4. The Second World War and After: The 1940s 143

JUDAH BEACH 145
The Wailing Wall on Archer Street 145

AVROM NOKHEM STENCL 147
Celebrating the Fiftieth Yiddish Booklet 148

KATIE BROWN 152
My Address Book 152

DORA DIAMANT 153
Solomon Mikhoels, the Man 154
At Yankl Adler's Funeral 157

SAMUEL J. GOLDSMITH 159
A Whitechapel Gallup Poll 159

5. Nostalgia and the Decline of the Jewish East End: The 1950s 167

L. BEYNESHZON 169
Chatting before the Afternoon Prayer 169
Between the Afternoon and Evening Prayers 1 172
Between the Afternoon and Evening Prayers 2 174
Between the Afternoon and Evening Prayers 3 176

ELLA ZILBERG 178
Gefilte Fish 179

RACHEL MIRSKY 180
A Sketch 180
OK 182
The Glass Hill 184

AVROM NOKHEM STENCL 188
At the Seaside 188
The *Idishe Shtime* 190

x   Contents

RAHEL DONIACH   192
Corrections   193

MOSHE DOMB   196
Petticoat Lane   196

Afterword   201

Appendix 1: Index of Feuilleton Sketches and Translators   203
Appendix 2: Newspaper Titles and Dates   209
Appendix 3: Artist Biographies   211
Notes   213

ACKNOWLEDGMENTS

FROM VIVI

The translations in this anthology are the result of a collaboration between me and Barry Smerin. The process of working on these—creating our own translations and working on each other's—has been rigorous, intense, illuminating, and joyful. We have each brought a range of different life experiences, ideas, energy, and vocabulary to the project, and the discussions of words and ideas on the texts, on translation, and on London have been a wonderful gift in the two years we have worked on this together.

This book came out of an Arts and Humanities Research Council two-year project at Queen Mary University of London called *Making and Remaking the Jewish East End*. The project leader, my friend and colleague Nadia Valman, has been ever supportive, and her comments are always insightful and challenging. I would also like to thank David Feldman for his interest and pertinent comments, Katy Petit for all the administrative bits and bobs and witty emails, and Pat Hamilton for helping me negotiate the university systems.

We have a small Yiddish circle in England who give me ongoing support, conversations, ideas, and help with Yiddish expressions and words. I would like to thank Steve Ogin, Sonia Gollance, Sima Beeri, Heather Valencia, Helen Beer, Bob Chait, Ester Whine, Haya Vardy, and William Pimlott. In the transnational Yiddish community, I'd like to thank Dovid Katz, Shane Baker, Itzik Gottesman, Dovid Braun, Sara Feldman, David Mazower, and Simo Muir. I am also grateful to Shachar Pinsker and Naomi Brenner for working on the editing of Winchevsky's "Reformed Noses" for the *Below the Line* website.

It has been a joy to make contact with the families of the writers and artists in this volume. Finding some of them has been a research project in

xii   Acknowledgments

itself, involving ancestry.com, emails to Facebook, London synagogues, and the Ben Uri Gallery! I have met with warmth and delight from all of you, and I am extremely grateful for that. My thanks to Francis Fuchs and Abigail Morgan-Fox, Geoffrey Shisler, Richard Kussman, David and Alastair Levy, Ruth and Iona Doniach, Tessa Rajak, Miriam Becker, Helen and Gabby Capitanchik, Dave and Dawn Skye Sochachewsky, Hazel Carr, Idan Diamant, Ruth Lask Kessentini, Lou Taylor, Dan, Denise, and Polly Jones, Josephine Gladstone, Jane Engelsman, Daniel Tabor, Gordon Wasserman, Julia McNeal, and Kathi Diamant.

Particular thanks to my most frequent reader, Sarha Moore, whose time, support and incisive comments are ever useful and appreciated. I'd also like to thank other family members and friends who have gotten bored of my conversation but at least now know the word *feuilleton*: Edith, Nicky, Ruti, Jude, Erin, Marketa, Liam, Kristina, Bradley, Maya, and Yishai.

Finding the feuilletons and getting to know the writers has taken me to the British Library, the YIVO archives in New York, and the National Library of Israel. Sincere thanks to the helpful archivists for their assistance in finding material and in digitizing images.

This is my third book with Wayne State University Press, which has become a pal. I'd like to thank Sandra Korn, who has made the process seamless, and the vibrant team of Kelsey Giffin, Traci Cothran, Emily Gauronskas, and Carrie Teefey. I was delighted at the careful, insightful, and useful comments of the anonymous peer reviewers. Particular thanks go to my copy editor, Mindy Brown, who continues to bring broad knowledge, creative thought, and careful research into her editing.

FROM BARRY

I am very grateful to Vivi Lachs for inviting me to collaborate in the translation of this anthology, particularly as several of the authors were known to me personally through my attendance at the Friends of Yiddish meetings in Whitechapel in the late 1970s and early 1980s. Working with Vivi has been a hugely enjoyable and enlightening experience, and I look forward to our continuing friendship and the pursuit of our mutual interests.

I'm also thankful for this opportunity to express my lasting indebtedness to the late Avrom Stencl, the creator and the life and soul of the Friends of Yiddish circle, for his support and encouragement of my early efforts in the teaching of Yiddish and the translation of Yiddish literature, and to

Majer Bogdański, the lifelong Bundist, composer, and performer of Yiddish folksong, who played a very active part in the Friends of Yiddish and took over running the meetings after Stencl's death in 1983. Majer made a powerful impression on me with his passionate rendition of Yiddish songs and greatly encouraged me to use Yiddish folksong as teaching material in the various Yiddish language courses I was conducting.

INTRODUCTION

Urban Sketches in the London Yiddish Press, 1884–1954

If you had opened a Yiddish newspaper in London any time from the 1880s to the 1950s, let's say *Der arbayter fraynd* (The Worker's Friend) in 1898 or maybe *Di tsayt* (The Times) in 1929, or even *Di idishe shtime* (The Jewish Voice) in 1952, and turned to page 2 or 3, you would have seen an article printed under a strong black line. The line clearly marked the writing as set aside from the news of the day, and the article beneath it was most often an urban sketch known as a *feuilleton*.[1]

The feuilleton sketches of the London Yiddish press documented and critiqued Jewish London and, in particular, the urban East End that surrounded the reader. The writers found their material on the streets of Whitechapel, Aldgate, and Stepney. The writers talked to locals and noticed small incidents that made them angry at the injustice or made them laugh at the foolishness. They watched the East End immigrant society's divisions and warmth, vibrancy and despair, and they responded to them with opinion and humor, story and satire, exaggeration and poignancy. Feuilletons gave newspaper readers a break from the annoying and depressing news of the day. They could be a topical laugh or an embellished fiction of a local event. They could be meandering thoughts or opinionated polemic; whatever the style, they were a part of London's Yiddish popular culture.

Local popular culture was not confined to the Yiddish press; it included the packed nightly Yiddish theatres and music halls. Locally written pop songs and theatre acts may have shared some of the themes of the urban sketches, but the feuilleton column in a daily paper was cheap, accessible,

2   Introduction

quick to read, and quick to be discarded. It was a source of shared entertainment and discussion—read on the bus, aloud to workers on their break, or at home in the evening with family; and, being published daily, the sketches could refer to up-to-the-minute news. Recently scholars have taken a greater interest in analyzing and translating Yiddish popular forms and exploring writing that cuts across the arbitrary boundary of high and low literature.[2] It is in this fuzzy area that popular forms have "hidden literary value" and offer historians and translators many new directions.[3]

This book is chock-a-block with London urban sketches, and they are a gold mine for exploring East End Jewish life as seen by the people who lived it. Even if you have not heard the word *feuilleton* before, the style will be familiar. As we look back at London's Jewish past, they provide not simply entertaining snippets of life but an oblique angle on an old chestnut, a mulling over of a new idea, a cry of pain and anger, and an eye-opener. Reading these sketches today gives us details of the domestic and community lives of Jewish immigrant Eastenders which are missing from the political, institutional, or social histories of Jewish London. Histories that relate to work, political ideologies, family, war, and religion are expanded by the personal and curious details in the feuilleton stories. For example, the sketch "An Evil Decree against Flower Sellers" by the writer Yankele not only engages with how the First World War affected London's immigrant workers but also shows how the wartime situation brought difficult decisions that had a knock-on-effect for the poorest families. Yankele describes how the income of a struggling flower seller outside a London hospital is suddenly put in jeopardy when the hospital raises a sign asking visitors to donate to hospital resources for wounded soldiers rather than buy flowers for their loved ones. This intimate sketch shows one instance of invisible hardship wrought by the wartime situation in the Jewish East End.[4]

In another sphere, a religious ceremony for a new Torah scroll appears not once but twice in sketches from 1924 and 1933. Bal Rekide's vivid narrative in "A Torah Scroll Procession in Whitechapel" describes a parade with ecstatic religious women dancing through the streets of Whitechapel, watched by the community's non-Jewish neighbors. In what would usually be confined to a Talmudic debate, the sketch voices Orthodox Jewish locals' concerns over whether the ritual wine would still be considered holy after it had been seen by gentiles. This sort of detail about a specific Orthodox belief and practice extends what we know about the multiple community prayer rooms and synagogues of the Jewish East End by showing how the religious

Introduction   3

presence in Whitechapel spilled unabashed onto the local streets and the various debating points it raised.

In a third example, Leon Kussman's tale, "The Whitechapel Politician" from 1912, takes us into a local restaurant and into a discussion of the politics of building a channel tunnel. Although these arguments from a Jewish perspective are fascinating and make up the majority of this sketch, there is another aspect that could be overlooked: The background location gives us a sense of the vital role restaurants played in the lives of local workers and the varying quality of the food they provided. Many workers, particularly single men in lodgings, relied on local food providers, whether cafés, restaurants, subsidized community kitchens, or soup kitchens. These details are as important as the political argument and less present in historical narratives than the arguments around the channel tunnel that were already a source of debate.[5]

Finally, the writer Katie Brown's letters column, *In froyen kenigraykh* (In the Women's Kingdom), portrays through an agony aunt style the atmosphere of change in the 1920s around the roles of men and women. The argument begins with a husband and wife squabbling over making room on the kitchen table and whether to prioritize the wife's writing materials and books or the husband's plate of food. Brown's trademark gentle but astute humor and satire place the large movement for equal women's suffrage into a Jewish domestic realm where tiny daily arguments were had. The humor allows men and women to engage with the debate outside more overt political arguments.

These fictional sketches have been overlooked partly because they deal with small or mundane aspects of life not deemed important when dealing with larger political and community events; partly because they are fictions from a subjective standpoint, full of emotions and contradictory feelings; and partly because they were written in Yiddish, which few social and cultural historians were able to access. These sketches are not simple texts. We see people's complex lives and motivations, which are not straightforward, and the sometimes uneasy relationship between individuals and community. Brought together, these fifty-three sketches from ten newspapers, two literary journals, and a chapbook offer us a broad and exciting new view of London immigrant life. In so doing they complement the political, cultural, and social histories of London's immigrant East End by adding surprising yet significant details from a grassroots perspective.

The twenty-six writers in this volume represent the majority of local feuilletonists of the period who, at the time of their writing, lived in

4   Introduction

London.[6] The choice of sketches was based on the quality of the writing, the importance of the local issues they raise, and the thematic connection to the lives of the immigrant generations and their children. These writers, whether they were aware of it or not, were a part of documenting the East End immigrant milieu from the expansion of the Yiddish-speaking community in the mid-1880s to its decline in the mid-1950s. They fill in gaps in the history of the East End, and are part of the creation of a Jewish East End identity and, later, mythology.

Each feuilleton was printed with a title and the name of the author. However, because the feuilleton genre covered an array of possible writing styles, the piece was often subtitled with a finer description: *A skits* (A Sketch), *A shtiferay* (A Prank), *Fragmentn* (Fragments), *A bild* (A Picture), *A humoreske* (A Funny Story), *Bashraybungn* (Descriptions), *A shtimung* (An Atmospheric Piece), *A shpas* (A Joke), or *A dertseylung* (A Story). Whatever the style of writing, the purpose of the piece was the same: to document and critique aspects of urban life. To this end, some pieces had more focused subtitles, such as *Bildlekh un tsenes fun gas* (Pictures and Scenes from the Street) or *Fun togteglekhn lebn* (From Daily Life). To underline that the urban sketches in the London Yiddish press specifically referred to Jewish immigrant community life in the East End of London, some stories employed even more clearly defined subtitles: *A bild fun der londoner geto* (A Scene from the London Ghetto), *A bild fun der vaytshepler idisher virklekhkeyt* (A Scene from Real Life in Jewish Whitechapel), *Shtraykhn funem yidishn lebn in london* (Sketches of Jewish Life in London). Sometimes the black line itself was enough to alert the reader that the sketch below was a feuilleton, and there was no subtitle. Sometimes, when the column was such a regular feature, there was not even a black line. Just occasionally, the sketch was simply subtitled with the word introduced to the Yiddish language from the French, *felyeton* (feuilleton).

*   *   *

The story of the feuilleton began in France just after the French Revolution. In the 1790s the French mass media underwent a huge expansion in readership, but Napoleon Bonaparte soon implemented censorship to curtail what the press could publish. Seeking to retain their larger reading audience, two Paris newspaper editors in 1800 brought in a style of writing that was accessible and nonpolitical as a contrast to the serious news of the day. They published it separately from the newspaper, as a loose-leaf sheet, or feuilleton. The feuilleton contained cultural material: book and theatre reviews, word games, and announcements. Its popularity was enough that within a few years, the loose sheet was moved into the paper itself; to set it apart from the general news and politics that filled the paper, it was printed on an inside page below a black line. This demarcation made the feuilleton easy to find in the newspaper and also pointed to the difference between the important reporting of political events and the more lighthearted literary and cultural material.[7]

As feuilletons became more common in the press, the genre broadened to include forthright opinion pieces on social issues, stories, humorous sketches, satire, reportage, and verse. The important aspect was their urban nature, their flexibility in incorporating high and low culture, and their connection between the writers and their audience. The genre further expanded in France in the 1830s, when serialized novels were placed into the space below the line, and multiple feuilletons began appearing in one issue of a newspaper.[8]

The feuilleton's creative embellishment of lived life and the connection between these urban sketches and local community issues and politics became hot topics for discussion. The feuilleton was no longer simply a guide to popular culture but an active site of debate and a forum for popular opinion.[9] Indeed, coffeehouses became one of the locations where readers chatted about, argued over, and debated issues raised in the features or stories of the feuilleton.[10] The distinction between news and culture may have been clearly defined in print by a black line, but the column's content was less clearly definable. It became part of the debate over what was factual news and where objectivity and subjectivity grazed against each other and blurred the borders of what constituted fact and opinion. The feuilleton not only commented on urban life but began to define it.[11]

Within little more than a decade, the newspaper feuilleton was adopted by the German press. The content was not new: similar cultural themes had been published in German journals from the early eighteenth century. However, the feuilleton's appearance as part of an ephemeral newspaper, to be picked up, read, and discarded, made the genre available to a much broader audience. By the middle of the nineteenth century, feuilletons were standard fare in the German daily press and were being written by known writers.[12] A number of key German Jewish writers, writers with Jewish heritage, and those who were seen as having Jewish connections, including Heinrich Heine, wrote feuilletons for mainstream German newspapers, and the genre became associated with Jews in the German public eye.[13]

6   Introduction

The feuilleton genre was not without its critics, who complained that it was trivial and empty of serious content; that it lacked sincerity, and the style was too informal; that the subjectivity of the writer was narcissistic; that the light, ironic tone that made it so accessible and captivating was decadent; and that it degraded the profession of journalism.[14]

The feuilleton's first appearance in the Russian press came in 1820, and by the 1840s, it was widespread. Here it also became the terrain of professional writers and was often written in the style of an essay. Russian feuilletons split into two trends: The "bourgeois feuilleton" was characterized by the use of wit and irony, lightly touching on social trends of the upper echelons of Russian society yet steering clear of issues that were too political or controversial. The "tendentious feuilleton" was the place for social and political criticism, challenging rather than supporting the status quo. These two styles of feuilleton coexisted until the Russian revolution, after which debate ensued over how satire and critique should operate in the new Soviet state.[15]

Although the British press did not use the term *feuilleton*, feuilleton-styled sketches and serialized novels were published in a variety of newspapers and magazines. From 1834 Charles Dickens, under the pseudonym Boz, wrote for the *Morning Chronicle* and the *Monthly Magazine* with sketches of observations and impressions of Victorian street life.[16] From 1893 "literary sketches" appeared in the weekly journal *The Sketch*, which offered entertaining and light reading (and which later published a host of short stories by Agatha Christie in the early 1920s).[17]

In the mid-nineteenth century, Eastern European Jewish writers and intellectuals with religious and secular educations were multilingual and literate. They spoke Yiddish at home and knew Hebrew from religious texts, prayers, and secular literature by Enlightenment writers. The Eastern European Jewish writers who had been educated in Russian had also been taught German, and could read a range of newspapers in different languages. So they were familiar with the now regular stream of feuilletons in Russian and German newspapers. Thus when the Hebrew weekly *Hamelits* (The Advocate) produced the first Yiddish supplement, *Kol mevaser* (A Voice of Tidings), in 1862, both the Hebrew and Yiddish sections simultaneously included feuilletons.[18] As the Yiddish press expanded in Eastern Europe, America, and Western Europe, feuilletons became standard fare.[19] Every day of daily papers, every week of the weeklies, there appeared different feuilletonists' names, pseudonyms, initials, or no name at all, but most if not all the writers were known, and in standard feuilleton style, they were often the narrators, alter egos, and active characters in their sketches.[20] On July 25, 1884, the first issue of the weekly leftwing Yiddish newspaper *Der poylisher yidl* (The Polish Jew) appeared in London, aimed at the Yiddish-speaking immigrant community. It was the first Yiddish newspaper in England to last more than a few issues, and it always included a feuilleton.[21]

* * *

This anthology contains urban feuilleton sketches in Yiddish from the early period of Jewish immigration to London from Eastern Europe to the declining years of the Jewish East End. It begins with Isaac Stone's description of seasonal work in the sweated trades, published in *Der poylisher yidl* in 1884. One of the later feuilletons in this collection appeared in *Di idishe shtime* in 1955, penned by the poet Avrom Nokhem Stencl as he sat with his fellow writer and editor Ben-A Sochachewsky, pondering their status as the last of the aged London Yiddish writers. Throughout the period from the mid-1880s to the mid-1950s, hundreds of feuilletons were published regularly in the mainstream daily and weekly London Yiddish press. In addition to those daily and weekly newspapers already mentioned in this introduction (*Der arbayter fraynd*, *Di tsayt*, *Di idishe shtime*, and *Der poylisher yidl*) there were also *Der idisher ekspres* (The Jewish Express), *Di velt* (The World), *Der familyen fraynd* (The Family Friend), *Di post* (The Post), and *Di tsayt*'s evening paper, *Ovent nayes* (Evening News).[22] Many of the sketches in the feuilleton columns of these newspapers were penned by Eastern European or North American Yiddish writers whom the British editors relied on to supply daily copy and to promote their papers with well-known names, such as Avrom Reyzen, Sholem Asch, Perets Hirschbein, Zusman Segalovitch, Anna Margolin, and Zalman Shneur.[23] The remaining feuilletons were written by dozens of local London writers. These writers had all been born in Eastern Europe, had maintained contacts there, and were cognizant of the wider Yiddish literary world in Eastern Europe and America. They aspired (sometimes successfully) to be published in the larger Eastern European and American Yiddish newspapers and journals, which had significantly larger readership than that of London. Yet most of their publishing output during the time they lived in London concerned London Jewish life.

Some of the local writers were well known internationally and lived in Britain for only a few years, such as the prolific socialist writer and editor Morris Winchevsky and the anarchist Yosef Haim Brenner. They both made substantial contributions to Yiddish culture in London before leaving

8   Introduction

for America and Palestine, where they continued their literary careers. There were other writers with international reputations who made London their home and are represented in this volume. Esther Kreitman, of the famous Singer family (Israel Joshua Singer and Isaac Bashevis Singer were her younger brothers), was a talented fiction writer, and Avrom Nokhem Stencl became known as the Yiddish bard of Whitechapel. Other popular local writers, although they later fell into obscurity, were household names in the Jewish East End of their time, such as the journalist Leon Creditor, the humorous sketch writers Katie Brown and A. M. Kaizer, the socialist writer and editor I. A. Lisky, and the aforementioned poet and editor Ben-A Sochachewsky.[24] In addition, the local Anglo-Jewish leader and celebrated English-born writer Israel Zangwill made his name in the Yiddish feuilleton column of *Der idisher zhurnal* (The Jewish Journal) in the serialization of his book *Children of the Ghetto*, which was translated into Yiddish by American immigrant writer Leon Kobrin as *Kinder fun der geto*.[25]

Not all writers rated writing feuilletons very highly. Yosef Haim Brenner felt deeply unhappy about writing in Yiddish rather than Hebrew, and in particular about writing what he saw as lowbrow feuilleton sketches, calling the feuilletonists talentless writers of "jargon" (a pejorative term for Yiddish) and decrying feuilletons about Jewish London as "a work of trickery" that lacked artistry.[26] Yet Brenner needed to make a living, and possibly it was for that reason that he chose to write his Yiddish work under a number of different pseudonyms, from the easily recognizable *Reb khayim* (Mr. Haim) to the less obvious *A farblondzheter* (A Lost Wanderer). Other writers also used pseudonyms. The writer Avrom Margolin used the pen name *Avreml* (diminutive of Avrom or Abraham), the writer Asher Beilin used *An'eygener* (A Relative), and the writer Leon Creditor used *Leybele Batlen* (Leybele Layabout). These were not pseudonyms to disguise who they were, because they were local celebrities whom the East End immigrant community knew and respected, but today it took some searching and eureka moments in primary and secondary sources to find this information.[27] Even the writers whose pseudonyms cannot now be traced were likely to have been known in the small immigrant enclave where news and gossip were quickly passed around. There are three writers in this volume who were clearly insiders in the community, but their identities remain a mystery today. These writers, known as Bal Rekide, Yankele, and L. Beyneshzon, wrote fascinating and sometimes controversial pieces engaging with local issues.

The use of pseudonyms disguised the writer, including whether they were male or female. The less overtly political focus of the feuilleton was seen by the male newspaper editors as a feature that could attract the growing number of women readers, and to this end they employed a small number of woman writers.[28] Of the handful of female writers in the London Yiddish press, Katie Brown (Gitl Bakon) was the only regular and prolific published author from the 1920s to the 1950s. Her work was seen as directed at women, but her popularity showed she was more widely read.[29] Brown was first commissioned to write specifically for women in a type of agony aunt column in *Der familyen fraynd*. This provocative column, "In the Women's Kingdom," an early part of which is translated in this volume, ran from 1922 to 1926 and aired a range of views. Following the example of the editors of European Yiddish presses in creating women's pages for their female readers, Brown was later commissioned to produce a regular women's page in *Di post*.[30] This section added a feminist voice to the often sexist portrayal of women in male writers' feuilletons. Another successful and important female fiction writer was Esther Kreitman, whose more literary stories appeared in the feuilleton section of *Di post* and *Di tsayt* and included a serialization of her first novel. In the 1940s, Stencl's journal *Loshn un lebn* (Language and Life) gave voice to other local female writers, such as essayist N. M. Seedo, sketch writers Rachel Mirsky and Ella Zilberg, and occasional writers, such as the librarian of the Jewish Reading Room, Rahel Doniach, and the actress Dora Diamant. Most of the female Yiddish writers for *Loshn un lebn* had no other publishing platforms for their work, but their writing offers us additional perspectives and shows the varying roles and struggles of women in the immigrant community.[31]

One of the strengths of the feuilleton column was its stylistic diversity. This anthology concentrates only on fiction forms, but the fictional element encompassed Avreml's sharp satire, Batlen's comic slapstick, Zilberg's nostalgic musing, and Diamant's personal memories. Frequently the writer him- or herself appeared as a character in feuilleton sketches, observing or participating in the action. This persona sometimes crossed over from the text and became associated with the writer in real life. Morris Winchevsky, acclaimed as one of the most talented feuilletonists, created a character of an older man that followed him around the rest of his life; he became known by his nickname, *Zeyde* (Grandfather), while still in his thirties.[32] His persona of *Der meshugener filozof* (The Crazy Philosopher) railed against inequality and class privilege among Anglo-Jews, immigrants, and British society in

10 Introduction

cleverly crafted satirical outbursts. The philosopher grandfather is often depicted in conversation with his grandson. Winchevsky's column in the socialist *Arbayter fraynd* newspaper was variously titled *Tseshlogene gedankn fun a meshugenem filozof* (Fragmented Thoughts of a Crazy Philosopher) and *Bilder un verter fun a meshugenem filozof* (Pictures and Words of a Crazy Philosopher), and it took its material from what was happening in local urban news. Winchevsky concentrated on East End workers, the wider Anglo-Jewish community, and English political figures, yet included international concerns that had an impact on the local community. In the amusing sketch "Reformed Noses," Winchevsky uses a news story about an American nose surgeon to comment on a range of behavior of politicians; and he satirically notes that this nose surgeon can fulfill the desires of Anglo-Jewish leaders who desperately wish to look English. His fast-paced sketches are packed with associations and references to people, events, and current affairs. His socialist polemic portrays the ferocity of ideological debate in London.[33] One reason for Winchevsky's popularity was the connection his philosopher made with his readers. This bond crossed the boundaries from the *Arbayter fraynd* to his own activism in the London milieu, where he could be found reviewing plays in the Yiddish theatre, speaking at socialist meetings, or marching at union demonstrations. Winchevsky provided topical anthems in Yiddish for Jewish union workers to sing at demonstrations that related directly to their demands. He also wrote ballads about London poverty that were declaimed from the Yiddish stage and sung across the world.[34] Winchevsky, the *zeyde* of the feuilletons, brought his persona into his own home community.

One final aspect of feuilletons was the way real events were fictionalized to emphasize details that were not reported in the news outlets. For example, Yankev Yitzkhok Capitanchik's *Der umfargeslekher donershtik* (That Unforgettable Thursday) is a moving representation of a massive demonstration by immigrant Jews marching across London to grieve over and protest Polish atrocities in recent pogroms.[35] The fast day of "Sorrow and Protest," as it was advertised in the Yiddish press, had taken place on June 26, 1919, a week before the feuilleton was published.[36] The sketch takes this memorable incident as its starting point, but it is not a news report. First, the character of Capitanchik appears in his sketch, and his reactions become central to the piece. Second, Capitanchik embellishes his narrative with the imaginative observations of bystanders watching the march go by. He describes the range of non-Jewish British observers lining the streets of

London to witness the event. He also shows the divisions within the Jewish community. When the march reaches the West End, we see wealthier Jews joining English spectators to watch rather than take part in the march. This points up the class difference between the working-class East End immigrants from Eastern Europe at the parade who passionately felt the pain of their Polish brethren, and the West End middle-class Jews who were anglicized and established in Britain. The latter may have felt empathy for the marchers but had little or no personal connections to Eastern Europe. At the end of the sketch, in a mass meeting at the end of the march, the stage is filled with the Anglo-Jewish aristocracy and leadership, including some members of the Rothschild family who, during the prayer for the dead, openly weep from the stage. The depiction of a Rothschild feeling moved by the pain of his East End immigrant coreligionists at the climax of the story becomes symbolic of the success of the mournful parade. The East End Yiddish-speaking workers have managed to touch the hearts of the West End Anglo-Jews. These nuanced details in the feuilletons give us a sense of a living community that is full of contradiction and emotion.

Reading urban feuilleton sketches from 1884 to 1954 provides a fascinating window into the Jewish East End's local politics and debate from a grassroots perspective. Whether satirical, funny, or serious, the sketches are entertaining and often surprising and intriguing. They aren't so much a history lesson as a trailer for a serialized drama hit: East End Jews.

1
THE GOLDEN YEARS OF LONDON YIDDISH

1884–1914

When later London Yiddish writers looked back on the period from the mid-1880s to the First World War, they saw it as a golden period of British Yiddish-language culture in London's East End. Morris Winchevsky and Yosef Haim Brenner were writing and editing Yiddish newspapers; the Yiddish theatre was buoyant with multiple plays a week performed by local celebrities; the popular music halls churned out new Yiddish pop songs; and the Yiddish language was vibrant and alive on the streets.[1] The explosion of London Yiddish culture created by Eastern European immigrants to Britain developed atop a number of political and social tension points engulfing the immigrant community.

The assassination of Tsar Alexander II in 1881 and the restrictive antisemitic May Laws of 1882 had led hundreds of thousands of Eastern European Jews to leave their homes in search of more economically stable lives free from the threat of violence. Most left for North America, but some headed for London's East End, traditionally an area of initial habitation for immigrant groups due to its proximity to the docks. The East End of London was transformed when between 100,000 and 120,000 Russian and Polish Jews settled in Whitechapel, Stepney, and Aldgate. Yet the number of Yiddish-speaking immigrants in the area at any one time was even greater,

14   Chapter 1

because large numbers of transmigrants on the way to America stayed days or months before traveling on.[2]

One of the fiercest areas of conflict within the immigrant East End was that between workers and bosses regarding labor conditions in the sweatshops. Jewish unions mounted strikes and demonstrations, marching through the East End to demand higher wages and shorter hours. These strikes sometimes won small improvements, but often the advantages gained were short-lived and reverted to older inequalities.[3] The situation for workers in tailors' workshops is the theme of Isaac Stone's socialist feuilleton sketches "Busy and Slack in London," written in three parts over consecutive weeks in September and October 1884. They show the fraught point of tension in the tailoring trade. Workers swung between the busy season, when work was abundant and there was huge pressure to complete jobs by working long hours late into the night, to the slack season, where there was no work. Stone described the slack season as synonymous with starvation, as the poorest workers received no government assistance to tide them over during the idle months.

Before the First World War, the established Jewish community of around 60,000 members who lived across London—with the wealthier Jews in West London—were thrown into helping coreligionists with whom they had little in common. They established charitable institutions to help the immigrants financially, provide for their immediate needs, and encourage them to acculturate into British, and indeed British Jewish, norms as swiftly as possible. However, the Anglo-Jewish leadership underestimated the difficulty of these tasks, the amount of financial support needed, and the desire of the immigrants to retain their Eastern European–style Jewish cultural life in Britain.[4] The immigrants wanted to keep speaking Yiddish, and not simply abandon it to become English.[5] Yiddish-language culture blossomed in the local cafés, markets, and a range of political and social organizations and cultural institutions. Yet these early years were fraught with the tensions between the Anglo-Jews' diligent and generous but paternalistic support and the real economic and cultural needs of the immigrant Jews.[6]

Anarchist Yosef Haim Brenner and socialist Morris Winchevsky both addressed the tensions between the Anglo-Jews and the immigrants. Brenner's furious feuilleton, "A Tale of Reincarnation," attacks both class inequality and the passivity of the workers. Winchevsky's sketch "Money" concentrates on the injustices that come from wealth. However, the leftwing socialists and anarchists disagreed over how to respond to the difficulties faced by the workers, and their ideological battles over strategy were vocal and fraught. Indeed, Winchevsky's socialist feuilletons were published in the *Arbayter fraynd* just as the newspaper was taken over by the anarchists, leaving the social democrats to establish new journals: the literary *Di fraye velt* (The Free World) and *Der veker* (The Awakener).[7] Not only on the left but across the board, immigrants were not a cohesive group, and they enacted explosive rivalries and passionately held differences over lifestyle and ideology between the religious and the secular, the religious and the socialists, and the socialists and the Zionists.

Some workers' strikes brought these groups together in momentary alliances, and they also brought Jewish and non-Jewish workers out in support of each other, despite the growing antisemitism fomented by Evans Gordon and the British Brothers' League, which campaigned for immigration restrictions. The league's anti-immigration push culminated in the Aliens Act of 1905.[8] The aliens bill had gone through considerable modification as it made its way through Parliament, and in the end the act was less exclusionary than its earlier incarnations. The legislation might have slowed immigration, but Yiddish culture continued unabated.

The 1890s and several subsequent decades marked the heyday of Yiddish on the streets of the East End, with the language audible everywhere and visible on posters and advertisements. The Yiddish music halls were churning out local popular songs; the Yiddish theatres were packed nightly, and Yiddish newspapers proliferated. Y. Finkelstein's sketch "In the Grocery Shop" draws characters that could have been in a domestic comedy on the London Yiddish stage. The feuilleton sketches were not drama, but they were a form of popular culture that became part of the heated controversy over the distinction between high and low art (*kunst* and *shund*).[9] The debate around quality centered on the Yiddish theatre, but at times feuilletons were tarred with similar criticism as being nothing more than cheap laughs that were devoid of edifying content.[10] Yet feuilletonists themselves—in particular Leon Kussman, writing under the pseudonym L. Izraeli in *Der idisher ekspres*—berated the popular theatre.[11] The editors and feuilletonists for the satirical arts magazine *Der bloffer* (The Bluffer), Kussman and Avrom Margolin (Avreml), made endless fun of the debate in their satirical sketches.[12]

"The Temple of Art," *Der bloffer* 1 (1911). "*Hamlet* is playing to an empty house. The only audience is a greenhorn. But *Shmendrik* is packed out with local Jews. So, take pride in the taste of our London intellectual public! The will of the people has triumphed." Collection of the National Library of Israel.

"The Tailors' Victory in the Fight for a 9-Hour Working Week," *Der bloffer* 17 (June 1912). "Scab (to the master): 'What? With really no more than 9 hours' work a day, where will I get money to bet on the horses?' Master Tailor: 'Don't worry, my friend. You'll work 9 hours before lunch and 9 hours after lunch.'" Collection of the National Library of Israel.

ISAAC STONE (1855–1916)

Isaac Stone arrived in London from Podolia as a youth. He worked in a tailor's sweatshop, and was a socialist and outspoken union activist, Yiddish writer, and journalist. Stone was a member of Aaron Liebermann's radical Hebrew Socialist Union and a comrade of Morris Winchevsky. He wrote extensively for *Der poylisher yidl* as well as for a range of other newspapers, journals, and pamphlets, including *Der fonograf* (The Phonograph) and *Der idisher zhurnal*, mainly in Britain but also in Eastern Europe. His main theme was the exploitation of sweatshop workers, but he was versatile in his style, producing opinion and polemical pieces together with feuilletons and novellas. One novella, *A Brief Account of the Life of a London Tailor*, was translated into English by Leonard Prager. A second serialized novella, *Di yerushe* (The Inheritance), is a fast-paced crime mystery of switched identities and Jewish–non-Jewish relations in the murky back streets of London.[13]

During the 1910s Stone published essays about the combative relationship between Judaism and Christianity: *Yeyshu hanotsri: An entfer tsu di neshome-fangers* (Jesus of Nazareth: An Answer to the Soul Thieves) and *Di eybike milkhome tsvishn yudentum un ir shtifkind* (The Eternal War between Judaism and Its Stepchild). Later in his life Stone moved to Leeds, which had a strong tradition of union activism, and he edited *Der lidzer ekspres* (The Leeds Express).[14]

• •

Busy and Slack in London

Der poylisher yidl, 1884

I.

FAT BELLIES AND HANDS

Just as people are sometimes beset by troubles, suffering, illness, and the like, so London's garment workers are afflicted by two evils, namely "busy time" (a time of much work) and "slack time" (a time of going hungry).

On the face of it, this statement raises a difficult question. Obviously, as even a little child knows, slack time is a curse that our teacher Moses forgot to include in his rebukes to the Children of Israel. It's like a bout of chickenpox or measles that every garment worker has to suffer twice a year. But, you ask me, why do you consider busy time a kind of a plague? That's a fair question, but I can assure you that I'm not drunk or crazy, God forbid. I mean it quite seriously. So let me explain clearly why busy time is just as much a plague as slack time, and perhaps even worse.

First of all, for the sake of my readers who have just arrived from abroad, let me give you some pointers to help you distinguish easily between the two times, busy and slack. For example, it's the Sabbath and you take a walk to the blessed spot that everyone calls the "pig market." There you'll see masters (you'll recognize them immediately by their fat bellies) scuttling about like poisoned mice among the weary workers. They bustle around in a great hurry, yelling: "Jack! Are you a machinist?" "John! I need a presser." "Jim! I need a hand." (That's what they call a worker—not a whole person, just a hand, a foot.) Finally, you'll see a fat belly grab a hand and drag him off like a wolf dragging a lamb, while all the poor souls left without a master look on resentfully, as if they would gobble up the fat belly and the hand along with him, angry at being left with their poor families for a whole week without work.

But even after witnessing this scene, you still won't know the proper name for such a time. So, as soon as the Sabbath is over, you'll have to come with me on a sick visit to a tailoring workshop. Once you've seen it, I'm convinced you'll know exactly what such a time should be called. On Sunday morning we'll climb on all fours up to a tiny attic, in darkness so thick that we could poke each other's eyes out. But don't be frightened, we'll easily find the hole we're looking for. The noise of the machines will rattle in our ears, and if we follow that voice, we'll enter the workshop.

II.
"BUSY TIME" IN THE WORKSHOP

It's already ten o'clock in the morning, and the lambs are feeding. They've been working since seven, and it's about time for a bite to eat. The machinist is still sewing, but he's eating at the same time. He's not an angel who can't carry out two tasks at once. He's just a sinful mortal, so of course he can sew and eat at the same time. He gives the wheel a turn and takes a bite of bread. A turn! And a bite! The master's wife is a good woman, believe me. She brings each worker a cup of coffee—or whatever you want to call it. The workers ought to be able to drink their coffee at ease, because English workers get half an hour off for breakfast and the same again for tea. But our quick-witted Jewish master tailors soon worked out that one half hour in the morning and another in the evening makes a whole hour,

The Golden Years of London Yiddish   19

and an hour costs money. So what did they do? Instead of giving the workers an hour off, which is enough time to stitch a coat, they get their wives to kindly bring breakfast into the workshop and practically stuff it into each worker's mouth, like you stuff a bit of grass into a horse's mouth while it's on the move so that it doesn't waste time.

The coffee—or the murky water that bears that name—stands next to each individual until it gets cold and full of dust, because he has no time to drink it. The master is standing over him shouting, "Finish the job! Look sharp! Where do you think you are? In a café? A restaurant? On the Sabbath you'll have plenty of time to drink coffee. That's not what I want here. Quick! Finish the job!"

That's exactly what a garment worker's breakfast looks like in busy time.

The workers slave away like horses without a break until ten or eleven at night. How much longer? The machinist glances at the clock. He's amazed. The little hand should be pointing to eleven, but it's still stuck at nine. And now the master's laying out a good three hours' work for him. "Hurry up! Hurry up!" he shouts. "It's only nine o'clock and the work has to be finished."

The master's wife soon brings in the tea and practically pours it into the workers' mouths, like a sparrow feeding her chicks: "Carry on working, little ones."

Now, dear readers, you have some idea of busy time. But that's not all. You'll get the full picture when you see those same workers bringing back bottles of medicine from various hospitals. That one has only one lung, another has heart failure, and yet another has lost both his feet. Then you'll know that now is the blessed period called "busy time."

So let me ask you. Am I not right to call busy time just as much of a curse and a plague for Jewish garment workers as slack time—not the slightest bit better? I hope you no longer misunderstand me and will agree that I'm in my right mind.

III.
SLACK WORKERS—BUSY "UNCLES"

Now we come to the second kind of time, what people call "slack time," and perhaps you'd like a clear indicator of this too. So let me give you one. It's not worth going to the pig market on the Sabbath, because there's nothing to see. All we'll find there are hands, feet, and the occasional head, starved, haggard, ill, and exhausted, but we won't see any fat bellies there during slack time.

Nor is it worth clambering up with me to the dark attic. We certainly won't be able to find the hole we're looking for in the dark, because the sound of the machines will have died away. The workshop is like a cemetery, a theatre for vermin. The master sits in his office, tucking into a piece of meat with his good wife. So what's for us to see there? It'll be much better for us to pay a visit to "Uncle," and stand outside his pawnshop with the three brass balls. That's where we'll witness scenes worth seeing.

Here comes a woman carrying things wrapped up in an apron: a pair of trousers, a petticoat, a child's jacket, maybe a few nappies—in short, a whole bundle of clothes. As you know, the uncle is a decent sort. He inspects each item separately to see if it's still any good, if it's worth anything. In other words, a good bloke like him wants to know whether an impoverished worker still has a shirt on his back. "How much do you want for this?" he asks the woman. "Three shillings," she replies, her eyes filled with tears. "Ha-ha!" the uncle laughs. A fine cause for laughter, indeed: a woman taking the last bit of clothing from her body and exchanging it for a piece of bread. "Three shillings," the uncle shouts, cursing a little and calling her all kinds of names—out of friendship, of course. "So you won't take one shilling for it?" "What choice do I have?" the woman replies. "Just give me the shilling. The kids are screaming for food. My old man is hungry, and I can't spit my soul out."

Do you think, dear readers, that she gets the shilling? Not bloody likely! The good uncle strews some money on the table, even more than a shilling's worth, then counts out the coins and gives her eleven pence ha'penny, keeping one coin for himself. I don't know why he keeps a ha'penny for himself, and even he couldn't say why. But whatever the reason, the woman grabs the money and rushes off to buy bread for the children.

In the street we see the wrecks of men, young garment workers hurrying along with their collars turned up, shivering from the cold. They run from one café to the next like hungry wolves, hoping to find an acquaintance who will take pity on them and buy them a cup of coffee to moisten their dry tongues.

These same young men once shone with sweat—during busy time, that is. In fact, they were really no better off than they are now, but with a few pennies in their pockets they laughed at everything. No one was doing as well as them. They played cards, went to music halls, and took no care for the future. Today, those same men go around in great misery.

So, dear readers! You think my indicator is quite sufficient, so that even a blind man can see that now is slack time. Nevertheless, let me show one more thing. Over there you see a whole group of people sitting on benches. One leaves and five come to take their place. They all hold a little book in their hand, and one by one they go inside through a narrow door where a secretary deals with them. He gives one of them a ticket to the committee, another a ticket for a loaf of bread, and yet another is simply thrown out. And all the while the shouting and pandemonium is absolutely deafening. A woman laments that she has had nothing to eat for three days, while a young man complains that he has been out of work for a month already. Holding her head in her hands, the woman screams: "You'll find me and my children dead from starvation!" The screams and shouts of people asking only for food to eat are nothing less than heartbreaking.

So now you know exactly what slack time looks like.

Translated by Barry Smerin

MORRIS WINCHEVSKY (1856–1932)

Morris Winchevsky was born Leopold Benzion Novokhovitch in 1856 in Yaneve (Jonava), a small town near Kovne (Kaunas), Lithuania. He had a traditional religious upbringing and a secular Russian education. At age twenty-two, working as a bookkeeper in Germany, he was influenced by the work of radical socialist writer Aaron Liebermann, then living in London. Winchevsky wrote for Liebermann's Hebrew journal *Ha-Emet* (The Truth). They corresponded, and Winchevsky was arrested under Bismarck's 1878 antisocialist laws for having letters from Liebermann in his possession.* He was imprisoned for five months before being released on bail.

Morris Winchevsky, 1880s. From Abe Cahan's memoir *Bleter fun mayn lebn*, vol. 3 (New York: Forverts Association, 1926), 110a. Mazower Private Collection, with the permission of the Forverts Archive.

---

* Otto von Bismarck, chancellor of the German Empire from 1871 to 1890.

22   Chapter 1

Winchevsky arrived in London in 1879 and spent the next fifteen years as a newspaper editor, radical activist, journalist, and poet, writing in Yiddish for the immigrant workers of the East End. In 1884 he cofounded the left-wing newspaper *Der poylisher yidl*, and later edited and contributed to *Der arbayter fraynd*. When that paper was taken over by anarchists, he left to create the monthly paper *Di fraye velt*, and later the social democratic *Der veker*.

Winchevsky wrote scores of editorials, articles, poems, translations, plays, and reviews. He is the author of the pamphlet *Der alefbeys fun treyd yunionizmus* (The ABC of Trade Unionism). His popular ballads concerned poverty in London. His first published poem, *Tsvey geslekh* (Two Alleys), about the consequences of gambling, was declaimed live on stage at the Princes Street Yiddish theatre by the famous actor Jacob Adler. Winchevsky's ballad *Dray shvester* (Three Sisters) was put to music and became popular across the Yiddish-speaking world. His workers' anthems were sung at demonstrations by Jewish sweatshop workers campaigning for better pay and conditions in London and New York.

Winchevsky was nicknamed *Der zeyde* (The Grandfather) after his popular satirical feuilleton column in the character of *Der meshugener filozof* (The Crazy Philosopher), where the three sketches translated here were first published.

In 1894 Winchevsky left London for New York, where political activism and Yiddish culture were higher on the Lower East Side's agenda. He was widely published, with at least two multivolume complete works to his name.[15]

How Do You Become a Poet?

Der arbayter fraynd, 1889

I was always doubtful about the story of God appearing to King Solomon and asking him what he wanted. I know you shouldn't blaspheme, but this story strikes me as a bit of a tall tale. I'd like to believe it, but I don't. All I can say is this: If God came to me today and asked me what I wanted, I'd only ask him to make me a poet. Solomon had been a poet since he was a child, but he wanted to be a sage, a philosopher. God fulfilled his wish and made him a philosopher, so the poet of the Song of Songs became the author of Ecclesiastes. For me, it's the other way round. I've been a philosopher from childhood (as evidence of this, let me tell you that from the age of thirteen,

I tried not praying!), but from being a philosopher I would like to become a poet. I wouldn't be timid and would say to God: Merciful father, I have enough wisdom, make me sing; I have philosophy, give me poetry.

And if he fulfils my wish, like they say he granted Solomon's request, then ah, with my poems I would comfort broken hearts and strengthen exhausted hands. My voice would raise up the fallen and straighten those bowed down. I would cheer up the despondent and enliven the miserable. I would sweeten the life of those embittered and encourage the fainthearted!

With my poetry I would give the oppressed courage and joy in life to those languishing. I would give the lonely friendship and defend those abandoned. I would console widows and stand orphans on their feet. I would make my poem a jubilant cry and my pen a powerful sword, and my verse would break the chains of tyranny, like our ancestors felled the walls of Jericho with their ram's horns—if that's really true.

Greek legend tells us that the Thracian musician Orpheus had such amazing musical powers that he could tame wild animals and pacify lions and tigers with his song. The story is probably exaggerated, and maybe it's all just a lie, but to be such a singer must be divine! I'd be satisfied with less. I'd be happy with the lesser power of poetry, but I would also perform wonderful deeds.

I would sing for those who are shackled in chains of money and transform their chains into cobwebs like the ropes that bound the mighty Samson. I would raise my voice to support those who are indentured and hire out their bodies, the overworked and worn out who want to become free, happy, and strong. With my poetry I would give them all courage and hope for victory. I would not rock them to sleep, as other poets do. I want my poetry to encourage them to fight for freedom.

So how do you become a poet? Just think of the present. Think of what's happening now in London. English and Jewish workers who are denounced, misrepresented, and silenced are opening their mouths, standing up straight, and coming to their senses. It's flammable stuff. It's endless and immeasurable and only missing a spark. Just one tiny spark could ignite hundreds of thousands of hearts that are warm, but not yet hot enough. Who will bring that spark? No humdrum person. What's missing is an inspired poet who can inspire other people.

What if I were that person? Tell me, good, dear reader: What if I were that person? If for just twenty-four hours I could be such a poet, the spark-bringer, the igniter of the holy fire, and then, when needed, burn in the fire itself.

Every beggar can have a fine life; what is enviable is to die well, like Rouget de Lisle. A man who composes a "Marseillaise" before dying dies better than a Jay Gould who makes millions of dollars and lives. And then ... wait a minute, I'll tell you a story:

This evening, I came in from the street very thirsty and tired.

"What are you drinking?" I asked my grandson.

"Let's make tea," he said, and went and brought the gas burner and the kettle and matches. I put on the water to heat up and waited impatiently for it to boil. It proved (if I can make a passing comment) that hunger or thirst tests the patience even of a philosopher. In short I waited very impatiently as five minutes passed.

"What's happened to the water?"

"It's warm," said my grandson.

"Warm, warm is not enough."

I waited. Never has time taken so long to pass as now. After another four or five minutes, I asked:

"What now?"

"It's hot now," said my grandson.

"Hot, hot is not enough."

I waited. A few minutes later, I impatiently picked up the evening paper and read the latest on the different arguments in the debate around the Great Strike.

"Granddad, the kettle is hissing," said my grandson.

"Hissing, hissing is not enough, it must boil. Have you seen, my boy, what is happening in London today?"

"What, with the dock strike?" he asked.

"Yes," I said, "with the workers—at first it was cold, then it got warmer, then hot. Now it is hissing, but it isn't boiling yet."

"It's hissing, but it's not boiling yet," the youngster repeated, lost in thought. He didn't understand what I meant. Do you?

Translated by Vivi Lachs

Reformed Noses

Der arbayter fraynd, 1890

My grandson came home from school today with an important piece of news. A friend of his told him that one of his other friends heard that his father had read in the paper that some clever bloke in America said that he had found a way to reshape noses. What an amazing place America is! The world's youngest daughter (if you don't include the baby, Australia) gets cleverer by the day, like her mother, Mrs. Europe, and her grandmother, Mrs. Asia, and she's growing in leaps and bounds. Every single day America thinks up something else new! A real success story, as sure as I am a Jew.

One day America realized that human ears weren't good enough. "There are loads of big ears," America said, "but they can't hear anything at a distance." So they got down to work and invented a telephone. But not completely happy with that, America said: "Human beings have got really long tongues and very big mouths, but what they say can only be heard when they say it, and no later." Again they got down to the task and came up with a gramophone. Now, America is starting on noses.

As my grandson says, the plan is not to make noses better at smelling (in this respect the Yankees don't need better noses) but to make noses more attractive. The nose reformer says he can make flat noses prominent and protruding noses flatter; he can make long noses short and short noses long; he can make pointy noses rounder, and noses that look like squashed potatoes a bit pointier; he can make wide noses narrower and narrow noses wider; he can make milky-white noses redder, and ruddy noses paler. To sum up, he is a sort of magician who can make your nose look however you like.

I don't know if you've heard of Cleopatra's nose or the nose of Napoleon the First, and many other famous historical noses, but I've just been thinking about them. Take Napoleon, for instance: He always chose men with big, long noses for his generals and liked people with long noses above all. Surely you must have heard of the Duke of Alba's nose: That was the kind Napoleon really liked. It could be that Napoleon, who wanted to lead the world by the nose, liked that sort of nose because you can grip it more easily with your hand.

Then many of my English Jewish acquaintances come to mind. Whether they are gentlemen or not, the most important thing is to look English, and what prevents them from looking English is their unfortunate nose. What a fortune the nose-reformer would make at the Eastern Wall of the Bayswater Synagogue!* For, as you must know, although the Jewish aristocrats are Jews in the synagogue, everywhere else they strive to be John-Bull

---

* Anglo-Jewish Ashkenazi "cathedral" synagogue in West London, established in 1862. One of the three large synagogues that formed the United Synagogue in 1870.

Englishmen, and their long, beaked noses torment them.* They console themselves with the fact that Gladstone has a big nose and that the chancellor of the exchequer, Goschen, has a long nose, and that the late Gambetta had a broad nose.† But Gladstone studies the bible, and it could be that he comes from one of the Ten Lost Tribes. Goschen is certainly descended from Jews, and Gambetta was too clever not to be Jewish. Just look at all the money he accumulated in his few short years; and don't forget that he was a friend of the people, a one-eyed friend who had to smell out with his long nose what he couldn't see with his blind eye. In short, it's not much consolation. The sideburns, the pointy laced-up boots, the clothes, the speech—everything is English apart from the nose. May it catch a cold!

And Alexander the Third's bloodhounds! If the great American nose reformer took this on, Tsar Alex would drown him in money!‡ Because there must be something wrong with the noses of his spies. They don't sniff everything out, and as many as they are, and as hard as they sniff, the revolutionary spirit grows, as the saying goes, right under their noses. If it's necessary to make his faithful bloodhounds' noses more pointed, or stretch them out—I don't know what because I'm no nose-reformer (not even a bog-standard reformer)—he, the American, would already know what needs to be done; he would find a way.

As you can see, because of my grandson's bit of news, I've been thinking a lot about noses. Believe me or not, I'm telling you that I've started to think that if the nose manufacturer comes over here to London, I might do a bit of business in partnership with him. We could publish a newspaper together. I would write the political items and he the scientific articles, because someone who can turn a beaky schnozzle into a beautiful Greek nose must be a very learned man. In five minutes, I've concocted a whole plan. First, I establish a newspaper called *The Nose*, and I write a lovely editorial in which I of course explain that the paper is called *The Nose* not because it is a national

---

* John Bull was a caricature of England, portrayed wearing a Union Jack, with top hat and cane.

† William Ewart Gladstone, Liberal politician. In 1890, he was between two terms as prime minister. George Joachim Goschen served as chancellor of the exchequer from 1887 to 1892; Léon Gambetta was a French republican statesman who proclaimed the French Third Republic in 1870.

‡ Tsar Alexander III, emperor of Russia, 1881–94.

The Golden Years of London Yiddish   27

Jewish newspaper, but because it campaigns for general nose reform. I've even composed a little ditty that you can see here in print.

Readers bring your noses
My partner here proposes
To reform them into what your heart desires.
Long ones shorter,
Narrow, broader,
He'll just do whatever it requires.
Large to slight,
Thin put right,
Amaze your sense of smell along the way.
Pale or glowing,
Straight or flowing
Never again ashamed from this day.
With brand-new flair
When sunk in prayer
Compliments will then fly to and fro.
So bring your noses
To smell the roses
But before you do that you must first . . .

Blow? That's not so poetic. Now, where do you get hold of this chap? We'll talk about this a bit more.

Translated by Vivi Lachs

Money

Der arbayter fraynd, 1890

With money you can get lots of things: with money a pauper can get a cup of warm, cloudy, semi-sweetened water in a charity café; with money a Jewish workshop master can get "hands" for a whole year and the honor of reciting a verse of the *Ato horeyso* prayer on Simchat Torah;§ with money a

---

§ Simchat Torah: festival celebrating the conclusion of the annual cycle of public Torah scrolls readings. The *Ato horeyso* prayer is recited before parading the torah scrolls. The honor to take part is accompanied by a monetary donation to the synagogue.

28   Chapter 1

rich Englishman can get a seat in parliament *and* a brainy assistant to concoct a speech for him; with money the Russian tyrant can get a supporter of his great leadership and an admirer of his horsewhip; with money Bismarck can get an old 1848 revolutionary to write a poem in praise of his dog and a long article about his long bellybutton; with money chauvinists can get supporters and the United Patriots a secretary;* with money an English reverend can get a *cheder* teacher to teach him to read Hebrew well enough to recite the tricky bits without choking;† with money a wealthy ignoramus can get a niche column in the best newspaper where he's allowed to prove, in black and white, what a goddamned fool he is; with money a rich woman can get some religious zealot to rule that although a skimpy ballet dress is not allowed in Jewish law, her sleeveless, low-cut ball gown is perfectly kosher; with money a wealthy greengrocer can become the Lord Mayor of London, make judicial rulings in Guildhall, and sentence people to four weeks' hard labor on the strength of his expert knowledge of fruit;‡ with money a murderer can get a lawyer, and decent society can pay a murderer to murder the murderer; with money you can get a bit of quinine and two quarts of clean water from any English pharmacy to treat every nasty illness from a cold to lung failure; with money a rich son can get a scribe to write a fiery eulogy for his father who only ever kept three of the Torah commandments: to eat well on the eve of the fast day of Yom Kippur, not to lay *tefillin* on the morning of the fast day of the Ninth of Av, and not to recite the Shema prayer on the first night of Passover;§ with money sweatshop masters can pay for a preacher to give a sermon against the socialists who say that "hands" are made both to work and to hit back when necessary; with money English Jews can own newspapers that prove that selling worn-out secondhand clothes, charging interest,

---

* The United Patriots National Benefit Society was involved in several financial scandals in London in the late 1890s involving raising money by dubious means at the expense of the workers who were supposed to benefit from its assistance.

† *Cheder*: after-school religion classes for elementary school children.

‡ Henry Aaron Isaacs, son of a fruit merchant, was Lord Mayor of London (1889–90) and was active in Anglo-Jewish affairs. The Guildhall was the administrative center for the City of London.

§ Yom Kippur is the Day of Atonement and a fast day. The Ninth of Av commemorates the destruction of the two temples in Jerusalem. The Shema is a prayer recited three times a day. *Tefillin*: phylacteries; two small leather boxes containing Hebrew texts, worn by Jewish men at morning prayer.

The Golden Years of London Yiddish   29

cheating on the stock market, and going to synagogue are typical practices of the Jewish community; with money capitalists can get half-baked philosophers to explain to the common people that drunkenness does not result from poverty, rather poverty from drunkenness; with money the old English monarch can get writers to prove that a woman who wears a crown on her head instead of a bonnet is the country's jewel, a jewel that is worth a million a year, if not more;¶ with money a person without a thought in their head or a tongue in their mouth can get an attentive audience that listens to their speeches and laughs at their insipid, superficial jokes; with money a person like Polyakov in Russia can get scholars who produce amazing, miraculous evidence that he is a human being;** with money anyone can get hold of pen, ink, and paper and write down whatever their heart desires, and then pay for a publisher who will print it all and even readers who will read it; with money any scoundrel can get philanthropic support, even though the word *philanthropy* comes from two Greek words *philos* (loving) and *anthropos* (human being), and he is neither one nor the other; with money a person can buy a dictionary where he can find out where the word *philanthropy* comes from, even though, like me, he has never learned Greek; with money every tyrant can get spies and sniffer-dogs to track down and persecute people who take a stand against him and his wicked power; with money a rich Englishman can get the title baronet and a bride with a dowry of tens of thousands of pounds for his son, who marries her but still plays around with other women, widows, divorcees, and other people's wives; with money a missionary can get charlatans who let themselves be baptized with water, and which brings the soul-saver more money than he paid out; with money the governors of every district can get teachers to instill in the children of the workers a world history that is cooked sweet and sour and conserved in religious honey, so that the children make good slaves for the governors for as long as they can work, and then patient prisoners in the workhouses when they are old; with money the rich man's wife can have jewels that she can wear, pawn when needy, and show off to the neighbors; with money people in America, at times even in England, buy votes for the country's leader, which will enable him to lead lots of people by the nose; with money people can make their children into officers, who murder short and sharp, doctors who murder slowly but surely, and

---

¶ Queen Victoria was on the British throne until 1901.

** Russian banker Lazar Polyakov (1843–1914) came from a Jewish family.

pharmacists who murder whenever the situation arises; with money you can buy all sorts of insipid poetry and dense literary junk, bound, gilded, and titled like the poets and writers are themselves; with money you can pay membership fees to various societies so that you can be treated with a bit of respect when you have the ague; with money you can get rid of flies, mosquitoes, and beggars in top hats; with money you can buy a ticket for a good performance at a London Yiddish theatre where, if you have a cold, you can sweat profusely and get better, or otherwise you can get ill from just being there; with money you can see all the kings, princes, and generals in Madame Tussaud's waxworks, and for an extra sixpence many of the common murderers.

In short, you can have everything, get everything, see and enjoy everything with money, except for one thing—and that one thing I'll talk about another time. Oh!!! I've grown tired writing, I'm old comrades, old.

Translated by Vivi Lachs

YOSEF HAIM BRENNER (1881–1921)

Yosef Haim Brenner by Chaim Topol, unknown date. (https://commons.wikimedia.org/wiki/File:Yosef_Haim_Brenner,_drawing_by_Chaim_Topol.JPG). Accessed July 28, 2024.

Yosef Haim Brenner was born in Noviye Mlini, in the district of Chernigov, Ukraine. He had an Orthodox education, studied Hebrew literature, and worked as a Hebrew teacher. He arrived in London in 1904 in a state of poverty; being a socialist and a Hebraist, he reluctantly found work in the Yiddish press. He took a job with the printer Israel Narodiczky, and he lived in Narodiczky's home above the Narodiczky Press printing shop in Mile End Road. From there Brenner established the Hebrew journal *Ha-Me'orer* (The Awakener). He worked with the Yiddish social democratic journal *Di naye tsayt* (The New Times), writing news items and translating and proofreading articles. He considered himself enslaved to the lowly pay of ten shillings a week and

The Golden Years of London Yiddish   31

was furious with the workers' inability to hold strike actions for improved conditions and pay. Although he was loath to write creative work in Yiddish, he began to write literary articles and feuilletons.

Brenner's Yiddish writing appeared in a range of London Yiddish papers: *Di naye tsayt*, *Di fraye arbayter velt* (The Free Labor World), *Der idisher zhurnal* (The Jewish Journal), *Di idishe folks literatur* (Jewish People's Literature), and the Yiddish supplement *Di idishe velt* (The Jewish World), mainly using a pseudonym or a version of his initials. In the piece translated in this anthology, he uses *A farblondzheter* (A Lost Wanderer).

Brenner became close friends with the writer Asher Beilin in 1906, and when the famous Yiddish writer Sholem Aleichem visited London that same year, he employed both Brenner and Beilin. In 1909 Brenner settled in Palestine, where he became a Hebrew writer and is considered one of the pioneers of Hebrew literature.[16]

•••

A Tale of Reincarnation

Di naye tsayt, 1904

Tell me, my friends, do you believe in reincarnation?

"In reincarnation, no less?" you reply in astonishment. "What on earth are you talking about? Reincarnation? Either you're joking or—begging your pardon—you're out of your mind. Us, believe in reincarnation? People like us don't believe in high-flown nonsense: we don't believe that a socialist can trigger an explosion simply by speaking;* we don't believe in either an earthly paradise or in a world to come; we don't believe there is any sort of creature that speaks one word of truth; we don't believe that anything in this world is more valuable than a shilling; we don't believe that anyone can get by without dirt, or that there's anything more pleasant than to be immersed, with all our senses, in a soft, warm rubbish tip; we don't believe . . . oh, who can make a complete list of what we don't believe? Should we, the descendants of a . . . a . . . civilization, believe in something as outlandish as reincarnation? Oh, for crying out loud!"

---

* This may refer to the Haymarket massacre of 1886 in Chicago or the Bloody Sunday demonstration in 1887 in London.

Okay, okay, take it easy! What are you getting so het up about? I'm only asking. So you don't believe in reincarnation. That's fine with me. But I do, and, let me tell you a secret, I live in fear of reincarnated creatures. Yes, indeed, actually in fear of them. I began to believe in it, in reincarnated creatures I mean, through a chance incident. Before that incident I didn't believe in it either. So, have I aroused your curiosity? Do you want to know? Really? Should I tell you? Yes? Okay, here goes . . .

In Lithuania, in the small town where I was born and brought up—and where I probably would have died, had not my lousy luck dragged me over here to London—there lived, from time immemorial, a man known as Ruthless Stefan. This Stefan was as rich as Croesus. And for his entire wealth he had to thank his large hunting dog, who was called Shmulik. (You don't think it's a suitable name? That's what it was like in those days: many dogs had human names. Believe me, I'm not making it up.) Without Shmulik, Stefan, with his fat belly, short, chubby legs, short-sightedness, and greasy little bloodshot eyes, would have been a rotten shot. He wouldn't have got very far without Shmulik. He even used to tell his friends (though not usually in Shmulik's presence because it wouldn't have been right; a dog is a dog after all, and dogs understand, in doggy fashion, what people are saying about them) that his modern rifle, bullets, and gunpowder would have been no use to him without Shmulik. Shmulik was such a darling, such a precious treasure with the following virtues: First, he was long and thin, with sunken flanks and thin but iron-strong legs, the marks of a good runner. Second, he was so loyal, so dedicated to his master. His eyes were often teary, reflecting deep, unbounded submissiveness. To be a really good dog, you had to have these qualities, and Shmulik certainly had them. When Stefan hit him, which he did very often—not, God forbid, for some sin, but just to show him who was boss—the submissiveness in Shmulik's eyes deepened and grew more intense, and his loyalty increased.

To be a good hunting dog it is absolutely essential that the dog has no idea what meat tastes like. First, because meat develops laziness and passion. Second, it can happen that a captured fox or hare, instead of being brought to the hunter, goes down into the dog's belly, and that would be totally against the interests of the hunt. Ruthless Stefan did what he could to ensure that Shmulik's taste for meat became atrophied: the only sustenance Shmulik received was a piece of dry bread, which Stefan would throw from his richly laden table over to the rubbish tip where Shmulik spent his time when away from work. And Shmulik accepted it with love.

The Golden Years of London Yiddish   33

Hunters are concerned that their dogs should not associate with other similar dogs, because society and company are not good for a hunting dog: they lead it astray. Roaming around with a pack, it will eventually come across a dead animal and get to know the taste of flesh. And then, well . . . you can wave goodbye to the dog.

And Shmulik was a first-rate dog. It wasn't enough that he didn't associate with other dogs, he hated every single other dog with a deadly loathing. More than one dog came away from him with its throat torn open. And people? They felt his teeth even more. How many times did he rip my coat? How many scars remain on my hands and legs from his teeth? And do you know why? Because I took pity on him. I was a boy then, and I thought that a dog could also understand human speech. I used to admonish him, saying:

"Shmulik, you're a dog, that's true, but you've got to understand that a dog can also live well. Look at your scraggy flanks, see how ugly the rubbish pile is where you lie exhausted after a day running. See how heavily you breathe. Your tongue is hanging out. What food have you had today? A dry scrap of bread, and that on a day when all the fresh hares, foxes, and birds that you caught are hanging in the storehouse, and you could easily have gobbled up all of them."

Shmulik would listen to me with such a look, as if to say: "You just wait with your complaints, I'll soon show you who's the boss." And he would leap at me, barking so furiously that it made me tremble, and it's a miracle that I managed to escape him with my life.

That's how Shmulik lived for many long years, satisfying his master in every respect.

Then one day, this happened: It was a lovely day, Ruthless Stefan had some sort of holiday and was entertaining friends at home and getting drunk. Shmulik was sitting on his pile of rubbish, chasing flies away with his tail. Suddenly a whole pack of dogs ran past, chasing a bitch in heat. This doggie wedding interested Shmulik, and he jumped up from his place, and in one second the long, thin figure of Shmulik was among the happy, jolly company. The whole pack wandered off behind the town, and there Shmulik tasted meat for the first time. The sharp nails on his strong legs bit into the carcass they had encountered, and his healthy teeth tore into the flesh with thirst and passion, bite after bite.

That night when Shmulik got home and stretched out as usual on his pile of rubbish, he began to howl sadly. Something was tugging at him, something he desired, and for the first time, instead of the deep submissiveness

34   Chapter 1

in his eyes, there was now a pitiful look of longing. When I walked past him that evening, Shmulik did not leap up on me as usual; he looked at me sadly and started to howl.

"Howl, howl, Shmulik," I told him. "Howling shows that you're beginning to feel and to understand that how you've lived up until now is not right. And because you've begun to feel that it's not right, surely now you'll change your life." And this time I left Shmulik with quite a different opinion of him.

The next day at dawn, Ruthless Stefan went out hunting with Shmulik. Stefan stretched out under a tree and made himself comfortable, smoked his pipe, and gave Shmulik a sign to get to work. Stefan waited an hour. Shmulik didn't come back. Another hour, and Shmulik still hadn't returned. Stefan became very uneasy. He got to his feet with an effort and went off to look for his faithful dog. And imagine what Stefan felt when he came upon Shmulik standing over a fox he had just caught, which was so totally devoured that even the fur was in shreds.

Stefan's eyes burned furiously. "How could Shmulik do such a thing?" Shmulik understood the look in his owner's eyes, but instead of getting up on his hind legs, as usual, and kissing his hand, he started to bark. Stefan could not bear such insolence; he picked up his gun and fired. A heartrending cry rang out, and Shmulik lay dead in a large pool of blood.

A long time has passed since that incident. Life cast me out of my small Lithuanian town into the big European city of London, where I live—or, rather, suffer—to this day.

One day I was walking along the street so ensconced in my own thoughts that I got quite lost. The loud barking of a dog roused me from my musings. I looked around. Hey? Where am I? A courtyard, a large courtyard. Some sort of noble, or as they say in England, a "gentleman," was holding a stick in his hand. Next to him stood a dog on its hind legs, looking the gentleman in the eyes as if to ask him:

"Gentleman, sir, what you are your orders?"

The gentleman gave a sign and, before I had time to look round, the dog's teeth sank into my leg. I gave a deep shout, and suddenly the dog jumped back, stuck out its tongue, and barked something in dog language which meant: "A *landsman*!"* I looked at him, and, oh, my God, I recognized

---

* *Landsman*: fellow countryman. Often used to mean a person from the same town in Eastern Europe.

Shmulik. Yes, this was Shmulik. I recognized him by his deep submissiveness to the gentleman, by his long, clumsy tongue, by his thin, sunken flanks, and above all from his bite. Oy, what a bite! Yes, this was Shmulik. It was him with all his features. But how did he get here? And thinking, I remembered a story my rabbi had told about the transmigration of sinning souls, which make their way across rivers and seas and are reincarnated in some other corner of the world.

From that day on, I am persecuted by Shmulik everywhere. Wherever I go I meet him, and every time he gives me the feel of his teeth.

There was a miracle worker here, a famous man who knows the secret name of God. He tried hard to drive out the reincarnated creature, but it didn't help.

So, my friends, now do you know why I believe in reincarnation? Do you understand why I live in fear of reincarnated creatures? May God protect and save you from it.

Translated by Vivi Lachs

LEON KUSSMAN (1884–1974)

Leon Kussman was born in Aleksanderhof, near Mitava (Jelgava), Latvia. He moved to Lithuania as a small child, attended school in Odessa, and received his university education in Switzerland. He immigrated to London in 1911 and became a journalist and writer for the London Yiddish press, often using the pseudonym L. Izraeli. Kussman wrote theatre reviews and critical, provocative articles about the quality of repertoire and acting in the London Yiddish theatre for *Der idisher ekspres*. His own play written in London, *Di veg tsu frayhayt* (The Road to Freedom), was performed only once in London. He also wrote feuilletons for *Ovent nayes* and *Der idisher zhurnal*.

Leon Kussman. Painting by unknown artist. Courtesy of Richard Kussman.

36   Chapter 1

He coedited the satirical journal *Der bloffer* with Avrom Margolin (Avreml). His humorous story *Der politiker fun vaytshepl* (The Whitechapel Politician), which he wrote as L. Izraeli, was published as a chapbook. In 1913 Kussman moved to New York, where he became a prolific journalist, critic, playwright, and poet, working on the daily newspaper *Der morgn-zhurnal* (The Morning Journal).[17]

The Whitechapel Politician

A Humorous Tale

Pamphlet, 1912

It was a warm day one summer in July. The sun mercilessly roasted London's inhabitants, and those who had the good fortune not to work in a "sweatshop" had a larger sweating shop on London's streets. Walking about in the sun that day certainly worked up more sweat than in a sweatshop.

Midday. Crowds of people were thick on the ground, spilling out of the factories and workshops. With smeared black, filthy faces from the sweat, they hurried to get their dinner. Whoever had a home, hurried there. Whoever didn't, dropped into his favorite restaurant and quickly found a seat.

Tired from traipsing around the London streets and saturated with the Whitechapel air, I dropped into *my* restaurant. It's only been mine for a week. I've eaten lunch and supper there for a whole week and have only got stomachache twice. In my previous restaurants I never had such luck. I even saved money because I couldn't manage to eat there more than once a day. I couldn't stand that London carry-on so I asked a *landsman* to show me a restaurant where you could at least eat twice a day.

My *landsman* took pity on me and pointed out this restaurant as the best in the East End. I soon appreciated its advantages and was willing to get stomachache there a couple times a week. I wouldn't give this one up for all the money in the world.

When I arrived at the restaurant, all the tables were taken. There wasn't one table with an empty seat, but there was one—right in the middle—that had only one person sitting at it with a bowl of beef stew. Leaning over his table, the man was totally absorbed in a London Yiddish newspaper, with his beef stew next to him and the newspaper spread out over the whole table, covering an empty plate. I seriously wondered how, in this sort of cramped

The Golden Years of London Yiddish   37

place, one person could sit there all by himself at the table and read his newspaper undisturbed. Of course, I wouldn't have disturbed the intense newspaper-reader in his absorbed reading either, if I hadn't been frightfully hungry. So I took a seat opposite the man and ordered a steak from the waiter, knowing from experience that Whitechapel restaurants make steaks from real beef.

And also knowing from experience that by the time the beefsteak was ready you could have eaten a whole meal and still be able to eat the beefsteak with a renewed appetite, I took a chunk of bread, cut it into small pieces, and smeared them with mustard and slowly ate them. At the same time, I took the opportunity to observe my neighbor. A long, narrow face, a long, straight nose, a long, overhanging ginger moustache, and a pointed, cleanshaven chin that proved he was no new immigrant. A worn-out, hard English hat sat askew on his large, balding, sweaty head, as he stared anxiously in front of him. He must have been close to forty.

At first glance it was hard to determine what interested my neighbor more at that moment: the newspaper or the bowl of beef stew. He was so absorbed in the newspaper, it seemed that his hunger to read was greater than his hunger to eat. Apparently there was something there that greatly interested him, because while reading he shook his head strongly, twitched, and mumbled words like "Hm, Oh! No, no! Tut, tut!" which are not so easy to put across on paper. And, of course, he also waved his hands about a lot.

Then suddenly he abandoned the newspaper, grabbed the bowl of beef stew, and got so immersed in eating it that he seemed unaware of the existence of anything else in the world other than the bowl of beef stew. But this didn't last long, and soon enough he abandoned the bowl of beef stew and returned to being engrossed in the newspaper, and this repeated itself several times. He then began to do both things at once, which wasn't easy because the bowl of beef stew didn't diminish, and his eyes didn't leave the paper.

Suddenly, my neighbor raised his two small red eyes and laid them on me. He apparently saw at once that I was a greenhorn and asked me:

"Been in London long?"

"A few days."

I'd actually been in London a few weeks, but I liked to answer this sort of question with "a few days" because I knew from experience that in London "a few weeks" had little appeal. By "a few days" people understood that I was a newcomer. "A few years" would mean the newness had disappeared, and you'd become a half or a total old-timer. Earning a few pounds a week,

38   Chapter 1

you were already a businessman, but being just a few weeks in London and still without a business is the sort of meal a Londoner's stomach finds hard to digest. The man exclaimed with pleasure:

"So! You're still a greenhorn! Are you Russian? Have you just come from Russia?"

"Yes, I'm Russian, but I haven't come from Russia."

"How so! You haven't come from Russia, from Germany maybe?"

"No, from France. I've come from Paris."

The man's eyes lit up. He moved his chair closer and exclaimed: "So! You've come from France, from Paris! How about that! Here's a chap who's come from France and he doesn't say a thing. Why didn't you tell me before? Well, well, well! What a thing to happen!" The man could not settle down. He quickly grabbed the newspaper from the table and looked me in the eyes.

"Here, read it!"

"I've already read it."

"Is that so? So what have you got to say about the plan to build a tunnel under the water between France and England? What are people saying about it in France, in Paris?"

"What should people in France be saying about it? The Parisians are very happy with the project. They say there's just one problem with it . . ."

"So!" my neighbor cheerfully interrupted, "people in France also see that there's a big problem?"

"What do you mean?" I said, defending the honor of *my* French people. "You think the French are schoolchildren or *cheder* teachers. Don't worry, you can rely on them. If there's some hidden problem, they'll find it."

"That's what I'm sitting here wracking my brains about." My neighbor breathed more easily:

"The French, with their great Napoleon, who, in his three-cornered hat, had more sense and strategy than anyone in the whole world, wouldn't see a dreadful mistake, so! Well now, you come from there, won't you tell me what the French think of the project?"

"They say that no one in the world has thought up a better idea than digging a tunnel under the English Channel so that one can travel to England on an underground railway, but the problem is this, that between Paris and the channel and from the channel to London you have to travel in a train that runs overground."

"Wha . . . t!?" My neighbor stared at me with bulging eyes, struggling to bring out the final "t" that stuck in his throat.

"What I just said!" I tried to calm him down. "The French say that since France and England will be connected by an underground train, the project needs to be completed by also building a tunnel from Paris to the channel and from the other side of the channel to London, so that they can travel directly from Paris to London on their splendid 'Metropolitan' without changing trains."

"!!!"

"Because, maintain the Parisians, there's no greater pleasure in the world than traveling on the Metro, because the beautiful, elegant Parisian women, they say, look a thousand times more beautiful and elegant in the electric light of the Metro, so it is easier to fall in love with them and altogether more piquant and enjoyable to engage in romantic affairs. But unfortunately the Paris area is too small. Therefore, they say, there should be a plan to build a tunnel from Paris to London, and install salons, buffets, and compartments in the Metro. That would be a life! Life above ground, they say, has become dull; we should start living underground."

"That's the French for you!" my neighbor angrily interrupted. "Since Napoleon died, they've totally lost their minds, they don't think of anything other than women. Don't they understand that in this project there's a hidden danger, a danger for the whole of France!"

"What do you mean?"

"What I just said!" he replied, in the tone of an expert in these matters, and, pursuing his argument immediately in the manner prescribed by the Mishnah, he bent even closer to me, leant his left elbow on the table, and with the same hand, held me tightly by the right lapel of my jacket.* With his right hand, he gesticulated with index finger and thumb in a circle, which he cleverly moved and twisted in the air to help explain the issue, and accompanied his gestures with these words:

"Exactly what I said!" the man repeated and began to expound his political ideas:

"France is in danger if it agrees to this project to dig a tunnel under the English Channel. Because of this tunnel France will be crushed like a peppercorn under a millstone, your beautiful France! And England will choke on it, like on the bone that lies here on my plate. Do you hear? Even England, who fears nothing in the whole world, will, I'm sorry to say, be turned completely

---

* Mishnah: the oldest collection of Jewish laws from an oral tradition, later written down.

40   Chapter 1

upside down! Yes, yes, that's how it is, do you hear? It's clear to me, clear as day, that this is how it will be. And you know who they will get their comeuppance from, France and England together? You know who from?"

The man paused for a moment, staring at me with his small red eyes, which had, at that moment, become even smaller and redder. Spittle had begun to appear around his mouth, clearly this speech had given him pleasure. He was getting me worked up and looked at me strangely, clearly waiting for me to answer. I felt the pressure of his heavy hand on my right shoulder, and sweat poured out of me.

"For God's sake! How can I put up with this, watching him with his steak!" was all I could think of in that moment.

"I see you understand just as little about politics as your French people!" the man exclaimed, having failed to get an answer from me. "You just don't get it that when they go and build a tunnel between France and England, England will lose its privileged situation and, together with France, it will fall victim to Germany!"

"Oh really?"

"What? You don't believe it?" My politician got excited and grabbed me tighter by the lapel. "You just don't get it! What a numbskull! Don't you understand that this is exactly what Germany is waiting for, this whole tunnel business?"

The man paused for a moment, wiped his brow with the edge of the tablecloth, leaned even closer to me, and not letting go of my lapel, continued to speak:

"Germany, as you must know, is today the strongest country on dry land, except possibly Japan, and it has long had its eye on England. But it can't get here because on sea, England is still the strongest country in the world. So how does the cat get across the water? Germany sends its agents to France and England to talk them into building a tunnel under the channel to establish friendly relations between the two countries and increase trade. But the fools don't understand at all that Bismarck's brain is still behind it. Yes, yes, that's how it is, none other than Bismarck's thinking is behind it. I know this from a reliable source from a London Yiddish newspaper which first uncovered the story that Bismarck had left the whole project in his will. And today the Germans want to carry it out. Once the tunnel is ready, Germany will smash France, then send its troops through the tunnel and make mincemeat of England. Do you see what I mean? Mincemeat! England will no longer have its privileged situation."

"OK now, have you finished?" I tried to free myself from my politician, finding it hard to breathe.

"What? You still don't believe me?" The politician jumped up as if bitten by a snake: "You're a complete fool, if you don't mind me saying so. You know as much about politics and strategy as a German Jew knows about the blessing after excretion and urination. You must have learnt geography at some point. Let me show you geographically and strategically that I'm right, and you'll soon understand what politics is all about."

The man let go of my lapel and went on to show "geographically and strategically" that his politics were correct. Thank God for the people who thought up geography and strategy! I began to breathe a little more freely.

The man took his bowl of beef stew and put it down on my side of the table, and in a sing-song chant as if reading the Gemara, he began to explain strategy to me:*

"Let's suppose this bowl of beef stew here is England, surrounded by water on all sides. This knife and fork, which I'm putting down over here, is, let us assume, the English Channel. The plate of bread on that side is your France, and let's assume this plate of pickled cucumbers is Germany, and the small saltshakers next to the plate of beef stew are the English 'dreadnoughts.'†

"Now look! When the plate of pickled cucumbers, I mean Germany, wants to invade and take over the bowl of beef stew, that is England, they can't get to England in any other way than through the water or through the knife and fork, I mean across the channel, but there is the bowl of beef stew with its little saltshakers, I mean with the 'dreadnoughts,' and they won't let the bowl of beef stew across. Now imagine that under the knife and fork, they decide to build a tunnel, and you can get to the bowl of beef stew just like it was on dry land. So what do you think? Will the plate of pickled cucumbers lie around and sleep when it had long set its heart on the bowl of beef stew? It will surely invade the plate of bread, i.e., France, and it will wipe up the crumbs, like I'm wiping up this bread here. And so it will send its soldiers through the tunnel under the knife and fork straight into the bowl of beef stew and turn everything upside down. So now do you get my idea of what political strategy is?"

---

* Gemara: the Talmud, exegesis of Jewish law. When studied by orthodox men, the text was sung, rather than read in a traditional melodic style.

† Dreadnought: turbine-powered British battleship.

I don't know how it happened, but the bowl of beef stew suddenly tipped over right onto me, and from me onto the floor. The crash of broken pottery and the splash of the beef stew could be heard across the whole restaurant, and I don't know if it was because my beefsteak was ready or if the crash from the broken plate had attracted my waiter, but he came running over with the beefsteak in his hands and cried out in shock:

"What has happened here?"

"Absolutely nothing, absolutely nothing!" my politician stuttered with a blushing red face: "Calm down—England overturned."

"What do I owe you?" I asked the waiter, getting up and looking for my hat.

The waiter looked at me, confused, and didn't know what to answer.

"How much do you want?" I asked again angrily, already holding my hat in my hand.

"Elevenpence with the broken plate."

I threw down a shilling and hastily left the restaurant, leaving my politician contemplating the broken plate and the beef stew still lying on the floor.

At the door I bumped into my *landsman*, who was coming to look for me in the restaurant.

"Where are you off to in such a state?" he said, grabbing me with both arms.

"Come on," I shouted, in such a tone that my *landsman* was shocked and stood back.

"Come on! Take me to a restaurant where I can eat! This one here that you showed me is some fine restaurant, my friend!"

"Not again! You don't like this restaurant?"

"It's very good! But it wouldn't be a bad idea for you to show me another."

My *landsman* looked at me and suddenly burst out laughing, which didn't please me after the lecture I'd just had on politics and strategy.

"Hahaha! You're still a greenhorn, sure as eggs is eggs!! You must've been caught by the Whitechapel politician. Yes, indeed, I don't envy you! But who told you to be such a greenhorn and sit down next to him? Now you've had it, my friend. You must never go in there again; once he's got hold of you, he'll not leave you alone, and he'll give you such a special daily lesson about Whitechapel politics that you'll remember as long as the exodus from Egypt."

"I've already had that. Come on, I'm terribly hungry."

"So tell me now. What was your first lesson about?" My *landsman* chuckled. "About politics, about diplomacy, or about both of them together? Did he tell you that he had at a greater understanding of politics and strategy than all the editors of the Whitechapel Yiddish press?"

"No, he didn't say that. But I saw that for myself."

"There's lots to tell you about him, my friend, but you'll have another opportunity to get to know him better."

"Thanks."

My *landsman* took me to another restaurant, saying:

"The food isn't as good, but here no one will bother you."

Poor Whitechapel politician! Clearly you were a victim of the absurd sensationalism of Whitechapel's cheap yellow press. And poor me, who, because of you, will have to eat in this terrible restaurant and throw up every day.

Translated by Vivi Lachs

Y. FINKELSTEIN

A prolific feuilletonist with the name Y. Finkelstein wrote a series of weekly pieces between 1913 and 1915. They are typical urban sketches set in the East End which sit somewhere between reportage and fiction. The pieces are humorous, with a sharp, critical edge, written for a series in *Di tsayt* called *Ibern yidishn kvartal* (Around the Jewish Quarter). *Di tsayt* also published his two-part essay *Scholarship* in 1913. Finkelstein wrote similarly styled feuilletons for *Di velt* in 1915.

Finkelstein knew the East End immigrant community and the wider London Jewish community. He wrote a particularly forthright article, "Hibru komedyes" (Hebrew Comedies), criticizing Jewish actors who played stereotyped Jews on the English music-hall stage, accusing them of being complicit in propagating antisemitic stereotypes. He also wrote theatre songs, including the cheeky music-hall ditty "Opgeklapte hoyshayne" (Beaten Willows). After 1915 no further feuilletons appear under his name.

Although prolific during these two and a half years, Finkelstein (a fairly common surname), cannot be traced with any certainty. The protagonist in some of his sketches is Yankl (Jacob), also a common name, and indeed there were a number of Jacob Finkelsteins alive at this time, but none are traceable.[18]

In the Grocery Shop

Di tsayt, 1913

If you want to get a true picture of the life of the Jewish masses in London, you should set up your camera behind the counter of a grocery shop in the densely populated Jewish quarter.

A Jewish grocery shop is more than just a place where housewives come to buy food. It is also a hangout, a kind of club where Jewish women meet to spend a few free minutes, get a bit of air, and take a break from their monotonous home life.

Many a family secret is uncovered in the grocery shop. Gossip is exchanged, and all kinds of disputes and feuds between man and wife, between engaged couples, and between lodgers and their landladies are discussed. In the grocery shop you'll find out who is "well off," whose earrings are with the pawnbroker, whose husband is a gentleman, and whose is a luckless good-for-nothing; which women is a lady, and which a busybody; which wife is faithful to her husband, and which gets up to monkey business with the lodger.

The grocery shop is the most interesting place for an overworked Jewish housewife. There she's in her element, and when she pops in for a chat, she forgets about everything else. At home the dinner may be burning, or a child may have had an accident, but she can't tear herself away from the shop so quickly. As for the grocer, to be successful in business he has to be a great diplomat and show iron patience. He must know how to treat his customers and not—God forbid—show disrespect to any of them. He must listen to everything, watch what's going on, and keep his mouth shut. He must tell no one how much that woman owes him, or that this one is a beggar, always haggling over the price. For him they must all be "good customers."

From the grocer's behavior toward a woman who comes in to buy something, you can immediately sense her circumstances and situation. In comes a chubby roundish lady with a mass of false hair on the nape of her neck, glittering earrings, and a powdered nose, wearing a black cutaway pinafore. The shopkeeper greets her with a broad "good morning" and invites her to sit down. She approaches the counter with a proud look on her face and orders a big box of salmon, half a pound of butter, and a dozen of the best eggs. Meanwhile, she sticks her pudgy white fingers into the box of biscuits and tries one, chewing it together with a piece of the Dutch cheese lying on the counter. The grocer's wife also comes running out of the kitchen and nods politely at the customer.

The woman is Mrs. Goldstein, the wife of a master tailor who is so busy at present that he's simply shoveling in the money like gold. That's why she's such a respected customer: The grocer knows he can make a pretty penny off her while the busy season lasts. He knows the Goldsteins aren't skinflints, and when things are busy, they don't ask how long it's going to last but live each day to the full, and a penny is worth nothing to them. And he knows full well that in a few weeks, when the short busy season is over and the long slack time begins, Mrs. Goldstein will draw in her wings and again buy things on tick. But for the time being, she's still in the saddle, and he has to put up with all her caprices and not offend her.

On her way out of the shop, instructing the grocer to deliver her purchases to her home, Mrs. Goldstein encounters Mrs. Cohen, a lively young woman with big, beautiful eyes. The young woman looks at the proud, fat master tailor's wife with a contemptuous smile. "What airs and graces she gives herself," she says, imitating Mrs. Goldstein for the grocer's benefit. "So stuck up. I'm sure she thinks the whole of Whitechapel belongs to her. They get a few orders, and she splashes out. Just wait and see: It'll soon be slack again, and there won't be any food to put on the table. Oh, yes, we know her only too well, Mrs. Moneybags."

Mrs. Cohen, you see, is not afraid of slack time. Her husband, a foreman baker, is paid regular wages, so she can afford to make fun of the "wealthy" master tailor's wife. The grocer twirls his moustache and smiles, but he's afraid to open his mouth. Mrs. Cohen buys what she needs, carries on joking and, on her way out, informs the grocer what's on at the theatre that night.

"Her husband works his guts out baking bread all night," another customer exclaimed, "and she's out half the night at the theatre, and God knows where else. She ought to have my old man for a husband, he'd soon . . ."

"Good luck to her!" the grocer's wife breaks in. "What's she supposed to do? Waste away her years like me, tucked up in the shop every night like a worm in horseradish, never seeing the bright world outside?"

More women come in. The shop gets lively and boisterous. Women haggle with the grocer over a farthing. They stand around laughing and kibitzing about slack time, shortages, troubles, family celebrations, and sweet hopes for the future. "My Esther is going out with a young man," a staid middle-aged Jewess relates, "and he's everything you could wish for: tall as a pine tree and radiant as the sun. He's a good earner with a contract, and all the girls in the workshop are crazy about him." "Oh, yeah?" another woman, who has grownup daughters of her own but no man in the house, interrupts her sharply: "Take a good look around. That's London for you, full of people from all over the world. That guy might well have a wife back in the old country. You've heard the stories." "Don't you worry," the future bride's mother retorts angrily. "My Esther's not a freak, thank God. She could find ten husbands to replace him."

Their conversation is interrupted by the breathless arrival of a woman with a pointed nose and blue lips. "What's up, Mrs. Krasner?" women ask her at once. Quietly, Mrs. Krasner starts to tell them: "Well, sure enough, Mrs. Zlatkin's had a miscarriage, if you get my meaning. I've just seen the doctor coming down. She kept denying she was pregnant, but who was she fooling? I don't know what the world's coming to. People put their lives at risk to avoid having children. She's only got two, not babies anymore, and her husband earns two pound ten a week in regular wages. So what would be so terrible if she had another child? Her husband went nuts when people began to say she was pregnant, so now we'll really be able to congratulate him."

"I don't like that kind of thing at all," a dark, pockmarked women with a child in her arms and another clinging to her skirt interjected, her eyes gleaming angrily. "I've got six kids of my own, and none of them—God forbid—is one too much."

Into the shop comes a young man with long hair, wearing a faded overcoat, and asks for half a loaf of bread and a half-herring. He knows all the women in the shop, and they all know him. He's a *cheder* teacher who rents a room from one of them, and he's still single. Apart from teaching, he works as a traveling salesman, peddling clothes to make ends meet. The women cluster round him like *hasidim* round a rebbe. One of them asks him to bring a suit for her "boychik." Another asks him for a pair of underpants for her husband, and a third woman asks for a pair of woolen socks. The young man writes the orders down in a notebook. He's got a good head for business and knows exactly when to pop into the grocery shop.

Translated by Barry Smerin

The Nationalist

Di tsayt, 1913

Back in the old country, in his Lithuanian shtetl, he had been known as a supporter of the Haskalah, a Zionist, and a fervent advocate of the Hebrew language.* But what usually happens to young men like these when they come to London? If they don't get a chance to become a tailor's machinist, they become collectors of lottery tickets and remain paupers for the rest of their lives.

Things turned out very differently for the bloke I'm talking about. When he arrived here, he started off on the right foot, went into business, and made a success of it. Some years ago he married a girl born in England to wealthy Anglo-Jewish parents, and now he has a large, flourishing business, lives in a fine house in a fashionable district, and enjoys life to the full.

He hasn't given up his Jewishness. He isn't religious, but he remains the same fervent Jewish nationalist that he was in his youth in his shtetl in the old country. You often run into him at Zionist meetings. He is actively involved in Jewish affairs and is particularly interested in the question of Jewish education.

His early love of Hebrew has not weakened in the slightest. He talks to you for hours on end about old and modern Hebrew literature. He will quote to you by heart whole stanzas of Gordon's and Bialik's poetry. He'll give you a lecture on Klausner's latest article, and he gets so inspired by the beauty of the old Hebrew language that he actually starts speaking to you in Hebrew.†

I recently met him at a Sunday morning lecture on Jewish history. The lecturer spoke in Hebrew, and my nationalist savored his every word. His face shone with rapturous delight as he listened to the exalted and pure biblical language. After the lecture he invited me, as an old acquaintance, to come home with him and see his collection of Hebrew books. All the way home he talked only about Hebrew writers and poets and the good old days of the Haskalah. He complained bitterly about the Jewish public's neglect of Hebrew literature and the fact that the best writers had to stoop to writing in the Yiddish jargon.

When we arrived at his house, he showed me into a large, beautifully furnished drawing room, whose walls were bedecked with portraits of great

---

* Haskalah: Jewish Enlightenment movement.

† Judah Leib Gordon was a leading Hebrew poet of the Haskalah. Haim Nahman Bialik was the Jewish national poet who pioneered writing in modern Hebrew. Yosef Klausner was a Hebrew editor and critic of the new Hebrew literature. All were influenced by the Haskalah and were at the forefront in the revitalization of the Hebrew language.

Hebrew authors and other famous Jews. I felt like I was in a real Jewish environment, and it awakened in me sweet recollections, half-forgotten memories of my own youth.

He introduced me to his wife, who soon proved to be the opposite of her nationalist husband. She came across as a true English "lady" who knew nothing about Jewish nationalism. She took no interest in the conversation her husband was conducting in Yiddish about Hebrew books and authors. She made her excuses in perfect English and retired to another room.

Meanwhile, their twelve-year-old son sat at the table looking at the pictures in a penny comic book. From time to time he raised his eyes and gave us a blank stare. It was obvious that he didn't understand a word of what we were saying. My nationalist interlocutor noticed me looking at his son and remarked artlessly: "My son doesn't understand Yiddish. As you know, my wife was born here. At home we speak only English, except occasionally to a guest, so how should he know Yiddish?"

"But surely he studies Jewish subjects—I mean Jewish history and Jewish literature—by the new Hebrew-in-Hebrew method?" I interjected confidently. "No," he replied dispassionately. "Unfortunately, he doesn't understand Hebrew either. We live a long way away from the East End; there aren't any Hebrew teachers here, and I am always busy at work. Once I tried to arrange for a Hebrew teacher to come and teach him here at home, but 'she' wouldn't hear of it. 'The boy's got quite enough to do with his schoolwork and music lessons,' she said, 'and we shouldn't overstrain him.' I didn't want to get into an argument with her, so I left it at that."

Then he resumed our discussion about Jewish culture and showed me the new Hebrew books he had purchased. However, I'd lost interest in the discussion and couldn't take my eyes off the boy, who was staring at the books as if they were something from another planet.

I left the house with a strange, uncomfortable feeling about my Jewish nationalist acquaintance.

Translated by Barry Smerin

An "Honest" Servant

Di tsayt, 1913

Of all the large welfare charity's employees, Rozman is considered the most competent and the most honest. For the better-paid senior staff, Rozman is a devoted, faithful servant on whom they can rely. And for the wealthy committee members, those who give out the money and decide who gets it, he is a man of great integrity whose word is biblical truth.

Rozman's work is highly delicate: He has to investigate whether paupers who apply for assistance really are poor and deserve support. For such a job you need more judgment than justice, and you mustn't be influenced by sentimental feelings.

Modern charities do not operate like the welfare institutions of yesteryear, which gave to anyone who stretched out their hand. Nowadays, giving charity is not simply a religious duty but a science. You have to understand the psychology of begging, to know who you can drive away by shouting and who you won't get rid of until you throw them a bone. And that's why the charity needs a competent person to investigate who should be helped and who not.

And Rozman is very well suited to the task. As soon as he took up the post, he understood that the only way to please his superiors was by delivering unfavorable reports on people applying for support. And so he began energetically finding fault with the paupers. Discovering a pauper's "sin" is an easy matter. As we know, poverty is the mother of sin, and a pauper is a sinner. Rozman's so-called reports are full of accusations against the poor: that applicant is too lazy to find a job; another likes playing cards; a third is too impertinent; a fourth is still a "greenhorn" without any family here to support him.

Rozman's reports are Bible truth to the committee members. Once he has reported unfavorably on a particular applicant, the person in question won't receive a penny in aid even if they starve to death. And when the committee members draw up their monthly account of all who have applied for aid and calculate how much has been saved thanks to Rozman's reports, they feel sure they couldn't wish for a better servant.

Translated by Barry Smerin

Antisemitism on the Tram

Di tsayt, 1914

The tramcars and motor buses running through Whitechapel are frequently the scene of ugly disputes between Jewish passengers and the conductor over a ha'penny fare. There are certain short stretches in the Jewish quarter where you can ride for a ha'penny: from Aldgate to Bedford Street, from the London Hospital to Globe Road, and so on. But the rule is that you have to get on exactly where the ha'penny ride begins, and not earlier.

However, our Jewish men and women—God bless them—are not all well versed in the matter, and if they have to travel, let's say, from Whitechapel to Stepney Green, they won't walk to London Hospital to get the tram; they'll get on at New Road and ask for a ha'penny ticket. Most of the conductors aren't bothered about such trifles and leave the customers alone, but there are some obstinate wretches who insist on the slightest detail and demand another ha'penny for the extra few yards. The Jewish passengers react angrily to the conductor's impertinence and argue with him loudly in an English that arouses much merriment from the non-Jewish passengers.

Yesterday I saw just such a scene. An elderly Jewish woman carrying a whole load of packages got on in Whitechapel and asked for a ha'penny ticket. The tram stopped at the hospital, but she didn't get off and traveled on. The conductor came over to her demanding she either get off or pay another ha'penny.

The woman jumped up angrily and in broken English began to complain in front of all the other passengers that she'd only just got on and was only going to Sidney Street, and it didn't cost more than a ha'penny. So what in God's name did a thief like him want from her? But the conductor wouldn't leave her alone and insisted on payment of the extra fare. The woman, seeing she had no choice but to cough up another ha'penny, turned to me and the other Jewish passengers and vented her bitterness on us: "Bloody antisemites, the lot of them! Screwing another ha'penny out of me for nothing! They should all go to hell!"

"No need for curses, Missus," the conductor said quietly in Yiddish. "I'm Jewish too, but I have to look after my job. Next time you'll know where to get on."

Translated by Barry Smerin

Flower Day

Di tsayt, 1914

Now hear what happened last Sunday, on Flower Day. The East End streets were swarming with pretty Jewish girls carrying baskets of artificial flowers, offering their wares to the passersby. Not all those accosted by the sympathetic young flower sellers were members of the Zionist movement.

The Golden Years of London Yiddish 51

Some didn't even know why the flowers were being sold. But hardly anyone refused to buy a flower. Who could find it in themselves to refuse a lovely girl with pleading eyes such a trifle as buying a flower from her for a penny?

The enthusiastic Jewish girls brandishing both the flowers and the blue collection boxes inspired high spirits in the Jewish quarter. There was talk of a Jewish future, a "safe homeland" in Palestine, and people walked the streets proudly, in a festive mood.

A young flower seller standing near Petticoat Lane market made a particularly pleasant impression. She was pretty as a picture, a tall brunette with a long face, rosy cheeks, large, flaming black eyes, and silken curls tied in a blue ribbon. She was so lively and animated, performing her task with such diligence and commitment, that everyone had to stop and look at her, whether they wanted to or not. She spoke the words "Jewish National Fund—a penny" so sweetly that no one even thought of refusing to buy a flower from her.* She didn't let a soul pass by without giving them a leaflet. She sold a flower to the man sitting on the ground polishing people's shoes, to the driver and conductor of a tram standing at the stop, to a Chinese sailor, as well as to an elderly Jew coming out of the Machzikei Hadas synagogue.†

Just then, an Irish gentleman with a thick neck and a reddish nose emerged from the Lane.‡ The girl ran up to him with her basket of flowers: "Buy a flower, sir!" "What's the idea?" the Irishman replied. On the spot, without a moment's hesitation, the enthusiastic girl gave him a short lecture on Zionism. In clear English and in simple words, she laid out the whole tragic history of Jewish dispersion. She explained our national consciousness and our plans for a home in the land of our fathers and forefathers.

The Irishman stood there with his mouth and ears open, listening to what the girl was telling him. When she'd finished speaking, he took a flower, threw a silver coin in the box, and said, in a serious tone of voice: "You're quite right, my girl. That's the only way. As far as I'm concerned, they can all go to Palestine!"

Translated by Barry Smerin

---

* Jewish National Fund: set up in 1901 to support the establishment of a Jewish state in Palestine. JNF activities began in England in 1905.

† The Machzikei Hadas synagogue was a large Orthodox immigrant synagogue on the corner of Brick Lane and Fournier Street in Spitalfields, Whitechapel.

‡ "The Lane" usually refers to the daily Jewish market on Wentworth Street and Goulston Street. It is adjacent to the Sunday Petticoat Lane market.

2
YIDDISH THROUGH THE FIRST WORLD WAR

1914–19

By 1914 many of the key Yiddish writers had moved away from London—Winchevsky and Kussman to America and Brenner to Palestine—but the satirical writer Avrom Margolin had arrived in London from Berlin. The East End was full of activity, and being central to the tailoring trade, Eastenders capitalized on the wartime opportunities for manufacturing uniforms, so business, at least in the tailoring trade, was booming. Many Jewish men of military service age were not in the army but were visible as workers across the East End.

At the start of the First World War, conscription to the British army was voluntary for British citizens. The Anglo-Jewish establishment was keen to show that British Jews were volunteering. Rabbis and reverends gave sermons in synagogues, and articles in the English Jewish press promoted the message that it was Jews' patriotic duty to sign up and show their loyalty to Britain.[1] Many boys from established Anglo-Jewish families living in West London enlisted, but naturalized East End immigrants were reluctant to volunteer for varied reasons: They had conflicted feelings about fighting on the side of Russia; socialists refused to fight for the tsar; they were put off by reports of antisemitism in the army and the recruitment process; they were concerned they would be unable to meet their religious requirements; and they were unwilling to forgo new job opportunities as the demand for tailoring increased.[2] In response, a Jewish battalion was established with the intention of combatting antisemitism and encouraging Orthodox religious Jews to conscript.[3]

In January 1916 the Military Service Act, demanding compulsory conscription for British citizens, was passed. However, many immigrants were unnaturalized and not eligible for army service. In mid-1916 the government allowed non-naturalized Jews to enlist, encouraging them by waiving the £5 naturalization fee for good conduct in the army. In 1917 a new government system, instituted with the assistance of the Anglo-Jewish establishment, demanded that Eastern European immigrants choose either to fight in the British army or to return to Russia to fight in the tsar's army.[4]

The lack of a visible presence of Jewish soldiers in the army, together with immigrant Jews' prominence in a thriving East End industry, put Jewish patriotism in question in the public eye and underlined clear divisions between Jews and non-Jews, between middle-class Anglo-Jews and East End immigrants, and, within the East End, among naturalized immigrant Jews, unnaturalized immigrant Jews, and English-born Jews.

Yiddish feuilletons written during the war almost all engage in some way with the effects of the war on the East End immigrant community. Leon Creditor's comic sketches, written under the pseudonym Leybele Batlen, show how unnaturalized immigrants, not in a position to enlist, felt like they held a precarious position in Britain. Yankele's writing describes the varied effects on those trying to continue their daily lives, whether it be selling flowers or dealing with strikes. Avrom Margolin, in his sketch "A Monologue of a Whitechapel Recruit," critiques how the army organized recruits, and how Jewish men made choices about how they engaged with the war with considerable "swank."[5]

After the war, violence in Eastern Europe became a focus, and pogroms against the Jews of Poland and Ukraine filled the Yiddish newspapers. In 1919 the immigrant community organized a march across London to sway British public opinion and pressure the government to help their Eastern European brethren. The march was attended by prominent members of the Anglo-Jewish leadership. Yankev Yitzkhok Capitanchik's moving sketch, analyzed in the introduction, describes a version of this event. It is interesting that, more than the feuilletons of other periods, most of the sketches

Yiddish through the First World War   55

in this section engage with contact between East End Jews and non-Jews. Indeed, the final sketch in this section by Ben-A Sochachewsky, "The Last Resort," relates a woman's desperate choice between her children's starvation or their conversion to Christianity.

YANKELE

Yankele is a diminutive of the name Yankef (similar to Jake as a diminutive of Jacob). This common name is the pseudonym of a writer for *Di velt* who published a series of feuilletons about East End life and politics during World War I, sometimes subtitled *Bildlekh un tsenes fun gas* (Pictures and Scenes from the Street). In the same period, Yankele also wrote a regular feuilleton column in *Di tsayt* depicting a man's endless mockery of his foolish wife using stereotyped gender roles.

• •

An Evil Decree against Flower Sellers

Di velt, 1915

In front of the colossal edifice of the London Hospital, there has always been a regular small market of flower sellers during visiting hours.*

Dozens of men and women with baskets of white and colored flowers surround the wide entrance to the hospital, offering their wares to the people visiting sick friends and acquaintances.

During these hours, the flower sellers used to do a decent business. Almost all the visitors bought flowers, and it was only rarely that someone haggled over the asking price. When a person goes to visit a sick friend in hospital, their heart is open, and their pocket is generous. They aren't bothered about an extra penny or two for a bunch of flowers that will make a sick child happy.

And now here we are in this vast, bitter, neverending war, which has destroyed the world, filled the hospitals with sick and wounded, and sent food prices rocketing. Flowers have their value and attraction for the healthy, and have become utterly superfluous for the sick. The places where these fragrant flowers grew now resound with the constant crashes of artillery

---

* The London Hospital was situated on Whitechapel Road, in the heart of the Jewish East End.

fire. The ground that was once adorned with the most beautiful plants is now seeped in warm human blood.

The large London Hospital has now partly become an infirmary for the victims of war, for people mutilated by enemy shrapnel. It now has an extraordinarily heavy burden to bear. The beds are full, and looking after the patients costs twice as much as usual. Every piece of food, every dose of medicine, every bandage is like gold.

The hospital needs money, and flowers are an unwanted luxury, a superfluous item, even for the sick.

A large placard hangs on the hospital wall with an inscription in clear, bold letters:

"As this is a very bad time for hospitals, with so many patients and everything so dreadfully expensive, we request visitors not to bring flowers to their sick friends. It would be better to give the money to support the hospital."

And the impoverished flower sellers see it as an evil decree. Visitors heed the sign and shake their heads in refusal when the sellers confront them at the entrance with bunches of flowers in their hands. Their income grows less by the day.

Over there stands an old, stooped woman wearing a white apron, gazing despairingly at the wilting and dried-out flowers in her basket. She is already hoarse from shouting, but her wares are still all there.

This woman walked a long way to get here, but no one wants to pay her a penny sale. It is as if her flowers have been excommunicated. Every now and then, she looks up at the notice telling her she has made a useless trip with her flowers, and that nobody needs them here.

The woman stands for a moment, sorrowfully pensive. She has stood here selling flowers for so many years, and now suddenly, without a why or wherefore, they are taking away the crumb of bread from her mouth. She can't believe it and automatically holds the flowers out and runs after a couple who aren't even looking in her direction.

Translated by Vivi Lachs

The Tramway Strike

Di velt, 1915

Troubles, they say, have no end. The war has flared up again and, as if that isn't enough, God has punished us with a tram strike. This is what the world has come to. Not only are our lives hanging by a thread and we're threatened with poison bombs; not only must we lie in the dark and do without a scrap of meat to eat. On top of everything, we now have to drag ourselves around on foot.

In just a few days the tram strike has cut us to the core. We would raise our hands to heaven if only it would stop, along with the crazy war itself. You might think it's no big deal. The trams have stopped running—so what? The fact is that the strike has caused great suffering in the Jewish neighborhood.

A lot of workers can't get home for lunch; they languish in the workshop all day without a bite of hot food. Many Jewish housewives have to trudge all the way over from Hackney to the Lane and back on foot, carrying heavy shopping bags.

On the few trams still running here and there, all kinds of comic and tragic incidents occur. A few days ago I witnessed an interesting scene at dawn on my way to work. A group of Jewish men and women were walking along Cambridge Heath Road. They were dressed up for a special occasion, the women wearing jewelry and the men in top hats and lacquered shoes. I could see right away that they were on their way home from a Jewish wedding party.

A pretty, graceful bride held her wedding dress in one hand and walked arm in arm with her bridegroom, who kept looking back every minute to see if there was any sign of a cab or tram. Clearly, he wasn't too pleased at having to walk back with his bride from their wedding celebration on foot.

"What a state of affairs," an elderly Jewish woman, apparently a close relative, complained angrily. "That's all we needed, in the middle of everything—a strike, and a long walk to wear our legs out!"

English workmen on their way to work stared at the dressed-up group of Jews, and some of them made unpleasant comments about foreigners.

At last the wedding party reached the corner of Mile End Road.* Just then, as luck would have it, a tram came along. A crowd of people were already waiting at the tram stop, so there was a lot of pushing and shoving and a great squeeze. The bridegroom somehow managed to push his bride onboard, but the tram moved off abruptly, and he himself was left behind. The bride kicked up a fuss, and the groom ran breathlessly after the tram. He was a very pitiful sight.

---

* Mile End is on the eastern side of the Jewish East End.

The few trams still running are not manned by trained personnel but by anyone the company can get hold of. The driver is often a school inspector. As for the conductor, he's often a road sweeper, no less. He doesn't know the first thing about the job, and you can feel quite faint watching him struggle to punch the ticket and give you your change. The inexperienced conductors don't know the routes well either, and you often witness sharp quarrels between conductors and passengers.

In Whitechapel a Jewish woman carrying a lot of parcels gets on a tram that's going to Clapton and asks what the fare is to a street somewhere in Bow.* The conductor thinks the street is on his route and takes a penny from her. The woman travels as far as Cambridge Heath, then looks around and realizes she's on the wrong tram. She charges up to the conductor and demands to know why he misled her. Utterly confused, the conductor stops the tram and asks the woman where she wants to get to. Other passengers help him, but the poor woman with the parcels has to trudge all the way back on foot, cursing the conductor to high heaven.

No doubt about it, the tramway strike is a punishment from God for our sins.

Translated by Barry Smerin

The Whitechapel War Office

Di velt, 1915

What? You're not happy with the war reports in the newspapers? You say you're fed up with them; it's hard to make out what's really happening. Well, here's a piece of advice for you: Just pop over to the war office. It's right here in Whitechapel. There you'll find out everything. They'll tell you not only what's happened on the battlefield but also what the German Kaiser himself doesn't know—that is, when the war's going to end, who's going to win, and so forth.

I'm joking, you say. No one is admitted into the war office, and no one is going to reveal any secrets.

---

* Clapton is north of the East End in the borough of Hackney; Bow lies to the east. The tram would turn onto Cambridge Heath Road on its way to Clapton.

Yiddish through the First World War   59

It seems you've completely misunderstood me. I don't mean the war ministry in Whitechapel. I'm sending you to the war office that really is here in Whitechapel.

They let anyone in, I can assure you. All you need to do is spend a ha'penny on a glass of lemonade.

No need to make a song or dance about it, the war office in question is a little lemonade shop on a streetcorner in the Jewish quarter.

In that shop, ministers and politicians meet every evening for serious discussions of all the issues connected with the war. The owner of the shop is the war minister. He worked his way up to that exalted position thanks to his great knowledge of military affairs.

A former soldier, he arrived from Russia a good few years ago, but he didn't abandon his military service here in England. Rather, he enlisted in the great army of the proletariat. For long years he fought for his existence in the workshop, with saw and wood plane.

It was hard, exhausting work. His strength grew weaker, but duty is duty. He did not leave the battlefield until the very end, until he could no longer stand on his feet.

So what does a military hero do when he returns from a war? Play a barrel organ in the street or beg for money, displaying his shot-off arm?

And what does a worker do when he has served his time in full and can work no longer? At best, his friends hold a benefit for him and buy him a lemonade shop—an easy business to run. And that's exactly what happened to my war minister. When he was no longer able to work at the bench, his *landsmen* scraped together and raised a few pounds for him, with which he bought a lemonade and newspaper shop.

The business barely earned him a crust of bread for his family, but he was helped by his expertise in military matters.

To his good fortune, the Great World War broke out soon after he bought the shop. By nature a persuasive speaker, he began arguing in detail with his customers about the war news, displaying great knowledge.

Gradually his shop stopped being simply a place where you bought a glass of lemonade. It became a center of international diplomacy for many Whitechapel politicians who are not content just to read the newspapers but want to get the war news from the very source.

Every evening the shop is besieged by inquisitive Jews. They drink lemonade and debate aspects of the war. The shopkeeper stands there with his sleeves rolled up and fervently delivers his opinions as a person of consequence, an authority.

Chapter 2

"Didn't I tell you Italy would have to enter the war? Didn't I say only recently that Chamberlain would now be the right finance minister? And what about Przemyśl?* I already knew it would fall. The Russians won't hold out for long, I can tell you."

Everyone listens to the shopkeeper's pronouncements with great attention, casting one ha'penny after another into the till.

The lemonade shop is now known throughout the neighborhood as "the war office." As for the shopkeeper, everyone refers to him as none other than "the war minister."

Translated by Barry Smerin

● ●

Wartime Livelihoods

Di velt, 1915

Say whatever you like, but thanks to the war, our East End has been invigorated. It's not anything like it was.

The Jewish quarter is richer, livelier, and, I would say, more interesting. There's been an enormous "boom" here. Everyone wants to move here even though it's hard to find a place to live, just like in the good old days. Lots of new shops and businesses have appeared which—I hope I'm wrong—will either all disappear after the war or be greatly reduced.

Not only has the war created an exceptional, continuous "busy season" in our Jewish quarter, it has also brought many Jewish workers out of the workshop and into the business world.

Apart from those who have now had an opportunity to try their luck as workshop "masters," many others have opened all sorts of small businesses.

The East End is flooded with refugees—a good clientele for the new businessmen.

Most striking of all is the number of new restaurants that have sprung up in the Jewish quarter since the war broke out. Tell me, my lovelies, when did Whitechapel ever have so many restaurants? Everywhere you turn you meet with the smell of a newly opened restaurant. Not much chance of dying of hunger.

---

* In 1915, Neville Chamberlain was appointed mayor of Birmingham; he later became British prime minister. Przemyśl was a fortress town in Galicia, which was under siege from the German army in 1914–15.

Yiddish through the First World War   61

In Whitechapel the restaurant business always used to be good for nothing. Who needed it? The workers earned little and made do with meals from their landladies. Now a restaurant in the Jewish quarter is a veritable goldmine, every bit as lucrative as a workshop making clothes for the army. So if a Jew was making nothing from his grocery shop, his little furniture store, or whatever miserable business he had, he just threw everything out and turned it into a restaurant. He was sure to make a living, if only the war lasted.

The eating places you now find all over the East End are frequented not only by refugees and single people but also by married men, heads of families. What do you think? Prices are sky high. A pound of meat is worth its weight in gold. A Jewish housewife demands a lot of money for housekeeping expenses. So isn't it better and cheaper to drop into a restaurant by yourself for a bite to eat, and let the wife and kids make do with whatever there is at home? After all, there's a war on, and prices have rocketed.

Apart from the new businesses that have sprouted up in Whitechapel like mushrooms after the rain, the war has also created special Jewish "wartime livelihoods."

Take, for example, the downtrodden and dejected insurance agent: the gloomy young man, umbrella in hand, who used to roam the streets aimlessly, knowing it would be hard for him to earn a penny. Of course it was. Who needed insurance? Who wasn't already insured, and who didn't already own a Singer sewing machine? Insurance agents were greatly to be pitied, having no one and nothing to insure.†

Now the insurance agent walks with his head held high. It's a new world. He raps on a house door with confidence and asks if you want insurance against bombs, against Zeppelins. This, it seems, is quite a different thing: it's new, it's needed. The companies don't discriminate and insure Jews too. The agents don't tire themselves out walking needlessly. They make good business from insuring against bombs, just like they did with the early Singer sewing machines. The insurance agents have nothing to complain about in this time of war.

Another new Jewish livelihood created by the war is writing letters in Russian and German for people who have relatives in the countries where

---

† The Singer sewing machine was often the most valuable item in many Whitechapel households, with immigrants working as tailors and seamstresses. An insurance agent could ask for a high insurance premium, but once the customer was insured, there was no longer a potential earning target for the agent.

the war is raging. In the Jewish streets there are Yiddish signs in the windows reading: "Letters written here in all languages." And, from what I hear, those letter writers are making good money.

A Jew wearing a yarmulke sits in an "office" separated off from a little shoe repair shop, writing "German" letters for people with relatives or prisoners in those parts, and he charges sixpence for a letter.* The so-called German in which he writes the letters is pitiful, but the main thing is that it looks different from Yiddish, and he assures his customers that their letters will "get there."

That is a special wartime livelihood that suits people who aren't fit for service in khaki.

Translated by Barry Smerin

LEON CREDITOR (1875–1966)

"L. S. Creditor, Assistant Editor 'Jewish Voice,'" sketch by Maurice Sochachewsky, *Di idishe shtime* (July 18, 1952). Courtesy of Dave Skye Sochachewsky. From the British Library collection.

Leon (Leyb Sholem) Creditor emigrated from Lithuania to England in around 1905. He became the first professional Yiddish language journalist in Britain, writing for many newspapers and periodicals, including *Der idisher ekspres* and *Der idisher zhurnal*. During the First World War, Creditor wrote a series of humorous, topical feuilleton sketches for *Di velt* using the pseudonym Leybele Batlen (Leybele Layabout) and the subtitle *Adventshers fun leybele batlen* (The Adventures of Leybele Layabout). In the 1920s he also wrote for *Di post*.

In typical feuilleton style, all of Batlen's sketches derive from news items to which his namesake protagonist responds.

---

* Yarmulke: skullcap.

Yiddish through the First World War   63

They are humorous but have a critique tucked into the storylines. All the sketches of 1915 are connected to the war, and later pieces from 1928 refer to the Epsom Derby and the English football cup final. Batlen's pieces are often set up as conversations between Leybele and his unnamed wife. Unlike in most male writers' depictions of husband-wife relationships, Batlen is often the butt of his wife's jokes rather than the other way around.

Creditor wrote a historical play, *Bereyshis* (Genesis), and coedited the theatre journal *Teater shpigl* (Theatre Mirror) in 1946–47. From 1951 Creditor edited *Di idishe shtime*. He wrote *Der rambam, folkstimlekhe monografye* (Maimonides, a Popular Monograph), which was published in book form in 1955 and serialized in *Di idishe shtime*, and a literary critique of the works of Chaim Nachman Bialik.

His daughter was the Labour Party politician Baroness Dora Gaitskell, wife of the MP and Labour Party leader Hugh Gaitskell.[6]

In Woolwich Arsenal

Di velt, 1915

I think:

If God would help me out with a couple of hundred pounds, I would then help the country where I live and work.

I would have an airplane built at my own expense and order a large warship to be made. If I had a few pounds left, I would order three or four 14-inch cannons that can spray cannonballs like peas.

But you see, I am just a poor Jew, but I really want to help my country when it needs it.

She says:

"Listen, Leybl, if you really want to help the country, why don't you go and help make shells? If you do things with your usual enthusiasm, like when you chop a bit of firewood from time to time, you could make enough shells to kill a hundred Germans, and end the war."

"You're clever as the day," I agree with her. "I do actually have time between the afternoon and evening prayers to make shells for the war effort."

Without thinking much more about it, I set off quickly that same day after reciting the afternoon prayers.

64   Chapter 2

But how do you know how to get there? I'm not a born Englishman who can read a map and with one quick look knows where to go. I am just a Jew who has to ask! And how can I ask people the way to Woolwich Arsenal? Won't they get suspicious and think I'm a spy—and kill me?*

There is a way, however. I will tell them straight away exactly what I intend to do, and then it'll be as clear as day that I'm not a spy and simply want to help England.

So I say the prayer for making a journey and head off. I go up to a policeman on the street and ask him the way to Woolwich. I don't mention the arsenal. I take it for granted, as they say here.

"You know, Mr. Policeman," I say, "you know that the king himself has asked people to help, and everyone must help in any way they can. You understand therefore, Mr. Policeman, that I would like to help you a little bit, a little drop, you know. I am a Russian Jew, a very honest, very honest person. Now tell me please the way to Woolwich, yes!"

The policeman glared at me, and I thought I would collapse with fear.

"Why are you looking at me like that, sir?" I asked boldly. "I'll report you, because I want to help the government and you don't want it."

Do you think he took his stupid eyes off me? No, he looked at me even more intently from head to toe. He even saw that I was shaking. But he didn't do anything to me. He didn't arrest me, thank God. He just looked down his nose at me and gave me a sharp reply:

"Getoutovit, clear orf!"

I got his meaning. It's not as if I don't know any English. A horrible policeman. Well, I'll just ask another.

By now the sun had set. It was getting dark, and the streetlights were even dimmer than usual. As always there were fewer people on the street—they were worried about getting robbed. I realized that it was time for the evening prayer. I ran into the first small synagogue I came across and thought: "I'll go to Woolwich Arsenal tomorrow. I'll even take my missus with me. Why, shouldn't she help the country as well?"

Translated by Vivi Lachs

---

* Woolwich Arsenal is on the south bank of the River Thames in South East London.

An Air Minister

Di velt, 1915

I heard that the powers that be are thinking of appointing an air minister. So I got myself ready to go out as usual, kissed the mezuzah, and was about to set off, when she who always wants to know what I'm doing stopped me with her standard question:†

"Where are you off to?"

I thought for a moment. Should I tell her that I'm off to become a minister? She'll just laugh at me and say, "A man who can't pin a tail on a donkey wants to become a minister! God help me, he's out of his mind."

"Don't just stand there thinking!" she interrupted my thoughts. "I'm asking you where you're going."

"I'm thinking?" I say. "How would I not be thinking? A minister has to think or he can't be a minister, and especially a minister that has to deal with the air above us, up in the clouds, high up where the eagles and the parrots nest. It's quite something to be an air minister!"

And as I said this, I looked up into the air toward the skies, working out in my mind a strategy for operating airplanes, seaplanes, and biplanes, and talking all the while.

"Oh dear," she said, tapping her forehead, "he really has gone mad. God be with you." She comforted me as if I had just fainted. "What are you going on about? Jabbering about planes and clouds? For pity's sake, come to your senses."

"No," I said, "I'm not coming to my senses. I have to go to the cabinet office and offer them my candidacy. Whatever you say, a person has to try. Like God says to us mortals—you try, and I will be your helper. Don't forget, this job may be worth a few thousand pounds a year. We'll live like the rich. We'll eat chicken every day, with a drop to drink before the meal, and I'll take our top room for myself because we won't need a lodger with such a royal income. I'll even give up teaching at the *cheder*. Instead of the time spent teaching, I'll think up a new design for an airship, and afterward we'll sit at the seaside without a scrap of work to do, and eat and drink and go to the pictures."

---

† Mezuzah: parchment with Torah verses inside a case that is attached to doorposts of Jewish homes.

66   Chapter 2

Hearing my words, my wife began to understand that this might be a significant job opportunity and gave me her blessing. And I went off to the cabinet office thinking: Master of the Universe, if this country really intends to appoint a new air and ammunition minister, I am surely the right person for the job.

What I mean to say is that I am a real man of the air. For generations and generations, we Jews have had nothing but air to our name. Since the time that our biblical land was taken away from us, we have been ethereal beings. We have no heaven or earth; we only have the air. We've wheeled-and-dealed in air, lived and floated on air. Could England have a better air minister than me?

With these thoughts, I arrived at the cabinet office, where the airheads and their staff actually work, and I presented myself as England's future air minister.

The porter looked me up and down incredulously. I pushed my hat back a little, so that he could see my wide forehead. A minister must definitely have a broad forehead, or else he has to resign.

The porter still didn't believe me. He smiled, the wise guy. He didn't know that as soon as I became the minister, he would be in my hands, and I could even dismiss him without notice. However, meanwhile, you understand, I was in his hands and had to convince him that I was the man who would be the best air minister because I am totally pumped up with air.

So I steadied myself and thought: Bounteous God, if you gave me right now a pair of strong wings, I would soar up and hover in the air beneath the heavens so that the porter would be flabbergasted. Then he would believe me and not laugh at me.

And maybe, I thought, if I really had wings and raised myself up into the heights of heaven, I would never come back down to earth again. Because, just between you and me, here on earth it's not so good. I wouldn't in the least long to return.

But, as there are no wings, one can only be an air minister, and if one can't be an air minister, one has to remain a *cheder* teacher. I'm damned if I know if the porter, with his *goy*'s brain, understood my reasoning.* Because

---

* *Goy*: non-Jewish man. For Yiddish-speakers of this period, the word *goy* could be a neutral term denoting the distinction between Jew and non-Jew. Although the word sometimes has negative connotations today, its use in this story simply emphasizes cultural differences. Vivi Lachs, "Good *Goy*, Bad *Goy*:

Yiddish through the First World War 67

if he had understood he wouldn't have thrown me out and slammed the door after me!

Translated by Vivi Lachs

I Settled the Coal Strike

A Short Description of Two Coal Strikes That Were Settled by Mr. Lloyd George and by Me

Di velt, 1915

So, here we are. It's just been the fast of the Ninth of Av, and it didn't go by without a fitting calamity.[†] I'll remember it my whole life. It's not so easy to fast for a day, but on top of that I had to deal with my wife going on strike. But I can now happily tell you that my colleague Lloyd George has settled his strike, and I have settled mine, so both strikes are over.[‡] I can now, in a cheerful state of mind, tell you everything that I had to cope with.

On Tuesday morning, just after the Ninth of Av prayers, I came home and, glancing at my wife, saw that she was out of sorts. I thought, well, it's a fast day, so because she's got an empty stomach, she's feeling lousy. Although it is forbidden to eat on a fast day, you can still talk about food. So I said:

"Will you prepare some food for after the fast?"

"Why should I prepare anything?" she answered. "Whatever there is, you'll eat."

"But we have your noodle pudding filled with cheese every year after the fast."

"Not this year," she answered curtly.

"Why?"

"Because I'm not using the stove. I hate the Coal Board, and I won't give them any more money. They have given us coal for years, but now I've been

---

Representations of Non-Jews in the London Yiddish Press, 1915–1930," *Prooftexts* (forthcoming).

    † Ninth of Av: Fast day commemorating the destruction of the First Temple in 587 BC and the Second Temple in 70 AD.

    ‡ In 1915 David Lloyd George was head of the ministry of munitions. The following year he became Liberal prime minister.

dragged over the coals by them. The Coal Board collector came here early Monday morning and demanded a shilling from me, whether I had one or not. He stood at the door, stubborn as a mule, and wouldn't go away until I gave it to him, the antisemitic son of a bitch. I'm not doing business with them anymore. The Coal Board will feel the pinch."

"So," I said, "are you on strike?"

"I certainly am."

"But can't we get coal from another company?"

"All the coals companies are just as bad; they all want to be paid out of the huge wages you bring in."

"But we'll freeze, God forbid. What will you do to them with your strike?"

"I'll teach them some respect," she said. "I'll teach them that they can't tear into poor people; they have to deal with us politely and behave properly. And if they don't, well, I need them like a hole in the head."

"But won't we freeze in the winter without coal?" I asked, shivering.

"Then we'll freeze!"

"Won't we die then, God forbid?"

"It's better than living."

"But then we won't be able to go to Chaykl Lachman's wedding the *shabbes* after the Ninth of Av!"*

That rather stopped her in her tracks. Startled, she asked with renewed energy:

"Why not?"

"Because we'll be dead. Have you ever seen a corpse at a wedding?"

"But isn't the wedding in a year's time?"

"Exactly, by then, there won't even be a memory of us left. We'll have frozen to death."

"Really?"

"Are you kidding me?"

"You think that I'm really going to go back to dealing with the Coal Board and with such a revolting collector that I couldn't even bear to look at him?"

I suddenly understood why the coal strike mattered to her. She wanted a better-looking collector! So I used all my political strategies. The whole day, we talked and worked at it until I settled the strike.

---

* *Shabbes*: the Sabbath.

Right then and there, she wrote a letter to the manager of the Coal Board on the card that the loathsome collector had left.

Going to the pillar box to post the card, I saw the posters with the news: "Coal Strike Settled" and thought that my colleague, Lloyd George, hadn't had it any easier than me, but thanks to God, both coal strikes were settled.

Translated by Vivi Lachs

AVROM MARGOLIN (1884–1961)

Detail from *Avreml shvimt tsum bloffer kontsert* (Avreml Swims to *Der bloffer* Concert), *Der bloffer* (December 1911). Collection of the National Library of Israel.

Avrom Margolin, who wrote under the pseudonym Avreml, was born in Bobruysk (Babruysk), Belarus. He received his secondary schooling from private tutors because the Russian quota for Jewish students in secondary schools had been exceeded. He later studied medicine in Berlin and practiced as a doctor for two years, after which he became a full-time writer. He arrived in London in December 1911 to coedit *Der bloffer* with Leon Kussman. *Der bloffer* was packed with topical satirical sketches and verse, somewhat similar to *Private Eye* magazine in the UK. Much of the verse was penned by Margolin and much of the humor was directed at various Yiddish theatre personalities and the debate around quality theatre. At the beginning of World War I, Margolin coedited the short-lived weekly paper *Der milkhome telegraf* (War Telegraph) with A. M. Kaizer before joining the British army medical corps.

Margolin was a prolific feuilletonist, writing sharply satirical prose and rhyming verse, and he was published in *Di velt*, *Der idisher ekspres*, and *Di tsayt*. Rather than targeting particular people, Margolin's satire used and reused stereotypes of groups as stooges for his wit, including immigrant workers, Zionists, communists, Anglo-Jewish reverends, and so on. This became his trademark and can be seen in "At the Ball." In his feuilleton "A Monologue of a Whitechapel Recruit," Avreml's repertoire of stereotypes to ridicule is extended to include British army recruitment teams.

70   Chapter 2

After the war Margolin moved to America, settling in Chicago in 1922, where he continued to write satire for the journal *Der groyser kundes* (The Big Stick).[7]

• •

A Monologue of a Whitechapel Recruit

Di velt, 1916

So you think that I'm really an Englishman, a real, kosher, naturalized citizen as the Lord hath commanded? Well, you're mistaken.

I'm not at all. I've been here in this country for, touch wood, ten years already. I have made a living by traveling to markets, would that one could say the same about Rothschild's grandson.* And I have saved in the bank a pretty few hundred. I'm single and a whisker off thirty years old, and to be brief, I've paid this country my grandmother's inheritance.

But apart from that, you know, I shudder at the thought of what the future holds for my fellow Russian citizens, because anything could happen in wartime.

So I just went out and enlisted in the British army.

I even duped them, like naive fools. When they questioned me about my identity documents with a surprised "British?" Without thinking I threw back a hearty "Certainly," and they were simply taken in like bloody idiots.

They then nagged me further for papers showing my profession, my ancestry on my mother's side, but I had absolutely nothing.

They searched in two thick tomes for my name, Henry Carson (which in Berdichev, may its memory be blessed, was Heynekh Kazarnovsky), my address, the longevity of my years, and, plonking an identity bracelet on my *tefillin* arm, that was it. I became a soldier and a fighter at the pleasure of the state.[†]

Imagine if I had done such a prank eight years earlier in Berdichev, people would have looked at me as if I was crazy, my father would have given me a round telling off and would have beaten the idea of patriotism right

---

* Lionel de Rothschild (1882–1942) was vice chairman of the Central Jewish Recruiting Committee during World War I. He was the grandson of Lionel de Rothschild, who became the first Jewish serving member of Parliament in 1848.

† Berdichev was sometimes called the Jewish capital of Ukraine, due to its majority Jewish population.

Yiddish through the First World War   71

out of my head. He would have sold the undershirt off his back and become bankrupt to save me from gentile hands. But here, in this country, it's something else!

Such a prominent man as Rothschild concerned himself with the recruiting business, as if it was, God forbid, his livelihood. And no one told him that this was against the natural order of things or not his status.

This is, as the Russians say, common practice.

I don't want to give you my whole life story here, but they put me through three months' training on the laws regarding war and combat—not in Jews' College I'm afraid, but in Victoria Park.‡ They put me through a long series of exercises for marching, running, acrobatics, twisting, jumping like a hare, and, indeed, shooting, too. You can't imagine, I enlisted as naive as a lamb until I had completely digested the army bible.

But I will tell you the main point of this story. The bottom line is that I was twice on the front line and had some rather unpleasant meetings with the Germans. Once, like our patriarch Jacob's struggle with the angel, I received an iron fragment in my sciatic nerve. I wouldn't wish it on anyone, as I was laid up with free meals for three weeks in a hospital, where not so much the bullet but the chronic catarrh French language of the nurse nearly killed me. The second time, during a charge attack with Mr. Velvl's thugs, I lost two fingers and was discharged from service, declared eternally unfit like some sort of loser.§

But if you think I felt sorry for myself, you're mistaken again. First, where is it written that a Berdichever synagogue under-beadle in England should, after ten years' hard and bitter drubbing and suffering, really have ten whole fingers? Several ill-fated individuals would, after such trouble, lose their head as well! Second, how many people have got my smart-ass head, my nous to fool the tribunal as if they were regular suckers?

Do you think that I'm possibly embarrassed to reveal the trickery of the whole secret? Not a jot!¶ When they dragged me to the hospital for the second time, with my eight fingers, and interrogated me about who I am and

---

‡ Jews' College, established in 1855, trained English Jewish boys to become reverends in Anglo-Jewish synagogues. Victoria Park, just north of the East End, was popular for leisure and as a venue for political rallies.

§ Velvl: Yiddish nickname for Kaiser Wilhelm II, who was the king of Prussia and emperor of Germany from 1888–1918.

¶ Not a jot: not at all.

Chapter 2

what I was, who was my father and what is my profession, I told them the whole story with great aplomb: "Your honor, you should know that I am, in summary, a Russian subject, that is, a Jew, born in Berdichev. Don't take offense, but if I hadn't taken your clever tribunal by the nape of its neck and fooled them that I am an Englishman, they would never have trusted me!" And so forth.

You can imagine how, when the commission heard my speech, they burst out laughing in delight. The older doctor, impressed, slapped me on the back, saying:

"You're a smart boy!"

And with that, the whole theatre show ended. Now I travel around again with my bundles, and I don't pay the country, God forbid, even one ha'penny. And when those godlike on high send me my disability pension, I'll have with my eight fingers more cash than another person has with twenty. What do you think? I'm naive?

But this is nonsense! Even I have to make a living! The tribunal should insure themselves by having slightly cleverer clerks who have the common sense to give religious Jews some papers or be warned of the outcome!

But tell me the truth, how did you like my comic turn? Did I fool them well?

Translated by Vivi Lachs

At the Ball

Di velt, 1916

If, one rainy Sunday, the "evil inclination" urges you to go to a ball, and, God help us, you can't resist the pernicious temptation, then make sure you go only to a "proletarian" dance evening, where you'll experience the real pleasures of earthly existence.*

The more "proletarian" and "conscious" the ball is, the less money you'll need. The tickets cost practically nothing, and even if you do want to squander a bit of silver at the bar, there's nothing to spend it on. Nor will you need to flash a lot of banknotes around: The women will understand from your intelligence what sort of a man you are. Your money is as secure

---

* The "evil inclination" is a religious term from the book of Genesis referring to human beings' innate inclination to do evil, which is in constant conflict with the inclination to do good.

as in a national bank—safe from all the Jewish National Fund collection boxes, national stamps, and other Zionist begging bowls—and your mind, like your breast pocket, is free to wander and fantasize, dream and waltz, live and love to your heart's content.

In addition to these dazzling advantages, which are invaluable to all ballroom habitués and Whitechapel ballerinas, a "proletarian" ball has another great virtue, namely freedom from formal dress and finery. A lady's white costume and a man's black tailcoat are the rarest of guests—indeed the least welcome customers—at a ball organized by "class-conscious comrades." You'd need a magnifying glass to find a piece of jewelry on a woman's breast or a pin in a man's tie, even in the busy season sewing army uniforms.

What in God's name do we need all that stuff for? Once, in Germany, so help me, even before the Jewish ladies of Lemberg became our deadly political enemies, I thoughtlessly attended a "bourgeois" ball organized by so-called Austrian merchants, that is, Galician traveling peddlers of secondhand clothes.† The event was dominated by Parisian fashion and Nowy Sącz luxury in its full glory.‡ Cracow Jewish "princesses" in gowns with long, white trains arrived in taxis, accompanied by pet dogs carrying leather handbags in their snouts, and young Austrian "gentlemen" from the tailors' district, in ball costume and top hats, took the hall by storm.

The "High German" dialect, with a delicious Bukovinan tang, resounded harmoniously throughout the hall, as in a parliamentary chamber.§ The ball got underway, with the master of ceremonies announcing the various dances. There were plenty of tangos and Apaches.¶ The abundant alcohol at the bar, the free-flowing champagne, the low-cut evening dresses, the romantic intimacy and modestly suppressed laughter, together with all the music, made it seem more like a night at Maxim's than a gathering of Galician Jews.**

---

† Lemberg in German and Yiddish, and Lwów in Polish (modern-day Lviv, Ukraine), was a town in Eastern Galicia with a large Jewish community.

‡ Before World War II, nearly a third of the Polish city of Nowy Sącz (Nay Tsans in Yiddish) were Jews.

§ Jewish intellectuals spoke Yiddish using many expressions and a pronunciation that was influenced by standard German. This sort of language was considered highbrow or posh.

¶ The Apache was a popular ballroom dance with close contact and spins. It was a toned-down version of a dramatic and misogynist vaudeville dance act.

** Maxim's, established in 1893, became one of the most popular and fashionable restaurants in Paris, drawing a clientele of celebrities of the day.

74   Chapter 2

The end of the story, however, was much more "communistic" and down-to-earth. When I got home at dawn, exhausted and half-drunk as a result of the Austrian merchants' liberal generosity, I discovered that, instead of my own hat and coat, I had come away with an old man's outfit from Napoleon's times, and my pocket was lighter by the weight of a watch and wallet.

Such was the outcome of a "bourgeois ball."

In case my Galician compatriots should, God forbid, feel insulted by my account, let me assure them that at a Russian bourgeois ball you may even get your ritual fringe garment swiped.

That's why I only like "class-conscious" proletarian balls, which don't require a large budget and contemptible fashions—ladies' ball gowns and men's funeral attire. With one half-crown piece in your pocket, you're a regular prince at a proletarian ball. It will buy you a ticket, plenty of sandwiches and coffee, a tram ride there and back, and still leave you enough for a small contribution to the cause. You may even have enough left over for a chocolate or a cigarette, or a fresh pipeful of tobacco the next morning. You don't have to give your hat and coat to a guard for safekeeping; you can keep them on or just chuck them down next to the band. No one will touch them, not even a mouse. If, on leaving, you take better ones by mistake, there's no need to tear your hair out. Let the owner worry; he's sure to get in touch with you. Proletarians, thank God, are not lazy. And the women at a "class-conscious" ball, whatever clothes they throw on, are simply delicious—real dolls, let me tell you.

The ugly women at Zionist balls wear a Star of David hanging over their lowcut necklines, and each one you dance with stares at you as if demanding that you spend a shekel, whereas you would willingly give two shekels just to stop her hassling you. At proletarian balls, you can spend an hour gazing at the "fair sex" from a distance through a lorgnette, an hour writing the women love letters and little poems, and three hours dancing. You can talk about anything you want and however you like: poetically, theatrically, or prosaically. You can speak Yiddish or any other language, gesticulate and wave your hands about if you feel like it. Nobody will tell you how to behave. You can joke as much as you like, and with whomever you want. If you send a woman a couple of anonymous notes, she immediately identifies the author and attends to his heart like a doctor.

But the main thing is that you are instantly on friendly terms with everyone. If there's a group singing in chorus, you can simply join in: No need for permission. If someone shouts "tango," you can shout "waltz," and no one will tell you to shut up. If you take a liking to a lady who is deep in conversation with another man, even her fiancé, there's no need to feel intimidated. Just butt in and ask her for a dance. No one will have a go at you.

God bless the proletarian balls! Everything is so relaxed and friendly, so very *heimish*!*

Translated by Barry Smerin

YANKEV YITZKHOK CAPITANCHIK (1882–1940)

Yankev Yitzkhok Capitanchik arrived in London around 1910, an immigrant from Eastern Europe, via Buenos Aires. He was a baker by trade and reported on news in the industry. Capitanchik also wrote feuilletons for *Der idisher ekspres* in 1913, and for *Di tsayt* and the evening edition, *Ovent nayes*, from 1914 through the mid-1920s. He also produced the one-act play *Slek*, which was published as a single playscript. The melodramatic play follows a family struggling as the slack season hits at the same time as a strike in the factory where the son works.[8]

This feuilleton, "That Unforgettable Thursday," was a real event, organized by London's immigrant population and starting in the East End. Yiddish and English newspapers of the time reported on it. In true feuilleton style, Capitanchik engages with aspects that were not in the news reports, in a fascinating examination of the non-Jewish English population who witnessed the event.[9]

• •

That Unforgettable Thursday

Pictures and Scenes of the Day

Ovent nayes, 1919

What was the matter with me that morning? In the course of the long morning stretching out before me, I felt more and more closed in and just couldn't sit still. What was wrong with me? At least it isn't raining, the thought struck me. It was like being caught up in a conversation you couldn't get out of. Today

---

* *Heimish*: homey, informal, with a warm welcoming Jewish family feel.

Chapter 2

is a fast day, but I can't fast because of my weak heart—but I also can't bring myself to eat. And another shameful thought bothered me, and what do *those* people do—there—who haven't got anything to eat? The sick who don't have a doctor? Those who are sleeping in the street?

I dressed in black and went out to the funeral. Yes! It felt to me like I was going to my own family's funeral. Wherever is my aged mother? Is the ninety-year-old woman, whom I haven't heard anything from for so long, still alive? Where? And what about my sister in Brest-Litovsk? And my sister in Warsaw? And my brother in Malaryta? My mind was wracked by those agonizing thoughts.

In Fulbourne Street, there was total tumult. Stewards, there to keep order, were busily handing out placards and black armbands, and people were hurrying to the meeting halls. We were arranged in rows of four with one person at the front holding a large old trade union flag, and we marched to the People's Palace. In the other direction, a second group marched to the Pavilion Theatre.*

When we got to the meeting places, there were already thousands and thousands of Jews standing on both sides in long rows, waiting to go in to express their deeply felt pain by protesting against the Polish hooligans.

A light drizzle fell in a thin spray, as if putting the Jews to the test. Would anyone run out of the rain? But nobody even thought of moving. Everyone stood there, enveloped in deep grief, thinking of those people in that other country wandering homeless in the rain, cold, hunger, and Polish brutality. High up in the sky, clouds were spreading across the sun, but the strong wind from the west chased them away, and the sun came out in the east and lit up the Jewish multitude.

A hallowed silence reigned in the meeting halls. People were motionless, quiet, and anxious. They were somehow afraid to move freely, as if they didn't want to awaken those murdered and slaughtered in Poland. When the cantors began to sing, with the customary melody, the familiar prayer for "the holy communities who laid down their lives for the sanctification of His name," the congregation began to weep.† It reminded me of the lamentation

---

* Fulbourne Street is a small road perpendicular to the wide Whitechapel Road. Just west on Whitechapel Road is the Pavilion Theatre. The People's Palace is farther east, as the main road changes into Mile End Road.

† This line comes from the *Av harakhamim* memorial prayer for destroyed communities, written around the late eleventh century and read in synagogue on the Sabbath and on the Ninth of Av fast day.

Yiddish through the First World War 77

at the funerals of pogrom victims in Kishinev, Odessa, Zhitomir, and other towns in Eastern Europe.

Meanwhile, the whole length of Mile End Road, Whitechapel Road, and the surrounding area was packed with Jews and the fluttering banners of all the Jewish organizations. At 1 p.m., like a storm wind sways the sheaves of corn in a field, the enormous mass of people stirred, and the march moved off. No music was played; the only accompaniment were bitter groans and deep sighs of anger and fury.

On Commercial Street, from Whitechapel Road to the Lane, all the shops were shut, like on Yom Kippur, and you heard lamenting, wailing, and heartrending cries.

In Old Street a non-Jewish coachman sat on his empty wagon and laughingly insulted the procession, until a Jewish ex-serviceman beat the laughter out of him.

In Clerkenwell the procession was loudly welcomed by the onlooking crowds, and an animated discussion broke out among the non-Jews about people and humanity and whether the British government could stop the wild atrocities of the Polish thugs.‡

In Oxford Street the compelling spectacle of the demonstration reached its peak: elderly Jewish men with long, gray beards and grief in their tired faces; small children from religion schools with their teachers; and rabbis and trade unionists. Every single person marched with one feeling to the rhythm of a pounding heart, resolute in their strength and determination not to be trampled on by their enemies any longer. The aura of hope that rose from the demonstrators attracted the attention of the wealthy West End.

Clerks positioned themselves at the doors of the rich non-Jewish businesses. Wealthy, well-dressed ladies adjusted their spectacles on their noses to read the inscriptions on the banners, and girls eyed the Jewish soldiers. The Jewish inhabitants of the West End, who hadn't been able to join the demonstration, came to pay their due. At Oxford Circus the sea of people became so crowded, it felt like the whole of West London was pushing and shoving to pay their last respects to the martyrs murdered by the Russkies.

---

‡ These locales and those mentioned in subsequent paragraphs are on the route walking west from the East End: Old Street and Clerkenwell are in East Central London; Oxford Street, Oxford Circus, and Queens Hall are in the West End of London; Hyde Park is west of Central London.

In Hyde Park the regular visitors wondered at the huge stream of Jews flowing through in the middle of a Thursday so unexpectedly. They ran toward it from all sides, asking, "What's going on?" And they found out from the speakers.

In Queens Hall, London's Jewish leaders gathered on the stage. And when the cantor began singing the prayer for the dead, "God Full of Mercy," even the Rothschilds wept. Something touched their Jewish hearts, and they felt the pain of their race and the fragility of the ground under their feet.*

"Rothschild is crying" swept like a breeze through the massive crowd that thronged the hall, and they felt something akin to relief: It had touched the hearts of the wealthy Jewish leaders; and the legendary Rothschilds, who "redeem" all Jews from Christian hands, came into their thoughts, and a murmur swept through them like wind, that if Rothschild weeps, then the Jews will be redeemed—redemption is at hand.

Translated by Vivi Lachs

BEN-A SOCHACHEWSKY (1889–1958)

"Ben-A Sochachewsky," sketch by Maurice Sochachewsky, *Di idishe shtime* (June 26, 1953). Courtesy of Dave Skye Sochachewsky. From the British Library collection.

Ben-A (Yehiel Meir) Sochachewsky was born in Lodz, Poland. As a youth he contributed poems to Polish and Yiddish newspapers and was employed by a Viennese journal. He arrived in London just before the First World War and worked as a journalist and editor for the London Yiddish press under the name Ben-A Sochachewsky. He worked as a journalist with *Di tsayt* until it folded in 1950, yet he also found time to edit two short-lived journals: the 1925 religious monthly *Der folks veg* (The People's Path) and the 1932 weekly humorous journal *S'hitl* (The Cap). In 1951 he founded the weekly *Di idishe shtime*, where he worked until his death.

---

* The *El malei rachamim* prayer for the dead.

Yiddish through the First World War   79

Sochachewsky was a passionate advocate for the Yiddish language. He was a Yiddish poet and author of feuilletons, Hasidic tales, song lyrics, and fiction, which were published in various London Yiddish newspapers and journals. His novel of immigration to Whitechapel in *Di mishpokhe lasker* (The Lasker Family) was serialized in *Di tsayt* in 1949.

In common with many other Yiddish writers, he wrote about the East End, but he lived in Hendon, in North West London. One of his sons was the artist Maurice Sochachewsky, whose work is featured in this volume.[10]

The Last Resort

A Picture of Whitechapel Jewish Life

Di tsayt, 1919

The large crowd of men, women, and children who had gathered in a poor, dirty backstreet in Whitechapel at the scene of an unspeakable calamity were shouting and waving their fists at a young woman, one of those "Russian" Jews, who looked down into the street in alarm mingled with sadness and contempt, waiting impatiently for the miserable spectacle to come to an end.

The crowd directed most of its fury at the driver sitting quietly on the carriage the missionaries had sent to fetch the four children of an unfortunate young mother who, unable to bear their misery and suffering any longer, had decided to give them away rather than watch them starve to death.

The crowd's patience was close to bursting point. Any minute now the carriage would be overturned and smashed to pieces, and hundreds of fists would pummel the head of the impudent little missionary, who had already found it necessary to call a policeman so as to be able to take charge of the four little Jewish children, the oldest of whom, a girl, was no more than nine years of age.

The woman at the open window was getting more sure of herself and bolder by the minute. Again and again she called to the missionary in a high-pitched, unnatural voice, demanding to know why he didn't ask the policeman to drive away the crowd blocking the entrance to the building, so that she could bring the children, who were dressed and ready to go, down to the street.

By now the mother was so angry and agitated that no one listened to the policeman's requests to clear the entrance to the building. On the contrary, they appealed to his sense of justice, demanding that he himself declare whether such a crime—taking innocent Jewish children to the mission home and forcing them to convert—could be allowed to take place.

Members of the crowd shouted that they were willing to take one of the children themselves, to prevent the poor souls falling into the missionaries' hands.

Suddenly the crowd's attention was caught by a young man, a well-known relief fund worker, who came running up, out of breath, hot and bothered, begging the crowd to clear the entrance to the building for him and to stay as calm and peaceful as possible. The young man was known to the crowd, which did as he asked and made way for him, following him with grateful looks as he entered the building. The relief fund worker reemerged a few minutes later and, informing the crowd that he was going to the Jewish Board of Guardians, he rushed off.

It wasn't long before the young man was back again. He explained the situation to the crowd and assigned the four poor children to persons among them who agreed to take the children home for a few days while the Jewish authorities decided what should be done with them.

Soon afterward the missionaries' carriage moved off. The crowd made way for it and accompanied it with bitter curses until it left the backstreet and disappeared into the noisy Whitechapel hubbub.

The relief fund worker went back up to the mother's little room. Now, for the first time, he saw for himself the dreadful poverty oozing from the damp, dirty walls. In the middle of the room stood a rickety little bed without any bedclothes, covered in rags. A little table, a chair, and two or three crates made up the rest of the furniture, and the dirty walls were decorated with a couple of old, scuffed photographs. Two children sat huddled together in a corner, one aged two and the other three. Half-naked, ragged, and hungry, they stared from their corner in terror, as if afraid of the stranger who couldn't take his eyes off them. The children's mother, calm and indifferent, sat by the open window, through which the noise and bustle of the street could still be heard. From time to time a cynical smile played on her pale, beautiful, calm young face.

The relief fund worker stood silently in the room for a long time, looking back and forth at the children and their mother, as if something was plaguing him. He didn't know whether to take pity on the woman or lecture her on Jewish responsibility and proper Jewish behavior, as was always the case whenever misfortune placed him in such a situation. Either from habit or simply to get everything over and done with, he began talking mechanically, asking her how she had reached the dreadful decision to have her own children converted.

The woman heard him out calmly, then she rose to her feet and said coldly: "Yes, indeed. What should I have done? Watch them starve to death?"

She went on to explain the reasons why she had acted as she did. Walking with outstretched hands, weeping, begging, and ringing doorbells to ask for help had become too much for her, and she had been unable to go on. And the few shillings a week she got from one fund or another hadn't even been enough for the bare necessities. That was why she had decided to give the four children to the missionaries—the only people prepared to fulfil her wish and take the children. And she would anyway have to manage by herself with the two younger ones somehow or other.

The relief fund worker made another objection. The unfortunate woman laughed bitterly and gave him a poisonous, cynical look. Then, suddenly, she began savagely cursing her husband, who had run away to Russia and was the cause of all her troubles and suffering. "Ran away to save himself!" she shouted. "And abandoned me, pregnant and with five little children."

The young man was unable to remain in the room any longer. Bewildered and confused, he left the building. The street was calm and peaceful, as if nothing at all had happened. He walked away, sunk in troubled thoughts. With grief and anger he thought of the rich, well-fed Jewish population in London and throughout England, who behaved with such indifference and lack of sympathy toward the suffering poor—indifference that drove no few "Russian" women to do the worst.

The relief fund worker's eyes burned from the passionate anger inside him, and he felt a tear run down his cheek.

Translated by Barry Smerin

3
INTERWAR YIDDISH CULTURE

1920–39

After the First World War, the East End continued to host a thriving immigrant community. There were Yiddish plays nightly at the Pavilion Theatre and two daily Yiddish newspapers, *Di tsayt* and *Di post*. There was still a plethora of immigrant organizations and societies, including synagogues, friendly societies, and cultural and political organizations from different ideological perspectives. The Workers' Circle still ran lectures, events, and concerts in Yiddish. However, the demography of Jewish London was changing in terms of its inhabitants' first language, leadership of the Anglo-Jewish community, and areas of habitation.

The children of immigrants had attended English or Anglo-Jewish schools and socialized in Jewish youth clubs where English was the functioning language. They may have been bilingual, having spoken Yiddish at home with their parents, but they were less likely to be literate in Yiddish, and the Yiddish press was becoming the preserve of an older generation. The immigrants' grandchildren were already growing up in a totally English environment.[1]

The communal leadership of the established Anglo-Jewish community was changing as many more Jews with immigrant backgrounds were taking on prominent roles. Institutions that had been established during the nineteenth century by the Jewish upper middle class and aristocracy, such as the United Synagogue, the Board of Deputies of British Jews, and the Jewish Board of Guardians, became dominated by Jews who had immigrated in the 1880s and their descendants. Although many of those in positions of leadership knew Yiddish, the business of the organizations was conducted in English.[2]

Movement out of the East End increased rapidly during the 1920s and 1930s. Upwardly mobile immigrants and their children moved to the suburbs of London, developing the Jewish communities in East London's Ilford and Gants Hill, North London's Stoke Newington and Stamford Hill, and North West London's Cricklewood and Golders Green. Those remaining in the East End were mostly an older generation of working-class immigrant tailors, cabinetmakers, and market-stall holders who still spoke Yiddish.[3] Yet the East End remained a part of ex-Eastenders lives, and they regularly returned to visit family, buy food in the daily Jewish market ("the Lane"), and attend the Yiddish theatre.

The worldwide depression of the 1930s affected London less than other areas of the country, but the East End tailoring trade was affected by the slump in the textile industry, which produced significant unemployment among East End Jews. The gap in income between the Jews struggling in the East End and those upwardly mobile Jews who had moved away was apparent.[4] Upward mobility created a growing distance between the middle-class immigrants who had left the East End and the workers who remained. So, despite greater participation of Jews with immigrant backgrounds, the Anglo-Jewish institutions still did not speak for the whole working-class East End Jewish community.

As Jews became more integrated into British society and British organizations, anti-Jewish discrimination increased.[5] In 1933 the British Union of Fascists (BUF), headed by Oswald Mosley, targeted the East End with street meetings, shouting antisemitic chants and holding offensive placards. Fascist activity led to clashes with Jewish workers and Jewish and non-Jewish communists defending the East End Jews. Some of the political organization occurred in Circle House, the Workers' Circle's headquarters in Great Alie Street. A huge demonstration of Jews in 1936, in an action mythologized as the "Battle of Cable Street," stopped the BUF from marching through the East End. The antifascist demonstrators used the slogan "They Shall Not Pass."[6]

In 1938 Avrom Nokhem Stencl established his Literary Sabbath Afternoons (later called the Friends of Yiddish) in a hall in the East End. These weekly meetings where writers would read their material often attracted more than a hundred attendees. All of the London Yiddish writers from this period attended. The jeweler Mosheh Oved often supported the gatherings financially, new writing was encouraged, and there was an ongoing stream of guest speakers visiting from Eastern Europe and America.[7]

Local Yiddish writers of the twenties and thirties continued to engage with the immigrant community's evolution in the feuilleton columns of the Yiddish press. From 1922, Katie Brown's first regular writing column focused on the changing roles of men and women. Esther Kreitman and Lisky told troubling tales of individuals struggling against poverty, abuse, and unhappiness. Asher Beilin's "A Jew Takes a Pleasure Trip" and Arye Myer Kaizer's "The Hanukkah Miracle on London Bridge" both created comedy around those who leave and those who stay in the East End. Yiddish newspaper editors seemed to take a leaf out of the Yiddish theatre stylebook in interspersing serious stories with belly-laugh comedy.[8]

KATIE BROWN (1889–1955)

Katie Brown, 1930. Courtesy of the Mazower private collection.

Katie Brown was born Gitl Bakon in Ulyanov, Western Galicia (today Ulanów, Poland). She moved to London with her family at the age of twelve, completing her schooling and becoming a seamstress. She began writing for the Yiddish press in the early 1920s with a satirical women's column in *Der familyen fraynd* titled *In froyen kenigraykh* (In the Women's Kingdom), which ran from 1922 to 1926. In the early 1930s she wrote a weekly women's page in *Di post*.

Brown moved on to writing humorous urban feuilletons in the 1930s, becoming a household name; she was dubbed Whitechapel's Yiddish "best seller." Brown was involved with the local Yiddish theatre, writing plays and songs and also acting. Her home became a regular meeting place for actors and theatre writers, both professional and amateur. She was an active member of the *Arbeter ring* (Workers' Circle), and she edited the organization's journal of

86   Chapter 3

the same name during the 1940s. After the war Brown republished many of her earlier feuilletons in *Di tsayt*, lightly editing them to fit their new context.[9] Her stories were published in two anthologies: *Lakht oyb ir vilt* (Laugh If You Want To) in 1944 and *Alts in eynem!* (Everything Together) in 1951. Translations of her stories have appeared in two collections.[10]

In the Women's Kingdom

Der familyen fraynd, 1922–23

What follows is a slightly abridged translation of three weeks of the regular column "In the Women's Kingdom" in the weekly newspaper *Der familyen fraynd*. The column displays Brown's trademark tongue-in-cheek humor, where letters to and responses from the agony aunt, *A poshete yidene* (an ordinary Jewess), are all penned by her. Here Brown appears as herself, her husband, her readers, and *A poshete yidene*.

On November 17, 1922, the column included a deliberately provocative article titled "How to Keep Your Husband at Home," which suggested that it was in men's nature to escape the house on long winter evenings to play cards rather than be bored and harangued at home by their wives. Women, *A poshete yidene* claimed, are to blame for this situation because they ignore their tired working husbands' needs and criticize them. She concludes: "So, it is the duty of every wife to ensure that when her husband comes home, the food is ready, the house is clean, she and the children are nicely dressed and washed and always in a cheerful mood. In this way the home will be so precious and loved by the husband that there won't be any trouble for anyone."

—Vivi Lachs

December 8, 1922—A Good Advocate

Worthy Mister Editor of *Der fraynd*,

I am writing in response to the article of the 17th November. I would like to know what sort of women the writer is describing, and to ask him or her whether the strategies suggested would indeed keep a husband at home. And whether it is necessary for a woman to do these things. If it refers to women in general, it is illogical.

There are two sorts of women—wives of businessmen and wives of workers. A woman living a well-off lifestyle doesn't have to do anything to keep her husband at home. When he comes home from his business, everything is in good order: the wife well dressed, the children happy, quiet, and looked after (by the maid and the nanny). After supper he usually goes with his wife to the theatre, to socialize, or they have people over. She doesn't need to stop him playing cards because she also enjoys a card game from time to time.

But, for the wives of workers, is it possible for her to organize everything to be done before her husband comes home from work? Let me explain her situation. Life is so limited, the income is so small, and everyone lives in terribly crowded conditions. Families have four, five, or even six children. The wife has to be the cook, washerwoman, children's teacher, and everything. The whole yoke of household chores falls on her alone, and often she has to help bring in an income as well. Can you imagine how unhappy the life of such a woman is? Now you tell her, if she wants to keep her husband from leaving the house, everything has to be in tip-top shape before he comes home, and be ready with a smile. How extraordinarily illogical!

Why don't men put themselves in the position of their wives for one moment? It would be better to tell the husband that if he comes home from work and everything is not neat and tidy, he shouldn't get angry and run out of the house. He should give a fleeting thought for what his wife has done through the day: how many imaginative ideas she's had to think up to entertain the children and the effort she makes to get by on the wages that he earns. And then he'll see that he cannot blame his wife. Then he'll have sympathy for her and help in the house in any way he can, and that is what can bring the peaceful home. Then the wife will deal with the struggle to survive with love. She'll see her husband as a true friend who understands her, helps her, and doesn't see her as his slave who damages her health by doing more than her strength allows out of fear. The wife would then sympathize with her husband, care for, love, and look after him when he is unemployed (which happens often) because he would deserve it.

Katie Brown
Chicksand Street East

Mrs. Katie Brown is somewhat right but not totally.

There is no doubt that many men are good-for-nothings. But it is exactly the same with us women. Katie Brown mentions that women

88   Chapter 3

must be the cook and washerwoman, etc., but you mustn't forget that the husband also has lots to cope with in the workshop.

Imagine, dear sister, under what conditions your husband works: fear of the workshop master, the vexation when the work doesn't go as it should, and thousands of other little things that make him anxious.

It is true that we women have a lot to cope with at home, but we are not reliant on a master who can threaten us with the sack. If there is no money, the husband feels it much more than the wife because he is responsible for providing for the family. The woman's work is solely housework, and her duty is to make the home a slice of paradise. Instead, however, many of our sisters go out gossiping when time would be better spent on housework. I'm not talking about men who don't care for their wives and treat them as slaves. They're not worth wasting your breath on.

I heartily thank my friend Katie Brown who wrote to me. It shows that she is interested in what she reads and that she is a good advocate for our sex.

Poshete yidene

December 22, 1922—Sorrow of a Husband

Just as Katie Brown bemoans the lot of women, here Haiml bemoans the lot of men. It seems like it is a never-ending story. Both men and women complain about each other, which is not very pleasant.

The editor

A WIFE, A DRAMATIST

Highly esteemed *Poshete yidene*,

I hope that you will be so good and let me write a little about my troubles.

Having read the letter by KB and your answer, I was so incensed that I had to write to you. But before I go further, I will just remark to Madame Brown that there are more than two types of women. The third is my wife. If Mrs. Brown knew my wife or that sort of wife, I am sure that she would save ink and paper, and in particular, the agitation.

Now listen: I am a milkman. That means I am up at five o'clock every morning. I make myself a drink, and if my wife is awake, I take her a drink in bed. Then I go off with my milk wagon until around 11. Hungry, tired, and very thirsty, I come home.

But as I open the door, I hear my wife's voice (from the bedroom):

"I'm so parched I'm choking." I know the remedy, a cuppa tea. After that I make myself something to eat. Then I take the milk cart and go off again until four or five o'clock. I come home hungry and tired like you always do after a day's work.

True, I find the house tidied and neat, the stove is warm, but the table is full of books: plays by Gordin and Shomer, joke books and other stuff, because my wife is a bit of a writer.* I sit down, fed up with my life. Sometimes she asks me a question:

"You must be hungry?"

"Yes," I answer.

"Be so good," she says to me, "take your food. It's on the stove."

So I go and get my food, but then where do I put the plate because the table is full of papers?

"What can I do," she says, half whining. "I've been sitting here since three o'clock and can't find the right name for my main character. Maybe you've got an idea? The husband is called Fayvl Yatsek, and I want her name to be something gripping." (I will here mention that my wife is writing a play that she says will break theatre records.) I complain to her:

"What does your play matter to me when I haven't got anywhere to put my plate of food down?"

I finish eating where I am and put the plate down to be washed. Then I sit totally silent, because I'm not allowed to speak while my wife is writing. I sit contemplating my dreadful problems, talking only to myself.

Oh, Mrs. Brown, what should a husband like me do? Sitting around at home is hell. Going out to grab a game of sixty-six is a sin.† It could mean I don't come home at all. And we husbands are not yet

---

* Jacob Gordin (1853–1909) was a Yiddish playwright of serious, realistic drama. He is pitted here against Shomer, the pen name of Nahum Meïr Schaikewitz (1849–1905), who wrote plays for the popular Yiddish theatre.

† Sixty-six was a popular card game that often included gambling.

so barbaric to leave our wives and get out of the house because every husband wants to be sure that his wife will have the best of him.

So be well, *Poshete yidene*. Please send my regards to Mrs. Brown, and I hope God helps her to have a generous heart toward men.

Yours with care,
Haiml

Being a woman myself, I have full sympathy with Mr. Haiml, with the troubles he endures with his dramatist wife—or should I call her a tragic wife. It is very sad for a husband to live such an active working life and when he comes home not be met with a loving wife who has everything prepared for him, which can compensate for his physical suffering.

I must, however, say to Mr. Haiml that he is an exception! Not everyone has such a wife who, rather than providing her husband with every comfort she can, gives herself over to writing plays. No, not all wives are like this, and not every husband is a milkman.

So, if your wife reads this newspaper, we would like to say to her that a husband's patience can explode. He may put up with it now, but if it's a situation that he can get himself out of, he won't stay suffering in it for long. So, it would be better if Mrs. Haiml dedicated herself to looking after her husband and throw out the playwriting idea, because later may be too late. I know a woman who sometimes deludes herself that she is an intelligent actress; she sometimes leaves her husband to go performing in the provinces. In the end it nearly came to divorce.

I therefore advise Mrs. Haiml that she should better devote herself to her husband rather than her playwriting because the dramas she writes could decline into tragedy. And you, Mr. Haiml, I order you to talk things over with your wife in a quiet and calm manner to show her that she is not behaving properly. If she is writing a play, she must be an intelligent woman, so she will certainly understand and comprehend the great injustice she has done to you.

Poshete yidene

Interwar Yiddish Culture

January 5, 1923—Ice Cream and Pickles

Dear *Poshete yidene*,

Your answer to Katie Brown is utterly insufferable. I admit that men, whether businessmen or workers, have a lot to put up with and many unpleasant things to do. But you must not forget, my dear *Poshete yidene*, that women don't demand that men get their faces made up, or that they always have a smiling face, or that they are always comforting when they hear of their wife's pain and dilemmas.

The sad thing is that men have made a women's question just as nations have made a Jewish question. When you think hard about the two questions, you see that they both stand on the same situation, both questions come out of jealousy. But that has nothing to do with us women; what do we know about politics? We only need to know how to make our husbands happy. Oh, how sad that is!

I'm not talking about ignorant women; they are only worth pitying. They don't understand anything about life. I am in agreement with you, *Poshete yidene*, when you slander women readers for gossiping. But we can't blame these women, because there are men who love gossiping, and with men it is so entrenched they don't even know they're doing it because it's such an everyday act. And so, my dear *Poshete yidene*, just as you have taken the energy to teach women how they should behave, might it not be better to start teaching the men?

And now, Mr. Haiml, I read your heartfelt letter to the *Poshete yidene*, and I am also a woman and, as you know, we all have soft hearts, and it made my heart grieve for a milkman who has a writer as a wife and who has the audacity to write dramas! Yes, it is sad, very sad! But not for you, my dear Mr. Haiml. The saddest thing is for the wife whose husband doesn't understand her or sympathize with her. Do you not know, Mr. Haiml, that not everyone is blessed with the ability to write?

Believe me, I myself am no foolish woman, but I wouldn't even be able to write a sketch, and if your wife feels she can write, do you know what it means to her? It is her life. Do you know how many men would go without a meal and spend those few pennies to buy paper to write down their feelings? No, Mr. Haiml, you don't understand that, and instead of taking the greatest care of your wife, you just complain that you just want a bit of room on the table to eat.

How can you compare milk with drama? It is like pickles and ice cream. You go off, Mr. Haiml, with your milk and don't demand from your wife that she should be just like everyone else.

Take care,
Nelly Bitterheart.

My dear Nelly, it seems to me that you have a very bitter heart concerning men. You probably have a very unhappy life. It is clear that your husband is a scoundrel and a rogue who is not decent or caring of his own wife; there are such men, and your husband is clearly one of those. Some men insult and curse their wives and sometimes even hit them as well! If you have such a husband, it is indeed very sad! But I can't get away from the fact that very often it is us women who are guilty in this. For example, I know a woman whose husband puts her down a lot and treats her like dirt, although she pampers him and defends him, and when he gives her one warm word, she is prepared to go "through fire and water" for him. So, in all their arguments, she herself is guilty. It is our female psychology.

It is also right that not every person has the divine feeling and talent to write plays and sketches and stories. But women, however talented they are, however skilled they are, must not forget that she needs to attend to her husband, her children, and keep the house, because that is the silent agreement between husband and wife.

There is no complete perfection in the world. Neither men nor women are so perfect that there will be no argument between husbands and wives. It lies, however, in the women's strength to avoid unpleasantness, and to lighten the husband's heavy responsibilities whether he is a worker or does business. I'm not talking about the very wealthy. I'm also not talking about the really merciless scoundrels. When I talk of husband and wife, I mean our sort of people, the regular working-class person who is no scoundrel in any way: neither husband nor wife. So I think the best thing is that both husband and wife should stop embittering each other's lives.

And you, dear Nelly, letting out your bitter heart by writing. You have my full sympathy.

Poshete yidene

Translated by Vivi Lachs

Interwar Yiddish Culture   93

The Cantor's a Presser!

Di post, 1932 (version from Loshn un lebn, 1947)

Shloyme the Cantor is a first-class presser. For a piece of his handiwork, you should kiss his every finger, because, as his close friends say, a garment pressed by Shloyme is fit to put on display in the shop window. Even his enemies have to admit that there's not another presser like Shloyme the Cantor in the whole of England. Never mind that he can't make a living and has to go without food one day a week; he's still a good craftsman.

"In London," Shloyme says, "you have to be a bungler, because no one here appreciates good work, and no one wants to pay for it." And he goes on to prove his point: "Take, for example," he says, "a good synagogue cantor. There's no place for him here. And if, with God's help, he does get an opportunity to lead the Sabbath prayers on one occasion (as a test, of course), the synagogue will be full of opinionated experts who will decide the poor man's fate. The cantor gets going and does his best to please the congregation. He stands at the pulpit sweating, God help him, and when he's finished and hopes to get the job, one of the so-called experts says he sings too high and another that he sings too low because he doesn't have the sort of voice a cantor should have. A third expert says he lacks 'coloratura,' meaning that he doesn't embellish his singing with enough trills and vibrato. Yet another, an old man who fell asleep during the service, says he doesn't know any Hebrew. In the end, the candidate is told to try again the next Sabbath.

"In my shtetl," Shloyme the presser continues, "I was considered the best cantor. The most distinguished residents paid me tribute. My singing was to their taste. Jews from the whole surrounding area attended the synagogue where I was employed. Even on an ordinary Sabbath so many people came to hear me that the place was jam-packed. Not to mention festivals and High Holy Days. More than one woman swooned when I sang Kol Nidre, and if it hadn't been for the wretched war, I would surely have lived there, well respected, for the rest of my life.* When people started fleeing from the shtetls back home, some of my fellow countrymen who were living in England brought me here, and thanks to them I and my family survived.

"They took me into their synagogue right away, and I thought I was already sure of making a living. But, as the saying goes, 'Man plans, and God laughs.' In the course of the many years they had lived here, my

---

* Kol Nidre: prayer on the eve of the fast day of Yom Kippur, the Day of Atonement.

94 Chapter 3

countrymen had become assimilated. On an ordinary Sabbath they came to the synagogue dressed to the nines, in top hat and tails, and wore expensive prayer shawls of the finest silk. Their children were taught the prayers in English, and when the Jewish New Year and the Day of Atonement came round, the synagogue was full of women and girls who came for the memorial service, then went home, and returned only to hear the final shofar blown. When I looked around me, I felt sick at heart. I'd never seen anything like it.

"There I stood at the pulpit, a cantor from the old country, wrapped in my ordinary woolen prayer shawl with a yarmulke on my head, chanting the prayers in the traditional way. You can imagine the contrast. In short, I saw that the match wasn't right, and I resigned from the job. They accepted my resignation gladly and assigned me a small wage until I should find another position. I subsequently tried to find another post in various small synagogues, but they too were full of 'experts' who immediately felt that I wasn't suitable for them. The end result was that I, a good, traditional prayer leader, had to learn a trade to keep my wife and children from starving. Had I been one of those cantors who treat the cantorial art as a business, who grow a little beard for the New Year and shave it off immediately after the Day of Atonement, I would certainly have got a post, if only for the High Holy Days. But since I'm not that type, I lost even that small possibility, and that was the end of it.

"Now let me tell you," Shloyme continued with a smile, "what happened to me last year. Shortly before the High Holy Days, an acquaintance came and offered me a business deal. He wanted to hire a hall, turn it into a synagogue—just for the New Year and the Day of Atonement—and have me as the cantor. He was sure we would make a lot of money out of it. To be honest, I didn't much like the plan, but being as poor as I was, I decided to accept his proposal. He went straight off and hired a fine big hall in the East End, and began to make all the preparations, and in the meantime I practiced singing the High Holy Day prayers. I decided not to let anyone know about the scheme because, to tell the truth, I felt a bit ashamed to tell people who knew me and knew how I feel about religion.

"But later, when I went for a walk in Whitechapel, I felt quite faint. There were large posters on the walls with my picture, announcing that the world-famous cantor would be leading the service with a large choir. I felt deeply ashamed of the fraud regarding my reputation. I am indeed a good cantor, but not world-famous, and I knew nothing about a choir.

"I went straight to my acquaintance's place and cursed him for his audacity. 'How in God's name,' I protested, 'can you tell such a lie?' He burst out laughing and called me an idiot who knew nothing about business. Then he told me he had already sold a large number of tickets and showed me a packet of banknotes he had received in payment.

"Well, I realized that my protests were in vain, and I would have to go through with it.

"A week before the High Holy Days, he brought me the choir, so that I could rehearse with them.

"I looked at my choirboys and felt sick at heart. A bunch of neglected brats with torn shoes, stained shirts, dirty faces, and runny noses. And with that gang, I, Shloyme the Cantor, was supposed to act as the voice of the community and get God to grant the congregation a good year.

"But whichever way I looked at it, there was no way out. I just had to get on with it. So I stood them all in place and started teaching them the prayers. I soon realized that my efforts were in vain. They neither listened to me nor were even able to repeat a Hebrew word. And their voices were no good for singing either. Some of them had brought fish and chips with them for their supper, and they tucked into it while I was teaching them.

"I kept them toiling at it for several days and nights, like pharaoh with the Jews in Egypt, but it was no use. They started blaming each other and ended up fighting. The uproar rose to high heaven, and I could hardly manage to separate them. And when the neighbors came running to see what all the noise was about, I threw the whole lot out into the street. But I still wasn't free of them. They started banging on the door, demanding that I pay them for the few days' work. They gave me a great deal of trouble until I finally managed to get rid of them. When my acquaintance came the following day to find out what had been going on, I spat in his face and on the whole business. No more cantor, no more choirboys, no more anything. Finished. The poor chap had to return the money for the tickets and lost the deposit for the hall. But I was out of it with a clear conscience.

"Realizing that here in London I would gain no benefit or enjoyment from my skill as a cantor, I decided to become a presser. Better a lucky workman, I thought, than an unlucky cantor.

"Now my fellow countrymen make fun of me. Shloyme the Cantor, they say, is a good presser. But who cares? I earn my daily bread honestly.

"And when I feel the urge, from time to time, to lead a prayer service, I get together a quorum of ten Jews on an ordinary Sabbath and chant the

96   Chapter 3

familiar Jewish prayers with such passion that they thrill me through and through. And since no one has to pay for it, I receive many congratulations on my singing after the service, and everyone goes home happy. But when the High Holy Days come round, I just can't sit still. My heart is pounding, I feel drawn to the pulpit. I long to sing *Kol Nidre*, pray the additional service, chant *Unetanneh Tokef*, the central prayer of the Day of Atonement, and all the other holy prayers, just as I used to in the old home country. But there's nothing to be done. Since there's no chance of getting an assignment in any kind of synagogue, I go to pray among pious Jews in a small prayer house and beg God to grant my prayers for the New Year and help me achieve my heart's desire. And I pray that all Jews be granted a good year, that there should be no more sorrow in the world, and that everyone be inscribed in the Book of Life. Amen."

Translated by Barry Smerin

BAL REKIDE

The name Bal Rekide is a pseudonym meaning "dancer." Between 1914 and 1918, Bal Rekide wrote a number of feuilletons for *Ovent nayes*, the evening paper of *Di tsayt*. Some are set in a domestic family home and others concern situations between courting couples. These early feuilletons seem to have been written by a young hand, in contrast to the 1924 Bal Rekide sketch translated here.

●●

A Torah Scroll Procession in Whitechapel

Di tsayt, 1924

That late afternoon was bright and sunny. The wide pavements of Whitechapel Road were packed with promenading people. Here and there you could hear happy laughter from Jewish couples.

Being Sunday, people were dressed in their holiday best. Some hurried to the Whitechapel Art Gallery, heading for the Jewish National Fund bazaar, which was about to close. Others streamed by in groups going to Aldgate and from there to the West End.

Even the clanking of the trams and the horns blaring from the buses and cars gave the impression of a holiday. They seemed to be moving along more leisurely, basking in the golden sunlight.

Interwar Yiddish Culture 97

The same Whitechapel that on the Jewish Sabbath is filled with the clamor and racket of the market now seemed peaceful, and the chatter of people passing by filled the air with other sounds.

Suddenly, from Brick Lane across the road from the Whitechapel church, a dense mass of people appeared, walking in the middle of the street. The passersby stopped, curious to see what was happening.

It was a Jewish celebration, a parade with a Torah scroll. A few policemen were walking at the front, keeping order, and right behind them came klezmer musicians playing a merry tune on a variety of instruments. Because of the din from the trams, the melody was subdued and so muffled by the noise that people could barely make it out.

The musicians' hats were askew, their faces flushed, and they reminded me of a local wedding in a shtetl in Poland, Russia, or Romania, where the Polish village lads used to play along with the Jewish bands.

There was no time to think about that, because immediately after them came a line of Jewish women bearing large lighted torches, their faces looking piously to heaven. They were basking in the honor of taking part in a celebration of a new Torah scroll, which a scribe had written for their synagogue.

Above the heads of the festive crowd, a wedding canopy had been erected, and under it walked the celebrant, the rabbi of the synagogue, the wardens, and other important members of the synagogue board. Their faces glowed with an inner light, and the Torah scroll being carried under the wedding canopy gleamed in a fine mantle with a silver chain hanging around it.

From Brick Lane, the Torah scroll procession moved straight through Whitechapel, and the Christian passersby stopped and stared in surprise at the remarkable celebration. Some shrugged their shoulders, some smiled, and some watched intently. The trams and cars stopped, and their passengers looked out of the windows with curiosity, not knowing what was actually going on.

Here and there, groups of Jewish spectators stood watching and commenting on the procession. Some said it was a desecration of God's name to parade our most sacred object in front of strangers. Others were keen to show that the English were a nation tolerant of other religions, were not prejudiced, and were respectful of such a procession.

"Do you remember?" said one man, "how careful we had to be with the wine, taking it home on a Friday for Kiddush?* The bottle had to be covered

---

* Kiddush is the name of the blessing made over wine at meals on the Sabbath.

so that a non-Jewish eye wouldn't see it, so that we'd be able to use it for the blessing. And now not only do we have a Jewish market here on the Sabbath, but we even carry about a Torah scroll in the street, plain as anything, to be seen by strangers."

"No, it's quite the opposite," another man interjected. "We've got nothing to be ashamed of. On the contrary, let people see how, even in London, Jews are still bound to the Torah. And in any case, the English aren't just tolerant, they're almost like a bible nation themselves."

By now the whole Torah scroll parade had emerged from Brick Lane and was proceeding along Whitechapel Road. From a distance it looked as if the wedding canopy was oddly bent, doubled over by the curious gaze of strangers. And only its gold-spun silk edges twinkled under the rays of the late Sunday afternoon spring sunshine.

The men and women involved in the celebration of the Torah weren't aware of anything happening around them. Joy shone from their pious eyes as they marched like proud parents at the wedding of their oldest son or daughter.

An elderly man was walking next to me, a childlike smile on his wrinkled face. Although we didn't know each other, he shook my hand and with a familial casualness asked:

"So, how do you like this?"

I replied that it was very interesting.

"Ha ha ha," the old man laughed. "You see, and people say that the Jews in the East End are no longer as religious as their parents in the old country. Wherever a Jew lives, he remains a Jew and has Torah scrolls written. This is a wonderful thing, a good deed that will buy you eternal life in the world to come."

When the demonstration was over, I remembered the old man's words, and I too began to marvel at the remarkable quality of Jewish life. The same Whitechapel that has a large Jewish market on the Sabbath, as on an ordinary weekday, had just witnessed a parade, complete with musicians and a wedding canopy, for a new Torah scroll for a Jewish synagogue.

Such are the great contradictions of Jewish life in exile, and even the creasing and bending of the wedding canopy over the Torah scroll are like symbols of Jewish life, a singular life of its own, even in foreign lands, in foreign cities and in foreign streets.

Translated by Vivi Lachs

ASHER BEILIN (1881–1948)

Asher Beilin, Wikimedia Commons, unknown date (https://commons.wikimedia.org/wiki/File:Asher_Beilin.JPG). Accessed July 28, 2024.

Asher Beilin was born in Kiev, Ukraine, and studied in Bern and Freiburg. He worked as Sholem Aleichem's private secretary from 1901 to 1905 before moving to London in 1906. Beilin published in Hebrew-language journals but was prolific as a Yiddish journalist, writer, and playwright. He worked for *Der idisher zhurnal* and *Der idisher ekspres* and wrote for the supplement *Di idishe velt*. He published books with various London publishing houses, including Narodiczky Press (1907), Progress Farlag (1911), and Der idisher Ekspres (1918). He was a friend of Yosef Haim Brenner, whom he wrote about in Hebrew.

In 1917 his four-act play *Pasportn* (Passports) was produced at the Pavilion Theatre in Whitechapel. Between 1923 and 1932, he wrote a regular topical and humorous feuilleton on London Jewish life for *Di tsayt* using the pseudonym An'eygener (One of Us / A Relative). He took part in a "Living Newspaper" event in 1930 along with Katie Brown and Arye Myer Kaizer. Stencl considered these three feuilletonists London's top trio of comic writers.

From 1920 to 1933 Beilin worked for the Jewish National Fund. He settled in Jerusalem in 1933.[11]

• •

My Neighbor

A Right Misery-Guts—A Weekend in Jerusalem—A Blessing or a Curse?

Di tsayt, 1927

God Almighty has honored me with a neighbor, a Litvak Jew!* Such a neighbor!

---

* Litvak: a Jew from (historic) Lithuania; a person steeped in strict, rational religious learning and observance, and often the butt of humor by Jews from other places in Eastern Europe, including Polish Hasidic Jews whose observance was more emotion-based.

100   Chapter 3

He's bitter about every single thing, and it's his nature to constantly see things as worse than they are. It seems to me that his greatest joy in life is to spread his melancholy around, may God have pity on us.

My neighbor came over to my place one evening at the end of Shavuot.*

"Have a good week!" he wished me.

"And a good year to you!" I replied. "Sit down and have a cup of tea."

"So, the festival's over," he began, with the mournful intonation normally reserved for the Ninth of Av fast day. "The festival's gone."

"Ah, well, no festival can last forever," I answered.

"Yes, and so your whole life runs away before you can look around," he consoled me.

"Did the cantor sing the prayers well in your synagogue?" I asked.

"Well or not well, what's the difference? Jewry is slowly disappearing, and in a hundred years there won't be any synagogues or any cantors."

"How are you, anyway?" I asked.

"How should I be? You muddle away your few years, and before you look around, you're already a stiff."

"You warned me about a horse last week," I remarked, "not to put any money on 'Jack of All Trades' because I'd lose. But I didn't take your advice, and actually I won a pound."

"Then you'll lose it on the next races," he said.

"But I'm not going to bet anymore."

"Well, if you don't lose it like that, you'll lose it, God forbid, by paying the doctor, or through some other catastrophe!" he consoled me and took a sip from his glass of tea.

I looked for a way to change the subject from personal to world current affairs. I glanced at the newspaper I'd put down before he came in, and asked:

"So, what do you think of the amazing success of those two new American pilots?† It's what you'd call human progress. It won't be long before

---

* Shavuot: Pentecost / the Feast of Weeks. A two-day festival in May/June commemorating the giving of the Torah at Sinai after the seven-week period from the end of Passover.

† The two American aviators in the news in early June 1927 were Clarence Chamberlin and Charlie Levine (a passenger), who flew nonstop from America, landing in Germany. This was following the first nonstop flight from New York City to Paris on May 20–21, 1927, by Charles Augustus Lindbergh.

we'll be grabbing a weekend in Jerusalem or Tel Aviv instead of Brighton or Westcliff.‡ The time is coming when we'll be able to eat breakfast in London, lunch in Paris, drink a glass of beer in Munich, visit our relatives' graves in Poland, attend an afternoon prayer service near the Kremlin in Moscow, and in the evening pop in to the opera house in Rome."

"You're having me on, eh?"§ he said, taking a big sip of tea and turning toward me with a tetchy look:

"For you it might be a cause for celebration, but I think it's the worst thing in the world. Human progress, eh? Do you know what it'll lead to? To more wars! Fifteen years ago people also welcomed our aviation pioneers with cheering and dancing and drums, but then the war came, and the pilots used airpower to kill innocent women and children. But the tragedies that aviation brought in the last war will be a trifle compared to what will be possible in the next war. You'll see—if you live so long! America won't have to send any munitions in ships, which take a week to get there and risk being sunk by submarines. They'll be able to send arms to Europe in one day in a more secure way, through the air. They'll be able to launch air attacks on any country they want to. America's success in the air will mean that all other countries will have to build better airplanes and develop their own air forces. And the sooner they develop their air forces, the sooner the next war will come. Instead of celebrating, the whole of Europe should be building underground tube lines, whole underground cities where people can hide in wartime and crawl around like worms. But I doubt whether hiding will help. The new explosive materials will shake the earth to its depths. If you live through the next war, you'll have to thank God that you've only had a hand or a foot blown off and not your head. Your only son is growing up to be a lovely boy. And you'll see that one fine day they'll take him from you, and God have pity on him. This will be a war of wars. You'll see if a bomb won't blast both of your eyes out of your head. You see, Russia is preparing, even though at the same time it's yelling about wanting peace because it has no intention of fighting. But in secret Russia's making preparations. You know what's happening in China, you've also seen what's happening in Egypt, and you know that maybe the whole Orient is unsettled. The whole world is preparing. The success in aviation is the world's downfall. The time is coming when all the divine curses in the bible will come to pass."

---

‡ Brighton and Westcliff are seaside towns near London.

§ You're having me on—you must be joking.

102   Chapter 3

I couldn't bear any more of this. I got up and yawned demonstratively. I said that I felt a bit out of sorts and would go to bed early.

My neighbor, calming down, got up, and, wishing me a goodnight, said: "Don't you feel well? It's probably double pneumonia or cancer."

And kissing the mezuzah, he left.

Translated by Vivi Lachs

•••

A Jew Takes a Pleasure Trip

A Neighbor with a Car—A Trip to Westcliff— We Need to Get Hold of a *Goy*.

Di tsayt, 1927

One morning, I could swear it was last Monday, no, sorry, maybe it was Wednesday, or was it Tuesday? Anyway, it doesn't make any difference when it was, the point is that it happened.

Well then, one fine morning I hear a car horn beneath my window. I look out and see my neighbor, the Litvak, and his wife, the Litvatshke in a car.* They were sitting there comfortably and invited me to come and take a look at their new secondhand car, which they had just bought for their business—a horseradish sauce factory.

I went down and was introduced to the car. A four-seater. It didn't look too good—a bit the worse for wear, if you see what I mean—but a car, like all other cars, with four wheels. What's the difference?

My neighbor, the Litvak, invited me to scramble into the car. They were going on a day's pleasure trip to Westcliff and wanted me to come with them. I needn't be afraid—he assured me:

"My wife says I'm a good driver." "Yes," she said: "He knows how to drive." I let myself be persuaded and jumped into the car.

My neighbor decided to drive via the East End. First, he wanted to go to the Lane to get hold of some food for the day (he'd brought a bottle of brandy and some glasses with him from home which he kept in his pocket). Second, he wanted to stop near the hospital, to pick up another person, a brother-in-law of his. And third . . . He didn't finish, but I understood that

---

* Litvatshke: Jewish woman from Lithuania. Feminine form of Litvak.

Interwar Yiddish Culture 103

his third meant that his friends and acquaintances would see that he had a car and would be eaten up with jealousy.

The car stuttered a bit, as if suffering from corns and limping on one leg. But my neighbor assured me it was nothing, nothing dangerous.

He drove the car really slowly, explaining that people generally drive more slowly inside London than outside London. When they got out of the city, he'd show me what sort of car this was and what sort of a driver he was. The Litvatshke was stretched out comfortably as if not only the car but the whole world belonged to her.

In the Lane, my neighbor bought herring, kosher meat sandwiches, and sour cucumbers. The cucumbers were for the Litvatshke, who you know, just like all married women, loves pickled cucumbers. And because my neighbor is a Litvak, he bought himself a head of garlic.

He drove through Whitechapel, and, not far from the London Hospital, he picked up his brother-in-law, a fair-haired man with a pointed beard— and also his wife, who was wider than she was tall, and her two sisters, who were as alike as two peas in a pod. So as not to confuse people, they had different names, Sadie and Fanny.

The car went on its way, but as well as limping along, it also began whistling, as if it were suffering with asthma. Maybe it was upset that it was a four-seater carrying extra people.

Near Bow, a policeman began to get angry with my neighbor and asked him if he knew the difference between right and left. My neighbor explained to me that the policeman's complaints were groundless. He was probably an antisemite. By the time we left London it was halfway through the day.

"Now it will all go without a hitch," the Litvak assured me.

Suddenly it rained, it poured, and the Litvatshke suggested pulling the hood over the car. But Mr. Litvak didn't want to. He assured her that it wasn't worth the effort because the rain would soon stop. And only when we were all thoroughly soggy and soaked through did he stop the car and say:

"Do you think it might be an idea to pull the hood on?"

We both crawled out and pulled at the hood, but it wouldn't move. The fair-haired brother-in-law offered a piece of advice:

"We need to get hold of a *goy*!"

We stood around for a while looking for a *goy*, and then saw one. The *goy* came over and pulled the hood on, we paid him, and on we went.

The car wasn't moving like it had been. It slipped this way and that like a drunkard. Now swerving right and now left. The other cars passing

104 Chapter 3

us hooted their horns in long blasts like the shofar at the New Year, and the drivers swore at the Litvak and yelled at him threateningly.* But he remained calm.

"Who listens to them?" he complained. "They can't bear it that a Jew has a car as well as them."

Suddenly a slide and a screech and a zooooosh! What happened? Oh, just a minor incident, a tire burst. We both crawled out. My Litvak got the spare tire out of the car, and we both tried to change the burst one for the good one. But it was no bloody use, we just couldn't do it. We were both covered in grease and stood with outstretched arms, not knowing what to do.

The fair-haired brother-in-law offered a piece of advice:

"We need to get hold of a *goy*!"

Eventually we found a *goy*. The wheel was put on, and we went on further.

A few minutes later the car stopped again. My neighbor yelled, "Oh, no!"

What was the matter? The back of his trousers felt wet. He had sat down on top of the bottle of brandy, had broken it, and was sitting on pieces of glass. So, we were without brandy, but if necessary we could get some on the way in a pub.

It was getting quite late, and we were beginning to feel hungry. The Litvatshke opened the box with the food. Suddenly, crash! There was a shudder, and we all grabbed each other. The windscreen shattered, and the glass fell on us. What had happened was that the car had plowed into a charabanc coach. Total chaos. Our passengers stumbled out of the car, and the coach passengers stumbled out of the charabanc. The Litvak and the charabanc driver swore at each other, each accusing the other. Finally, they swapped names and addresses.

When the charabanc had driven off, the Litvak boasted:

"When we hit that coach, we could have all been killed. Thank God I'm a good driver, and it's only the car that is damaged. And that doesn't matter because it's insured."

We continued on our way, but we couldn't touch the food because it was full of glass. As we went farther, I thought to myself what a fool I am. Only last week I sent away three insurance agents, one after the other. It would have been better to have had a life policy.

---

* Shofar: ram's horn, blown ceremoniously as part of the prayers during the High Holy Days.

Interwar Yiddish Culture 105

A while later, the car stopped again. My neighbor turned the key, groaned, the car wouldn't go. We both stumbled out. My neighbor opened the bonnet, looked at the car's guts and innards, put a hand here and there, bloodied a finger, but it didn't help. We stood there despondently for a long time. It was getting dark; the rain began to stream down as if a tap had been turned on. What were we to do?

The brother-in-law offered a piece of advice:

"We need to get hold of a *goy*!"

We eventually found a *goy*. He came over, tinkered with the car and shook his head in despair. He told us that there was a garage at the top of the hill. We should drag the car up there, and they would have a look at it.

My neighbor and I began to push the car. It was slippery and steep. We sweated and realized we weren't strong enough. The fair-haired guy, however, had a piece of advice:

"We need to get hold of a *goy*!"

We got a *goy*. With great effort, we pushed the car to the garage. The mechanic explained that it was a big job, and it wouldn't be finished today. The fair-haired guy offered a piece of advice:

"Get a *goy* with a car to tie our car behind his and tow us to Westcliff and get it fixed there."

Finally, we found a *goy* with a car. We were towed along very slowly in the slippery rain. The journey went on and on, but eventually we got there. And I was lucky enough to catch the last train back to London. What a trip it was. What a pleasure!

The next day my neighbor invited me to go with him to Brighton the following week on a pleasure trip. He assured me that since the repair, there was no better car in the whole of England.

Translated by Vivi Lachs

Fun at the Theatre

England Is a Free Country—Jews Keep "Order"—"Haim, Are You Also Here?"

Di tsayt, 1927

"Alas, we have sinned more than any other people!

"Alas, we have shamed ourselves more than any other nation!"

Why say the penitential prayers in the middle of July? No real reason. I was just remembering my visit to the Yiddish theatre.

My fate as a journalist landed me in the Yiddish theatre a few days before it closed for the season: a visit I'll remember for a long time.

I don't mean for the enjoyment of watching the actors, I mean for the pleasure I had thanks to the honorable audience. This is what happened:

The music finished and finally the curtain rose. On the stage an actor and actress began to perform. But you couldn't hear a word from the stage, instead you heard the voice of the usher:

"Order!"

And another voice from the stalls:

"Keep quiet!"

A voice from the pit:

"Quiet!"

A voice from the gallery:

"Shurrup!"

And this continued for ages, with everyone shouting for order. A couple sitting next to me, seeing that the curtain had risen, took sandwiches and oranges out of a bag and tucked in to their meal, as if they'd come from Hungerland for a picnic.

Another couple came up to the couple having a picnic and showed them their tickets, demanding that they move because they were in their seats. The picnicking couple, however, refused to get up. The man calmly swallowed a piece of orange and argued that "England is a free country" and he would not give up his seat. The other couple went to get the usher, who also demanded that they move, but they wouldn't. In the ruckus, people yelled from all sides:

"Quiet!"

"Order!"

"Keep quiet!"

"Shurrup!"

Meanwhile the performance was happening on the stage, but you couldn't hear a thing.

Eventually it did quieten down a bit. The picnicking couple didn't move from their seats, but other seats were found for the ticket holders.

The two actors finished their sketch, and another two came on stage: a man wearing a police uniform and a woman dressed as a princess.

Prompter (yelling from his box): Princess, you are arrested.

Actor (repeats): Princess, you are molested.

Prompter (shouting louder): I won't go!

Actress (repeats): I don't know!

A little while later a child started crying in front of me. Its mother rocked it, singing to help it fall asleep:

"Hush, hush, baby, hush, hush baby!"

Again the shouts were heard:

"Quiet!"

"Order!"

"Keep quiet!"

"Shurrup!"

The prompter said something I didn't hear, and the actor repeated it and the audience laughed. Perhaps it was a good joke, a spicy one.

A bloke leaned over to me and asked:

"What did he say?"

I shrugged my shoulders, and he asked someone else and burst out laughing until he got a fit of coughing. The joke got passed from seat to seat and people laughed. Meanwhile you couldn't hear anything else.

The picnicking couple had finished their sandwiches and oranges, and now started on the monkey nuts. They cracked them and threw the shells down, on and on. I pleaded with them:

"Please stop cracking those nuts."

The woman answered:

"If you're on edge, go home and take it out on your wife."

And they kept on cracking, over and over again.

I really was on edge. I felt the heat rising in my face.

Luckily, a chap near me opened a bottle of lemonade, which spurted out and sprayed my face, cooling me down a little.

Meanwhile on the theatre stage, there was a dance. The audience loved it. A girl next to me was so enthused by it, she danced sitting down, dancing all over my corns.

After the dancing there was more prose. A chap sitting in front of me stood up to see better because the woman in front of him was wearing a large hat that was blocking his view. Standing up, he noticed someone he knew in the circle and shouted: "Haim, Haim, dammit are you also here?"

So now I couldn't hear *and* I couldn't see. Bored, I shut my eyes. There was no point keeping them open. And I sung under my breath:

"Alas, we have sinned more than any other people!

"Alas, we have shamed ourselves more than any other nation!"

God, I thought, why are we more sinful than other people? Why, heavenly father, do we have to shame ourselves in front of every non-Jew? Even in front of the usher and the theatre's fireman?

And as I was thinking, suddenly again:

"Quiet!"

"Order!"

"Keep quiet!"

"Shurrup!"

In the intermission, I bumped into one of the actors at the bar. The bar was packed. People were pushing to get to the drinks and sandwiches, making a racket and yelling.

"Doesn't this give you the impression," he asked me, "that the theatre doesn't have a bar but the bar has a theatre?"

He smiled, but it was a very pained smile. Things had to be different in future!

Translated by Vivi Lachs

"The Jewish Book Shop," lithograph by Pearl Binder, 1932. From Tom Burke's *The Real East End* (London: Constable, 1932). © Estate of Pearl Binder.

"The Yiddish Theatre," lithograph by Pearl Binder, 1932. From Philip Godfrey, *Back-Stage* (London: Harrap, 1933). © Estate of Pearl Binder.

"The Chalking Squad," lithograph by Pearl Binder, 1933. © Estate of Pearl Binder.

"Outside the Union," line drawing by Min Tabor, circa 1970s. Courtesy of Jane Engelsman.

"Untitled," line drawing by Min Tabor, circa 1970s. From Charles Poulsen, *Scenes from a Stepney Youth* (London: THAPP Books Ltd., 1988). Courtesy of Jane Engelsman.

"Untitled," line drawing by Min Tabor, circa 1970s. From Charles Poulsen, *Scenes from a Stepney Youth* (London: THAPP Books Ltd., 1988). Courtesy of Jane Engelsman.

ESTHER KREITMAN (1891–1954)

"Esther Kreitman," sketch by H. Szriftgiser, Antwerp, 1936. *Loshn un lebn* (June 1954).

Esther Kreitman was born Hinde Esther Singer in Bilgoray (Biłgoraj), Poland, the older sister of Israel Joshua Singer and Isaac Bashevis Singer. After an unhappy childhood, where being a girl left her feeling abandoned and unimportant and struggling with her mental health, she agreed to an arranged marriage with Avrom Kreitman. The couple moved to Berlin and then Antwerp. At the start of the First World War, when Germany invaded Belgium, the Kreitmans, with their baby son, Moshe, left Antwerp for London, where Kreitman lived for nearly forty years.

Kreitman translated works from English to Yiddish: Charles Dickens's *A Christmas Carol* in 1929 and George Bernard Shaw's *The Intelligent Woman's Guide to Socialism and Capitalism* in 1930, both published in Warsaw. She wrote two novels that were published in London: *Der sheydim tants* (Dance of the Demons) was published in 1936 in book form, having first been serialized in *Di post* in 1934 with the title *Dvoyrele* (Deborah). Her second novel, *Brilyantn* (Diamonds), was published in 1944. Both novels have strong autobiographical elements. She also produced a collection of short stories, *Yikhes* (Lineage), some of which were set during the Blitz; the volume was published by the East End publishing house Narod Press in 1950.

Both novels and the short story collection have been translated into English. Her stories also appeared in *Di post*, *Di tsayt*, and *Loshn un lebn*. The two stories translated here were never published in book form, and are newly discovered in the London Yiddish press. Her son, Maurice Carr, wrote a biography of his mother's life in London.[12]

• •

The Question
A Humorous Tale

Di post, 1928

Rabbi Borukhl, the town rabbi, sat wrapped in his prayer shawl and phylacteries, with his skullcap a little askew. The *tefillin* box on his scholarly forehead gazed down proudly.

114   Chapter 3

Rabbi Borukhl stroked his long black beard interwoven with silver strands. His keen brown eyes perused a religious tome lying on the table as he prepared to start his prayers.

The door opened, and a small, thin, elderly woman entered, draped in a tattered shawl.

"Good morning, rabbi."

Rabbi Borukhl lifted his eyes from the book.

"Holy rabbi, I have a question."

"So," said Rabbi Borukhl and gestured with his hand, as if to say "ask."

"A question, God help me! Everything happens to me. Well, who else would it happen to if not to a pauper? Not to wealthy Chava Leah; she has, thank God, someone looking after her. Well, never mind!"

"What's the question?" the rabbi asked.

"The question? What should it be? It's nothing, just a tiny thing. If it had happened to a wealthy woman, it wouldn't be a big deal, but then it wouldn't happen to a wealthy woman. I'm telling you, all the hard and bitter things only happen to the poor. I wouldn't wish it on you, it should only happen to scoundrels. God in heaven, have I got a cough! It shouldn't be such a big deal. I mean, what pauper doesn't have a bit of a cough? But I just can't sleep with it. I've done everything I possibly can to get rid of it, but nothing works. I can't go to the doctor because—that is, I can go, but, God damn him, he won't see me unless I pay him in advance, like it's my fault I still can't pay the debt I owe him for my late husband, may he rest in peace.

"People ask me why I don't go to the clinic. Oh, my goodness! If they were in my shoes, they'd know what it's like going to the clinic! They don't listen to you there, so when I start telling them the details of what and when and how, the only thing they say to you is 'be quick' and 'make it snappy.' If you want to say something particular about your cough, because who knows more about your cough than the person who has it, he tells me that if I don't spit it out in just a few words, he'll tell the nurse to throw me out. I hope he gets ninety-nine fevers thrown at him, dear God! So, what can I do? I drink milk. Fine, I have to drink milk; I hope Leybl the milkman has as much trouble earning his crust of bread as I have getting a drop of milk out of him.

"He gets all high and mighty! He said that it isn't worth him selling me just a half a pint of milk. You hear that? It wouldn't be worth it at all. It would cost him his grandmother's inheritance if she'd left him one. Who

Interwar Yiddish Culture   115

doesn't remember when that scoundrel Leybl slept in Berish's barn, thanking God that Berish let him deliver the milk for just a crust of bread? He used to bring me a half pint of milk a day because then my husband, may he rest in peace, was still alive! But those were different times. Now he acts like he doesn't know me anymore. I hope he forgets how to feed himself as well, merciful God in heaven!"

Rabbi Borukhl kept his kind, gentle eyes lowered and waited for the woman to finish asking her question. He didn't want to interrupt her. He sighed quietly for the poor Jewish soul who was pouring out her heart.

"In short, I had such a night, I wouldn't wish it on my worst enemy: endless coughing, sounding like I was chopping wood the whole night long. I barely survived until dawn, when I dragged myself out of bed to heat up my little bit of milk. I picked up a piece of kindling, but it was wet through. I started to make a fire but, no bloody use, it wouldn't burn. I blew on the fire but began to choke with my cough, God have pity on me. Blow blow blow, and the bit of milk was cold as ice. If I'd had decent shoes, it wouldn't have been so bad, but how does a pauper get decent shoes, how? I went to a neighbor to ask her to lend me a piece of dry wood, but it was pouring with rain and my shoes were torn to pieces. Rabbi, you should live long, just look at these shoes I go around in."

And saying this, Genendl Dvoshe took off a shoe to show the rabbi, and sand dropped onto the rabbi's table. The rabbi saw what was happening, but it was already too late, the sand was on the table, and Genendl Dvoshe was back standing in her two shoes.

The rabbi became impatient, but Genendl Dvoshe was apparently reaching the point of her story. She told the rabbi that while she was blowing on the fire to make it burn stronger, the milk, which was slowly warming up, boiled over onto a pot used for meat dishes and unfortunately soaked the little bit of Sabbath cholent.*

Rabbi Borukhl ruled that after twenty-four hours she could kosher the pot, and Genendl Dvoshe went home happy.

Translated by Vivi Lachs

---

* Cholent: traditional stew with meat, beans, and potatoes. Cooked on a Friday before the Sabbath eve and kept warm to eat on the Sabbath day (Saturday).

116   Chapter 3

The Dowry

A London Tale

Di idishe shtime, 1951 (reprinted from an
unknown earlier source, c. 1930s)

Although Mr. Harry Barnet had been married for twenty years, he never for
one moment forgot the debt his wife owed him.

He was owed a thousand pounds! It was actually owed by his father-in-
law, but because his father-in-law was long dead, he claimed the debt from
the daughter. However, as the daughter, his wife, didn't even own a thousand pence, she paid him in another way.

Paying him back was hard, but Mondays were harder than ever, because
on Mondays the landlord came round to collect the rent.

The landlord was a gentile who hated "foreigners." He said he didn't
care that the Barnets were Jews, but he didn't want any "foreigners" in his
house. What's more, they paid him very little rent, otherwise he might even
have got used to "foreigners" too. And while he couldn't throw them out
because the house was under legal control, he took revenge in other ways.

On Monday morning Mrs. Barnet dragged herself back and forth from
the bedroom to the kitchen, limping on her bad leg. She woke her husband

"Harry, it's already nine o'clock! You'll lose another customer!" she
called to him from the kitchen while she washed the dishes, saw the coffee didn't boil over, boiled the milk, cut the bread, and spread a checkered,
starched tablecloth over a white wooden table, all the while glancing into
the bedroom to see if there was any movement—but no such luck!

Harry was happily snoring away, smacking his red lips and blowing
steam through his nostrils like a horse. Mrs. Barnet wrung her hands.

"Mrs. Michael needs those things. He'll lose another customer, and
there aren't too many of them."

Finally, a creak from the bed and a loud yawn informed Mrs. Barnet
that Harry had got up at last.

Harry sat down on the bed, dangling a pair of legs like thick white logs.
His stomach protruded over the edge of the bed as, lazily and sleepily, Harry
scratched his soft, almost womanly breast. He gave a long, drawn-out yawn.

His wife came in.

"Just look at you. You'll catch cold like that, God forbid. Why don't you
put on your slippers?"

Interwar Yiddish Culture 117

She took out a pair of leather slippers from under the bed.

Harry didn't pay any attention to her. He immediately put his large square skullcap on his thick head and muttered something, then, realizing that his wife was right, he slipped into his slippers.

Remembering it was Monday, he started getting dressed. His trousers had got a bit too tight for him, his braces were too short, his shoes squeezed him, and the corn on his left foot hurt.

He washed his hands and face. He wiped his face with one hand, and with the other he took out his prayer shawl and *tefillin* from the wardrobe. The leather straps of his *tefillin* also seemed to have shrunk. His red lips began muttering. He yawned and mumbled on. Reaching the *Aleynu* concluding prayer, he spat on the ground according to custom and finished praying.

He went into the kitchen where the boiled egg, black bread thickly spread with butter, and the smell of freshly boiled coffee made him feel happy.

"Go and wash, Harry. You'll be late!"

"Mind your own business! Don't presume on your miserable little dowry! A right fool you made of me! I dragged myself round yeshivas and split my head open with algebra and German, all for that lousy dowry. But you couldn't catch any young peddler with your gammy leg, huh? Oh, the ground should fling him out of his grave, the thief. He promised me fifteen hundred pounds and gave me five. And what became of the five? Huh? I'm asking you! Have you lost your tongue? A nightmare!"

They heard a knock on the door. Harry turned as white as the walls. His puffy cheeks began to shake like jelly.

"Listen Mr. Barnet. I'm giving you notice for the very last time! I'll put you out onto the street if you don't clean up the flat. I won't have any foreigners here, and that's it."

Harry nearly choked on his food. He simply couldn't answer him. It was no use picking a quarrel with a gentile—furthermore Bob, the landlord's big brown dog, suddenly leapt forward. With his shiny long lion's mane, Bob gave a jerk toward the table, trying to rub up against Mr. Barnet.

Mr. Barnet jumped backward, nearly hitting the wall.

The landlord, a tall, sickly man with three deep wrinkles in each of his shrunken cheeks, took his pipe out of the corner of his mouth. A sly, angry smile appeared on his thin-pressed lips, and he cheerfully ordered the dog:

"Go on, Bobby! Get hold of him!"

The dog barked and put both its front paws on the table, almost knocking the breakfast to the floor.

Meanwhile Mrs. Barnet paid the rent. The landlord signed the rent book and left.

Harry sighed, wiped the sweat from his face, and set about finishing his breakfast despite everything.

"Yes, I had to get married to a cripple," he thought, cursing his father-in-law, his wife, and the gentile landlord.

His wife shuffled over quietly from the stove to the table and poured him another cup of coffee. She thanked God that he was silent.

After finishing the grace after meals, he picked up a suitcase stuffed full of goods and left the flat without saying goodbye. He lowered his heavy body quietly down the stairs, listening anxiously in case the gentile came out again.

Once on the street, he felt relieved, and on the 47 tram he bumped into a young man he knew:

"Hey, how are you doing? I was planning to come and see you. How about a game of chess this evening? What, you're not playing chess anymore? Never mind, we can play dominoes. You don't find dominoes interesting? Sure, chess is more intellectual. You know what, we can play sixty-six. Cards are better, actually. You get absorbed, and the evening flies by! You won't be at home tonight? Where will you be? So, I'll come round to your friend's place! A group of three is more cozy."

The young man saw that he wouldn't be able to shake off Harry, so got off a stop earlier.

"What, you're getting off already? Just give me your friend's address!" Harry jumped up, trying to grab the young man's sleeve, but he was no longer on the tram.

When the conductor shouted "Whitechapel," Harry got off and set off down the narrow streets. Here he felt at home.

Nearly all his customers were outside. In these narrow alleys it seemed like with outstretched arms you'd be able to touch the houses on both sides. Fat women stood on the front doorsteps with close-shorn, thinning hair and deeply lined faces. And there were young women standing around with shining faces and tight-fitting dresses that revealed triple-layered bosoms and other disproportionate parts of their bodies.

Harry licked his lips, threw a cheerful "good morning" to the young women, and began unpacking his wares. A circle of women surrounded him,

Interwar Yiddish Culture   119

their eyes beginning to shine. The colorful rayon and knitted underwear appeared enticingly from his suitcase: light green, red, yellow, purple, and pink.

The women pulled out the wares: this one a pair of pajamas, that one a petticoat, another held a swimsuit to her bosom, each asking the others if it suited her.

Harry kept a vigilant eye open. A Jewish man, sitting astride a squeaky bench with his legs wide apart to give his stomach more room, became angry:

"Hey, hey mister, beat it! Get out of here or I'll call a policeman! Look how crazy they get when they see him!"

The man knew that Barnet was a pest who sold his wares on installments. The women flocked to him, lost their heads, and took more than they could afford. So Harry went there once a week without a suitcase, with only his payment book, and refused to leave until he was paid his installments. He didn't even go when they threw hot water over him. Now even the angry Jew's wife was trying on a pair of pajamas!

Harry paid no attention to the man: He wasn't a gentile, after all. Harry helped the young women try on silk blouses, took hold of their bare arms, and asked other women for their opinions.

The women helped him, praising the goods:

"It really suits you, Mrs. Michael—I should be so lucky!"

"She looks like a queen in that jersey, bless her!"

When he got home, Harry crept up the dark staircase as quiet as a mouse and, over a piece of roasted meat and a large plate of grated potatoes, told his wife that he hadn't made a penny all day. She didn't answer, just sighed and carried on knitting a pair of socks for Harry. He remembered how pretty the women had looked wearing his clothes. It just annoyed him that the young man on the bus didn't want to have him round. He took out his chessboard, set up the pieces, and played on his own, cursing his dead father-in-law bitterly as he made the moves.

"That's all I needed—a cripple for a wife! With a dowry like that, she couldn't even have got a young peddler! Oy, gentiles or Jews, they're all the same. Is he any better?" And remembering the young man, his face burned with resentment. He threw over the chessboard in resignation. "That's all I needed," he said aloud, "a cripple for a wife!" His wife didn't answer him. She was used to it.

Translated by Vivi Lachs

YEHUDA ITAMAR LISKY (1899–1989)

"I. A. Lisky," sketch by Maurice Sochachewsky, *Di idishe shtime* (June 12, 1953). Courtesy of Dave Skye Sochachewsky. From the British Library collection.

I. A. Lisky was born Yehuda Isomer Fuchs in Yezerne, Eastern Galicia (today Ozerna, Ukraine). He was a younger brother of the fiction writer A. M. Fuchs, whom he followed to Vienna, where he joined the city's literary circles. He changed his name to Lisky so as not to be confused with his brother and published as I. A. Lisky. Lisky moved to London in 1930 and was active in leftwing circles and the Workers' Circle. He wrote articles and short stories for *Di tsayt* and coedited *Ovent nayes*. A collection of his short stories, *Produktivizatsye* (Productivization), was published in book form in 1937, with a version of some parts of the stories published earlier in *Di tsayt*.

Lisky wrote two novellas: *For, du kleyner kozak!* (On Your Way, Little Cossack!), from 1941, is set during World War I in a small village in Eastern Europe. *Melokhe bezuye* (A Humiliating Profession), published in 1947, concerns the London Yiddish literary circles and depicts well-known personalities thinly disguised with pseudonyms.

Along with his wife, Sonia Husid (the critic and essayist known as N. M. Seedo), and Stencl, Lisky was on the editorial committee of the literary journal *Yidish london*, and he was published in *Loshn un lebn*. Two of Lisky's Eastern European stories and all the stories from *Produktivizatsye* have appeared in English translation.[13]

• •

A London Girl's Secret

A Sketch

Di tsayt, 1931

It was already long past the time when people are released from their daily work, and Grandma Leah's eyes were ceaselessly searching for Sybil. And

Interwar Yiddish Culture   121

the more the hour hurriedly advanced toward night, the more worried Sybil's grandmother became. Something frightened her: It was so late, and Sybil wasn't home yet. She mused and brooded, until the noise of the city filled her head, and her thoughts began to spin a dark web.

Standing there with her brow framed by a ragged matron's wig, Grandma Leah looked like a transplanted wilting sheaf of rye that longed to return to its own earth. She used to tell people how she had arrived in London's foggy East End many years ago on an old-fashioned wagon drawn by two big horses, but those memories had vanished from the forefront of her mind. They had been stored away in a hidden cell. She no longer thought about all the days, weeks, months, and years that had been swallowed up by the great city, like plankton by a huge fish. She wandered about the flat, straining her eyes to catch the slightest movement outside.

By the time Sybil came home, the gas meter was already demanding a second threepenny bit to keep the lights on. Sybil's eyes were weary, like stars covered by clouds. She looked dejected, as if the whole weight of the London streets lay on her shoulders, with all the ancient churches, great prisons, castles, cemeteries, monuments, towers, and manifold rare antiquities that were England's greatest pride.

Sybil was strangely silent and looked at her grandmother very gently. She would have liked to draw close to her, sit down beside her, and unburden her heavy heart. Her grandmother would have sighed and groaned like only she could. But Sybil spoke no Yiddish, and her grandmother knew only a few words of English. So she remained silent, turning the whole day over in her mind. Her secret remained intact for the time being, and if the London lad who worked with her at the same table making dresses were to ask her once again to take him home and introduce him to her mother, she would again remain silent, take no notice, and lower her eyes.

Grandma Leah handed Sybil something to eat, as pleased to have her back as if she had found a lost treasure. "Vhy so late? Vot iz de matter?" she asked, mumbling the broken English phrases she knew by heart. There was so much more she wanted to ask Sybil, but her attention was suddenly taken up by the old family pictures hanging on the damp, dusty walls. She thought about her daughter, Sybil's mother, who had died a few years ago—a tall, stately woman with pale cheeks and the worried eyes of someone who gladly worked hard for a living despite a whole pack of troubles. She had been her own mistress, sewing underwear for unknown ladies and earning barely enough to meet her daily needs. Sybil's father was a bitter type with sinister eyes. All day long he pushed a cart around, selling old clothes. On his way home he would stay out late, drinking in pubs with his mates. He liked to sit with his legs crossed, pull ten-shilling notes from his inside pocket, and bet them on the horses. Afterward he would shout a lot and count his money, till his thick lower lip suddenly drooped, as if he had committed a great sin. He went on betting and losing money for years, while Sybil's mother sewed and sewed, till she sewed herself to death. Thus Grandma Leah sat ruminating, unable to free her mind from the dismal thoughts, gazing at Sybil with a pair of watery eyes that could have drowned her whole secret.

Days passed, and Sybil remained silent. She had no one to tell about her blond boyfriend. At work she felt his gaze on her as she sewed, and she seemed to hear him asking: "Will you introduce me to your mother?" When work was over they would walk home together at sunset, watching London turn its lights on. Crowds of people made their way through the blackened streets and houses, now lit up in bright colors, and the night spread its wings over light and shadow.

Then once, as they walked together along a London side street, Sybil suddenly felt the brightly illuminated night enfold her in a warm embrace, and her lips broadened in a girlish smile. And once again she managed to get her companion to ask that same question: "Can I go home with you this evening, darling? Will you introduce me to your mother?"

Sybil hesitated no longer. Her secret erupted in a sudden "Yes!" Trembling with excitement, the couple hurried through the quiet, dark East End streets till they came to her house. Sybil rapped twice on the knocker of the narrow front door. Together they climbed the dark staircase and entered the small, dark, but homey flat. Sybil looked at her grandma Leah a little strangely. In a damp, broken voice, she said to the blond young man: "This is my grandmother." And she burst out crying.

Translated by Barry Smerin

Mendl and the Torah Scroll

Sketches of Jewish Life in London

Di tsayt, 1933

An iron bridge stretched between the high walls, separating a few small, weary-looking houses from the rest of the street.

Interwar Yiddish Culture   123

It was close to Whitechapel.

Mendl walked through the passage under the bridge twice a day, once in the morning on his way to work and once in the evening on his way back.

On his way there he brought with him the noise of the street, the electric fever that throbbed on the ground and in the air, driving and rushing everything along at today's crazy pace. On his return, he brought back clouds of damp smoke from the ships docked in the Thames harbor.

Mendl was a docker. He worked loading and unloading the ships. He had broad shoulders. The skin on his face was as rough as bark, and his eyes were sunken. He wore a broad-peaked cap on his head and a scarf buttoned round his neck.

Mendl looked his age. He lived and worked unmoved by the passage of time, spending the passing years with his mates, the dockers, in the little pub on the other side of the bridge.

The local Jews called Mendl "the *goy*." And although the streets around Whitechapel are inhabited only by Jews, he was not the only "*goy*" among them.

Under the bridge, in the deep, damp recesses, coarse-faced Jewish stall-holders stood hawking their wares by the wet stone walls, anxiously pointing out the goods on display to every passerby. Opposite them, exhausted Jews with haggard cheeks displayed similar items on tables and boxes, hawking them, like yesterday and the day before, in the same weary tones.

One evening the men under the bridge grabbed Mendl on his way back from work. There were dark shadows under his eyes, his rough forehead was damp. Like yesterday and the day before, there was a smoking cigarette stub between his thick lips. The Jews under the bridge needed Mendl. They were waiting for him.

"How're you doing, Mendl?" they greeted him. They didn't inquire about his family, because Mendl had no wife or children. His years stretched out around him like the empty branches of a leafless willow tree.

The men began by drawing him into a conversation about the greyhound races, which also brought in a bit of money from time to time. Then they gradually got down to brass tacks. "What do you think? We won't have to ask Mendl for long, He's sure to contribute. The rabbi's been looking for him."

"So what about it, Mendl? Do you want to have a share in the Torah scroll? You won't have to put much into it, and it will definitely stand you in good stead."

The men under the bridge had been talking about the Torah scroll for weeks, and today there had been an especially big discussion. Jewish rag dealers with timeworn, troubled faces, carrying sacks of secondhand clothes, had suddenly gathered from the surrounding streets. They were telling each other excitedly that the rabbi had promised to celebrate the Torah scroll with a party. There would be plenty of brandy.

It was cold under the bridge, the air thick with smoke from the trains passing overhead. Mendl mumbled something in reply. You could tell from the look in his eyes that he was deep in thought. Who knows what was running through his head? Perhaps he was only thinking about his mates, the dockers. He got on very well with them—all those years working together in the docks, lugging those heavy loads to and fro. Or maybe Mendl was wondering whether he should give money for the Torah scroll, and how much he should promise the men under the bridge.

His eyes began to wander, and the men with the sacks and the stalls were also starting to leave. The old down-and-out women who came night after night to sleep under the bridge were approaching in the distance. They came whether the air was thick with fog or bright and clear, and settled down to sleep hugging kittens to their bosoms.

"Don't forget what you promised, Mendl. We'll soon have to come up with the money for the Torah scroll." The words died away under the bridge.

It was also cheerful today in the pub where Mendl was a regular—cheerful but dark. The weary dockers with the gray, worn-out skin on their long, dark faces and the bulging blue veins on their narrow necks, drank standing up, staring vaguely at the old arrows, spears, rifles, and other trinkets hanging on the old, blackened wooden walls. The circular lamps hanging from the low smoke-ridden ceiling cast a pale light.

Mendl knew all the drinkers well. Some drank in silence, staring in front of them as they drained their tall beer mugs. Others liked to play with the feet of the parrot in the cage on the bar. The bird used to push its thick beak through the wire walls of the cage so they could give it something to nibble on.

George, an old Englishman with a long, thin, gloomy face, was the one who paid most attention to the parrot. With his clay pipe stuck in the corner of his crooked mouth, George would always bend toward the cage, stare into it with his deep, gray, bloodshot eyes, summon the bird, and with a long, dry finger, tickle the soft feathers on its short, thick neck. George proffered the parrot a peanut kernel, and a delighted shriek issued from its half-open beak. "Mendl-endl, Mendl-endl," George muttered, giving him a strange dark look and a foolish smile.

Mendl was also prone to bare his broad yellow teeth and laugh for no good reason, without inner conviction. He too had known the parrot for years, ever since he had settled in Whitechapel and begun working in the docks, inhaling the dust and fog that covered the large warehouses, heavy buildings, and huge ships in the Thames harbor.

Today, however, he was unable to smile at the parrot. He seemed to be a different person. One of his mates approached with his usual twist of the lips. "Eh, Mendl," he said. "You were wrong about horse no. 3. It came nowhere." Mendl made no reply. He wasn't even listening. He stood there with his head in his weathered palm, his mind heavily burdened. He looked like a tree in a storm with worm-eaten apples falling from its branches.

He drank his beer, this time not to fill his stomach but to drive away the restlessness that had suddenly come over him. You could tell from the look in his eyes that, deep inside, he was far from silent.

Mendl had paced back and forth under the bridge till late in the evening, like a man who needed to vent his pent-up anger. A crowd of cats and dogs had congregated round the stall that sold pet food.

He had come to confront the Jewish peddlers and have it out with them. The lamps under the bridge cast a shimmering yellow light.

People walked by, children rushed around playing and shouting, but the men he was looking for didn't show up. They had gone off to parade the Torah scroll through Whitechapel, where the procession was already advancing through the narrow streets. At its head, the rabbi, dressed in a long glittering robe, with thick black hair adorning his pointed chin, carried the Torah scroll pressed to his heart, under a bridal canopy. He gazed into the distance, his large eyes moist under quivering lids.

The crowd moved slowly forward. Dressed up for the occasion, gray-haired workaday women with sagging yellowish cheeks and long proud noses loudly rejoiced. Right at the back, between the bare smoke-blackened houses and the little churches on the streetcorners, Mendl walked to and fro, like a man remote from the celebration.

Suddenly a feeling of resentment was added to the little bit of joy he was entitled to experience. Nobody was paying him any attention. He hadn't been placed in the circle around the Torah scroll, although he had contributed to the cost of having it written. But Mendl was not one of those morbid Jews constantly weighed down with beliefs created by hotheads who had spun them out and passed them on from generation to generation. So the twofold feeling didn't last long. His mood, like a sky in which rain and sunshine mingle, soon resolved itself. His rough cold, dark face retained the expression of resentment with which he had run to confront the men under the bridge, and later to the pub, where he now stood open-mouthed with a full glass in front of him, watching old George playing with the parrot and puffing on his clay pipe.

Just then, George shot him a friendly look. Mendl could no longer contain himself and exclaimed to the world in general: "George, you old rascal, you're a good bloke." His tongue lolled limply in his mouth, and he could say no more.

Unable to tell George about the business with the Torah scroll, he stood there uncomfortably, feeling the loneliness that had long been building up inside him enter his eyes. He got well and truly drunk, and the thoughts reflected in his eyes like in a mirror fell away and disappeared from his memory. He could see the street that led back to his home, with its single window swaying before his eyes. The noise in the pub buzzed in his ears.

An old English beggar was playing a concertina and singing a song of hardship and sorrow. Drunken women with caps on their heads were drinking heavily, while a poor haggard black man with large bulging eyes and a face as dark as the world danced before them.

Mendl stood there in the pub till closing time. When the workmen who had been playing darts, throwing the sharp, pointed little wooden arrows at the dartboard, started to leave, making their way to the door with heavy sagging shoulders, Mendl was already outside. His head was throbbing madly. His tall figure looked like a tar-covered pillar under the weight of a huge building.

The night loomed before him like a dark tunnel, accompanying him to the iron bridge. He walked through the passage and disappeared.

Translated by Barry Smerin

ARYE MYER KAIZER (1892–1967)

"A. M. Kaizer," sketch by Maurice Sochachewsky, *Di idishe shtime* (July 3, 1953). Courtesy of Dave Skye Sochachewsky. From the British Library collection.

Arye Myer Kaizer was born in Yordanov (Jordanów), Poland, in 1892, the son of a Hasidic kabbalist *rebbe*. In 1895 the family moved to London, where Kaizer had a religious upbringing in the East End: first in Sidney Square, Whitechapel, and later in Tredegar Square in Bow. He spent World War I in the Jewish Legion in Palestine, returning to London in 1920 and becoming a journalist for *Di tsayt*.

He was general secretary of the Federation of Jewish Relief Organizations of Britain. He regularly traveled to Eastern Europe as a journalist to report on the situation of the Jewish communities there and find out what they needed to be sent from London. On his return from the Ukraine in 1930, the federation published his report as a pamphlet, *Mir zenen hungerik* (We Are Hungry), and reports from other trips were published in *Di tsayt*.

Kaizer was the chair of both the Association of Jewish Journalists and Authors in England and the London branch of the Yiddish Scientific Institute (YIVO). He arranged many events, chairing some in his own home. During the 1930s and early 1940s, Kaizer was a regular writer for *Di tsayt* as one of its main feuilletonists; *Di tsayt* published more than 150 of his humorous feuilletons of Jewish life in Whitechapel. A selection of thirty-seven of these were published in the book *Bay undz in vaytshepl* (This Whitechapel of Ours) in 1944. Later stories appeared in *Loshn un lebn*. There have only been a handful of translations into English.[14]

• •

A Free Hand!
Di tsayt, 1931

"Give me a free hand," MacDonald demands of the public, "a free hand to do whatever I like!"*

---

* Ramsay MacDonald was leader of the Labour Party and British prime minister in a second Labour government (1929–35). In 1931, when this sketch was written, he formed a national government to oversee spending cuts.

128   Chapter 3

Well, that's fine with me, because I, poor wretch that I am, simply don't have the strength to read all the complicated manifestos, programs, and pledges, let alone work out whether they have any substance to them or are just a load of rubbish. My head is sufficiently weighed down as it is, what with all my money problems; so what I say is this:

"Take my hand, MacDonald, and lead me on the right path—with God's help, or maybe Baldwin's.* And if you should, God forbid, get stuck in the mud, at least make sure it's a decent sort of mud that's suitable for both you and me. At least do what that tram driver did when his tram ran off the rails. He drove it straight into a chemist's shop so that, although the passengers were badly injured by the glass from the shattered windows, they had bandages, cotton wool, iodine, and other medication available on the spot."

But my fellow countryman, Yeruchem the *cheder* teacher, the one they call "the philosopher," scratches his chin despondently as usual and declares: "Definitely not! A free hand? May God preserve us! My shrew of a wife has 'a free hand,' and just see what I look like. Giving someone a free hand is like handing a whip to a Cossack. No!" he shouts. "That is not the way! If you want to be a synagogue warden or treasurer, tell us, the shtetl householders, what you intend to do. You can see the roof is broken, the stove smokes badly, and the sink leaks, so let's hear what you intend to do about it."

"So what good will it do you, Yeruchem, if they promise you heaven and earth, and in the end it's all a lot of talk and little action? Didn't they promise us a 'national home' in Palestine? And you can see for yourself what's come of it."

"A promise is at least some sort of a contract," Yeruchem argues. "But as for that 'free love' of theirs, I won't have anything to do with it."

"Don't be silly, Yeruchem. When Passfield published his white paper, do you suppose he looked in the law books first to see what's allowed and what isn't?† All those promises are as worthless as a father-in-law's undertaking to maintain his son-in-law 'until he sprouts a beard.' If he likes him, the father-in-law will go on providing for his son-in-law even if he already has

---

* Stanley Baldwin had served as a Conservative prime minister through the 1920s.

† Lord Passfield (Sidney Webb) wrote the Passfield white paper (1930) outlining British policy in Palestine. It seemed to limit Jewish immigration by protecting the land of the Arab population living there. It was contested by Zionists, claiming it was backtracking on the Balfour Declaration.

Interwar Yiddish Culture   129

a beard as thick as a forest. If he doesn't like him, the young man's face can be as smooth as a pumpkin, but the father-in-law will find a hair on his mug and—that's the end of the maintenance!"‡

But Yeruchem the philosopher is as stubborn as a mule. It seems like his missus has given him such a hard time with that free hand of hers that he just goes on saying: "Give him anything you like, but not a free hand!" This despite his good opinion of MacDonald, whom he considers the most decent of the whole bunch. "As the saying goes," he continues, "of all the cobblers, the best tailor is Yosl the carpenter. But just give him a free hand and you'll ruin him, and then we're all done for. Take for example that bloke in Italy (his name escapes me for the moment, not that it matters). He was a decent person until only a short while ago—a socialist, a justice seeker, a liberator. But as soon as he got a free hand, he lost all his godly traits and all his humanity.

"And you know why? It's written in the holy books that in every animal there is something of the human being. Likewise, in every human being there is something of the animal. As long as a human being is fenced in, the animal within him lies dormant. But as soon he's free, the animal breaks loose and you can fear for your life.

"Give them a free hand, and they can come tomorrow and put an end to my *cheder* teaching. For him—MacDonald, I mean—my *cheder* will be too cramped and stuffy, not clean enough. He'll tell me to open the windows, wash the floor with carbolic acid, and other crazy nonsense.

"And he's not the only one. No sooner do you give someone a free hand than 'free hands' spring up overnight on all sides. And I won't be too surprised if, one fine day, that real free-hander, Kid Lewis, bursts into my place and orders me: 'Yeruchem! Teach me to recite the concluding Torah portion in one week, otherwise my free hand will give you such a whack that you'll see your great-grandmother and save yourself the trouble of reincarnation.'§

"Does such a free hand appeal to you? Not to me, it doesn't!"

So says Yeruchem. Maybe he's right.

Translated by Barry Smerin

---

‡ It was traditional in Orthodox Judaism that, as part of a dowry agreement, the father of the bride would provide room and board for the new couple so that the man could study full time in a yeshiva.

§ Kid Lewis was an English Jewish professional boxer from 1909 to 1929.

130   Chapter 3

•••

The Hanukkah Miracle on London Bridge

Di tsayt, 1936

> A true story that happened to Yeruchem
> on his first Hanukkah in London,
> just as he told it to me.

I.

If you're quite finished with your story, let me tell you a story of my own—my Hanukkah miracle or, as I call it, "the Hanukkah Miracle on London Bridge."

It happened about thirty years ago, when I had only just arrived in London. Still a newcomer, I came across an acquaintance from the old country, Shaye the woodworker. He had been a member of our carpenters' synagogue.* He was our prayer leader, our shofar blower—a veritable rabbi. And it was with him that we deposited our mourners' money and dowry portions. A turner by trade, he made furniture legs. He went on making those legs, till one fine day he took to his own legs and disappeared with everything, all the mourners' money and dowry portions, leaving nothing behind, not even a hair. Come to think of it, he did leave one thing behind: his Russian soldier, his wife—a tall, hardened, obtuse woman, a real trooper.

Where did Jews run to in those days? To America. There was a ship that left from Bremen, but it stopped in London, where they examined your eyes, looking for trachoma. If they found trachoma, you couldn't go on to America. All the trachoma cases stayed here. That's why England is a country full of people who can't see. But as well as the trachoma sufferers, the king of the pauper's grandchildren also stayed behind—all those who didn't have enough money in their pocket to get to America.†

Shaye was one of the trachoma sufferers. He didn't have a decent pair of eyes, but all in all, as I said, he was in pretty decent shape. He wasn't short of work. He soon got a job at a carpenter's shop on Virginia Road, but he didn't stay there long.‡ After working on Virginia Road for a couple years and getting to know the furniture business, he concluded that planing planks

---

* Some synagogues were established by particular trades.

† A reference to the novel *The King of the Schnorrers* by Israel Zangwill.

‡ Virginia Road in Shoreditch, just north of the Jewish East End.

Interwar Yiddish Culture 131

all day, wading through wood shavings, would get him nowhere. It was a job for those donkeys just off the boat. He would become a furniture dealer. He had a bit of money—you already know where he got it from—so he went over the water, over London Bridge, found himself a little shop with a window, and opened a furniture store on "weekly payments." Business started well, so he brought over his wife, the faithful trooper, and the children—the whole regiment! And they all lived in the two little rooms at the back of the shop. It was cramped, but they could breathe.

When Shaye ran into me here in London, he embraced me like a member of his own family. After we had exchanged all the news from the old country, he began insisting that I come round to his place on Hanukkah (which was in a few days' time) for latkes and a game of sixty-six. And I wasn't to come alone, but to bring my wife, Rasha-Gitl, with me. The thing is, whenever I hear the words "sixty-six," I get all excited. Wake me up in the middle of the night with the word "sixty" and you won't have to add "six." I'll already be shuffling the cards in my sleep. With me, it's like an illness—a disease, my missus calls it. To cut a long story short, it was agreed that I would come round to him on Hanukkah, God willing, and we went our separate ways.

II.

When Hanukkah came round, we started getting ready to leave. Although, to tell the truth, my missus hadn't wanted to hear of it. When I told her that he lived over the water, she said no to the whole thing. Since coming to London by ship, she hated the sea. As for the Germans who had dreamed up Bremen and the crossing, she cursed them to high heaven: "Dear God," she begged, "may the sea hurl them about, like it hurled me!" Ever since then, she gets seasick whenever water is mentioned. Once she even felt sick when there was some talk about installing a bathtub in our place.

On hearing that we were to go to Shaye's over the water, she declared that she wouldn't budge for anything in the world. Finally, with great difficulty, I manage to overcome her fears and anxiety and persuade her to make the journey with me, swearing by all that's holy that she would not throw up. But, as no wife believes her husband, she didn't believe me either and armed herself with provisions for the trip: half a dozen lemons, half a bottle of brandy, a variety of smelling salts to bring her round—in short, a whole chemist's shop. Loaded with all our medical baggage, we left Whitechapel by bus and set out over the water.

Chapter 3

But as soon as the bus reached the Minories, with Hanukkah just beginning, my missus started grimacing and said she felt sick.* She said she could already feel the water, the lousy sea. "You fool," I said. "Where do you see a sea?" But she didn't want to know. "I'm done for!" she cried. "I'm going to faint." And she really did begin to faint, tossing her head and clucking like a hen. I rubbed her temples with the brandy, gave her a sniff of the smelling salts, and shoved a lemon in her mouth. She sat up and opened her eyes. "Are we over the water yet?" she asked in a feeble voice. "What? Still not?" she moaned, and fainted away again. I rubbed her temples again, gave her another sniff of the Yom Kippur salts, and we drank a little more brandy. Who's "we"? you ask. Me and the conductor. What do you think? Do you imagine I was feeling all right? I also had myself to revive, and you can't be a greedy pig, especially when the *goy* helps you open the bottle.

A few minutes later, my fainting missus asked me, "Are we over yet?" and fainted away again. In short, what a jolly bus ride. And soon I had no lemons and no brandy left. I could see it was a waste of time, so I let her get on with her fainting. She'd surely have had enough of it sooner or later. But she kept on fainting and shouting "I'm done for!" all the way to Shaye's place. Arriving there more dead than alive, my missus started telling him about the great "Hanukkah miracle," how she had almost died crossing the sea, and how she had suffered. As for the return journey, she swore she wouldn't go back the same way to Whitechapel, across that damned sea, even if she had to travel round the whole of England.

"We'll see," said Shaye with a smile. "Meanwhile, let's have a little drink, eat a latke, and have a game of cards in honor of Hanukkah."

"We won't see!" my missus replied.

And just as she said, we didn't "see." Here's what happened.

III.

Without more ado, we sat down to play cards. We played such a frenzied sixty-six that smoke rose in the air. Actually, the smoke came from the burnt latkes frying in the room. The little room had become more of a "bake room" than a "back room." Our eyes were smarting, so Shaye went and opened a window. Outside there was "darkness over the land of Egypt"—a fog so

---

* The Minories is a street in East London just west of the Jewish East End and just north of Tower Bridge.

Interwar Yiddish Culture 133

thick you could touch it.† As my missus put it, "You couldn't see your hand in front of your face." We would soon have to set off home, but she wasn't happy about it. She said she would go via Manchester, Leeds, or Glasgow, if need be, but not back over the water.

"Don't be so stupid!" I said. "At night the water's calm, nobody feels sick." But she wouldn't budge. She wasn't going, she said. Anyway, you couldn't trust a London bus driver on a night like this. He could drive off the bridge in the fog, straight into the water. I argued with her so long that it got too late to go anywhere at all.

Then Shaye said, "Well, then, you'll have to stay the night!" I knew he had only two little rooms. "Where on earth are we going to sleep?" I asked. "We'll just squeeze up," he said. "You'll see. Don't worry, we'll soon make you up a comfortable bed." Then he showed us into a magnificent room, a king's palace, with fine furniture and a truly luxurious bed. "Shaye," I said, "why didn't you tell me right away that you have such a spacious spare bedroom? It would have saved me arguing with the wife." Shaye smiled, said goodnight, and slowly left the room.

"Shaye, you old devil!" I thought to myself. "God alone knows how many more furnished rooms you own." And he lets people think he lives in two little holes.

We got undressed and went to bed. We slept like the dead. We hadn't slept so well for ages. I don't remember who woke us, but when we opened our eyes, where do you think we found ourselves? You'll never guess. We found ourselves in the street! You hear me? In the street, no less! That's what it looked like at first glance. But I quickly realized we weren't exactly in the street, but almost. We were sleeping in front of a large, wide window, with a crowd of people outside. They were banging on the window and chanting "Time to get up, lazybones!" With their laughing and joking, we had certainly livened up the street.

Where do you think that devil Shaye had put us? If you had a thousand heads you'd never guess! He'd put us to bed in his shop window—a display window with a bedroom suite! If we had asked him earlier where he was putting us up, we would at least have known where we were. We were ignorant newcomers, but he wasn't! He knew what he was doing. Had he wanted to give us a surprise, or simply play a joke on us so that we

---

† "Darkness" was the ninth of the biblical ten plagues with which God afflicted the Egyptians.

wouldn't feel like coming to see him again and not want to go back "over the water"? God only knows. But at that moment, we knew only one thing for sure: We were lying wounded in a shop window and the blood was dripping.

What on earth could we do? We clearly couldn't just get out of bed. And every minute we lay there felt like an hour. It seemed like the whole of London was standing there at the window—like a theatre! And where was Shaye? Where were they all? Why were they sleeping so long today? There was nothing to be done. We would just have to stay in bed till someone came to our rescue.

"Rasha-Gitl, pull the bedspread up over our heads," I told the wife. "Let's at least not see them laughing at us."

So we pulled the bedspread up over our heads and snuggled down. But then they laughed at us even more. They were probably laughing at the holes in our socks. Pardon me for mentioning it, but they were well worn down at the heels at that time.

To cut a long story short, the two of us lay there in confinement until a policeman came in, lowered the shutters, and told us to get dressed. You think that was the end of it? Just listen to this.

IV.

As soon as we got dressed, he asked us to accompany him to the police station. "What have we done wrong?" we implored him. What great sin have we committed? We had already gotten what was coming to us when we were lying there in the window with the whole world laughing at us. But the policeman didn't want to know. He told us we would be charged with outraging public decency, no less! "Rasha-Gitl," I told the wife, "a fine mess you've got us into with your fainting. Why are you so silent?" "Who's silent?" she shouted, and fell down in a faint. The policemen caught fright and took to his heels. I thought I'd got rid of him and raised my hands to heaven. But it was only two minutes before he was back with two other policemen. He must have seen that my Rasha-Gitl was too much for one man to handle. For her, two are needed at least.

And that's what happened. No complaints or excuses helped, not even her fainting for a third time. They took us to the police station in grand style, holding us by the arm like a bride and bridegroom led to the marriage canopy, accompanied by jeers from the wretches gathered in the street to watch. Don't even ask! We were brought to trial in court.

Oy, vey! What we only went through! The judge, a nasty piece of work if ever there was one, wanted to have us locked up and deported. It was a miracle, a real Hanukkah miracle, that our lawyer managed to get us off with a fine. We were fined ten pounds each, plus costs. Oy, the trouble that rotten night's sleep had caused me! I had no idea where I was going to find the money.

I managed to scrape my ten pounds together and took it to the court. I didn't bother about my missus's ten pounds, to tell the truth. Let her sort it out, I said to myself. And if she can't, a short spell in the nick will do her good.* I'm also entitled to a bit of peace and quiet. Doesn't she give me enough trouble? Would I have found myself in that whole mess if not for her, with her seasickness and her fainting? But the judge turned out to be a real antisemite who wouldn't do a Jew any favors. He ruled that either we both pay up together or we go to jail together, because we had committed the offense together. Did you ever hear of such a thing? In the end, Shaye took pity on us and lent us the money, so we avoided going to jail.

That's my Hanukkah miracle or, as I call it, the Hanukkah Miracle on London Bridge. Not a bad Hanukkah miracle, eh?

Translated by Barry Smerin

MOSHEH OVED (1885–1958)

Mosheh Oved (Edward Good) was born in Skempe (Skępe), Poland, and came to England in 1903. He was a poet, a writer, and a staunch activist for Yiddish, becoming Stencl's righthand man in the Friends of Yiddish. A jeweler by trade, he ran a small shop called Cameo Corner, at 1 New Oxford Street in the West End, which attracted many Jewish and English customers, including Queen Mary. After World War II the shop moved to Museum Street, near the British Museum. Oved was a generous benefactor of Jewish art and Yiddish literature, supporting creative works and book publications. He was involved in running the Ben Uri Art and Literature Society for many years and was the president of the Friends of Yiddish. His poems and prose were published in the art journal *Renesans* (Renaissance), *Di tsayt*, Stencl's *heftlekh*, and *Loshn un lebn*.† His memoirs, *Vizyonen un eydlshteyner*, appeared in English as *Visions and Jewels*.[15]

---

* Spell in the nick—time in prison.

† Stencl's *heftlekh* (singular *heftl*): literary pamphlets published from 1936 to 1946. Afterward they continued under the title *Loshn un lebn*.

"The Jewish Poet Mosheh Oved in His Cameo Corner on Museum Street, WC1," sketch by Maurice Sochachewsky, *Di idishe shtime* (November 16, 1951). Courtesy of Dave Skye Sochachewsky. From the British Library collection.

Ben-Eli

Vizyonen un eydlshteyner, 1950 (first published [location unknown] 1931)

Of the many colorful characters who crossed my threshold, one of the most interesting and distinctive Jews was the poor, old, yet beautiful Ben-Eli.

I've known him for eighteen years, dragging himself around the dregs and leftovers of various present-day and old-time arts and crafts. He knows a little about everything, and a great deal about London pubs and their clientele, about antique dealers and how they got rich, and about the background of every prominent thief and the thieves' den that gave birth to him. No wonder he told me Charles Dickens had got a lot of firsthand material about the London underworld from him.

He has such a fantastical and romantic imagination that he'd suffocate within the narrow confines of realism and truth. He would have rotted away long ago in his squalid existence if he had stuck to facts and not deliberately

Interwar Yiddish Culture   137

indulged in outlandish flights of fancy. When the spark of genius flares up in him, he gets completely carried away. A genius can never keep his hat on!

As he sweet-talks you, he strokes his silky white beard contentedly. And when he tells you an ingenious made-up story, his face shines, bright and fresh as the first page of a new calendar. He smacks his lips after each delicious sentence, like a wine connoisseur after a drop of a really good vintage. He sips away at the bright imaginings that exude from his pores, bathing his face in a divine light.

"Good morning, Mr. Good!" he chants, in four warm baritone notes that ring out from his broad chest. "Good morning, Mr. Ben-Eli," I respond, like an alto, pronouncing his name with a soft "l."

"Well, Mr. Good, how's business?" he asks. He raises his eyelids sharply, and his eyes pierce me to the quick, as painfully as my business itself. "Alright, thank you," I reply, as if his question has not caused me any anguish. "Have you got something to sell?"

"I have a gold-plated chain for you. I bought it only yesterday at the pig market. To you, ten shillings. If I sold it to any old junk merchant, it'd cost him a pound."

"Spare me all the talk. Will you take eight shillings?"

"I can't, by my life! May I not live to see my grandchildren, if I take eight shillings. I paid eight shillings for it myself."

"Will you take nine shillings?" I ask.

"Alright," he replies. "Because it's you."

Then he spots six Yemenite silver buttons in the counter display case. "Aha! I know where you got those. Mr. Smith, from the Elephant and Castle, sold them to you—the dirty dog! I've had my eye on them for years. Now he's grabbed them from me."[*]

"Are you sure they're the same ones?" I ask. "Am I sure, Mr. Good? On my word of honor, I remember those buttons from thirty-five years ago. They were hanging in the window of Raphael's pawn shop in Kensington.[†] He was a fine piece of goods, that Raphael. Never gave a penny to charity in his whole life. Slept under the counter and kept all his money sewn up in his bedding. Whenever he had to give some change, he tore open a pillow and stitched it up again afterward. Before he died, he made a will leaving his mattress with five thousand pounds sewn up in it to a *shiksa*, a barmaid, and

---

[*] Elephant and Castle: an area of South London, in the borough of Southwark.

[†] Kensington: an area of West London.

the pillow with the small change to his wife.* His wife threatened to throw a big party with music on every anniversary of his death. That scared him, and he made a new will switching things round: He left the pillow to the *shiksa* and the mattress to his wife. As for those buttons, Raphael had wanted six shillings for them. Before he died, he held a sale. He wanted to die with cash in hand, and he sold the buttons for five shillings. After his death, the buttons hung for twenty years in Mr. Lou's shop in Wardour Street. He wanted no less than ten shillings for them. Last week I saw them in Farringdon Road, with Mr. Martin, the watchmaker.† Martin, no less! You've never in your life seen such a good-for-nothing as Martin. He had a shop over the water in a wonderful position, a gold mine, but he couldn't make a living. Along comes a smart guy from Manchester who knows London like I know the planet Mars, drops into Martin's shop, and asks him how much he wants for it. That idiot Martin goes and shows him, in black and white, that the shop cost him 149 pounds, and tells him he only wants five pounds' profit. The guy from Manchester bought the shop and got stinking rich, and Martin opened a sausage bar and lost every penny. The cook stole from him, the customers stole from him, and Martin ate the leftovers with no bread to go with them. The clever dick from Manchester is in thick with Jimmy and Morris, the two smartest crooks in the Minories. He'll either die in jail or in a Park Lane mansion.‡ Let me tell you—but keep it to yourself!—there'll soon be a court case and a huge scandal. I've seen the lights burning in Scotland Yard at two in the morning. They're wide awake, planning what to do with him. Poor old Martin. Such an honest watchmaker would have starved to death long ago, like most watchmakers, and said goodbye to all his troubles, if he hadn't taught himself to do magic tricks and play the trumpet. Now he does tricks on stage and accompanies the performers in the cheapest music halls. And in his spare time, he repairs watches and wireless sets. From all those three professions he makes a pitiful living."

The fact is, I bought the gold-plated chain from Martin out of pity. I gave him a plaster head of Apollo for it. The plaster head had cost me a Spanish leather decanter that was worth a dollar at that time.

I ask him: "How are things with you, Mr. Ben-Eli?"

---

* *Shiksa* (or *shikse*): non-Jewish woman. Often pejorative.

† Wardour Street, West Central London; Farringdon Road, East Central London.

‡ Park Lane: One of the most expensive locations in Central London.

Interwar Yiddish Culture 139

"I'm doing very well. I've got two sheds packed to the roof with goods. I can hardly get into them, so I've made doors in the roofs. I'd be the happiest man in the world if not for that serpent, that hag, that drunken cow, my son's wife. She, she . . . but better not ask. It's a pity he wasn't killed in the war. He would've been better off. She has ruined all our lives. But . . . better say nothing. Oy! A good day to you."

Old Ben-Eli dropped in on me like that for years. He would sell me a trifle, pick up an article in my shop, and link it with his burdensome reminiscences. As his powerful imagination took flight, he would invent one episode after the other, interspersed with laughs and groans, always ending with the same heartrending sigh: "Oy! A good day to you."

Around midnight on a pale, insipid night just before the end of the war, when the battlefields were already soaked with the blood of London's best, I saw two moons at the same time: the old, familiar moon, wandering through the sky among the watery clouds, and Ben-Eli's figure wandering through Holborn. The two stars in his bright face were leading him from Kensington to Stepney. A bag hovered above his shoulders like a cloud. In it were secondhand shoes for his grandchildren. He was striding along like a hero ascending a mountain hill to defend the weak.

So who is Ben-Eli?

He is descended from a wealthy, artistic family that has lived in London for generations. He says his father was one of the architects of the Houses of Parliament. I am sure he is descended from an aristocratic tribe of our people. He is always talking about his trifling losses and recalling foolish incidents. As for his national and religious losses—these he has long forgotten.

But when London was asleep, when all the factories and banks were shut, and daytime concerns had vanished, Ben-Eli's soul was wide awake. And he, the old prince, together with his princess, the moon, floated aloft from Kensington to Stepney. Not long afterward, Ben-Eli stood at my counter, dressed in rags, and made the following suggestion:

"Mr. Good, you've known me for many years. You know I'm an honest man and never ask for charity. The only houses in London that I don't frequent are the almshouses of the Board of Guardians. I want you to give me a few pounds' worth of goods on commission. As soon as I sell something, I'll bring you the money. You would get rid of some rubbish, and it would help me out."

"Listen, Mr. Ben-Eli," I replied. "You have always earned something from me, and I value your visits. I don't want to lose you. But you will sell my goods and the money will disappear, and—"

"No, no!" he interrupted. "I swear by my grandchildren!"

"I know you love your grandchildren, and it's for them that you work, live, and suffer. Do you mean to tell me you would repay what you owe me rather than buy your grandchildren something to eat? I can't believe you would behave so meanly."

"I swear I would."

"Enough swearing. There's no need. I'll give you the goods, although it's a great pity we should lose each other for the sake of a little rubbish."

And I gave him a few articles.

Summers and winters passed, and all the seasons in between, and I didn't see Ben-Eli again.

Then, about a year ago, I was sitting on a red bus that was making its way through the narrow streets, when I suddenly saw Ben-Eli sitting on the same bus. He must have seen me, too, because he turned as red as the bus itself, blushing like a young girl who had committed a sin.

I turned my head away, pretending I hadn't seen him. I jumped off the bus as soon as I could and caught another one. Good of me, wouldn't you say? Just read on a bit.

As I sat in my shop a few weeks ago, writing this very book, I saw an eye peering through a split in the curtain. I recognized Ben-Eli's eye. I stood up, drew back the curtain, and motioned for him to come in. We chatted as if nothing had happened, and I bought several gold-plated bracelets from him. He told me a few stories, entrusted me with a few secrets, and left.

After he left, I had a suspicion that one of the bracelets was not gold-plated but real gold. I tested it with nitric acid, and it turned out to be pure gold, with a melted value of thirty shillings.

When he returned a few days later, do you think I told him about the bracelet? No, not a word!

He left, and I couldn't believe I had been capable of such a despicable deed. That thirty shillings' worth of gold now weighed as heavily on my conscience as if I owned all the gold in the Bank of England. It squeezed my heart like a sponge clamped in a vice.

I would have told him and apologized, but he didn't come back again. I would have written, but I don't have his address. And I'm too busy with my business and my writing to run around Stepney making inquiries. If he has already passed away, God forbid, I don't know the language of the world to come well enough to communicate with him, even though I can think up stories and write books.

And now, just as I finished writing this, Ben-Eli came in, to my great relief.

I told him about the bracelet and handed him a pound. "Mr. Good," he said in a trembling voice, "I had no idea. This will do you more good than you know. Yes, it will, it will."

Although my customers are more or less decent people, he managed to sell me a beautiful, useless Turkish metal horse for six shillings. But he paid me in full with stories—each story a window into the innermost chambers of his soul.

"Why haven't you been round recently?" I asked.

"Oy!" he said. "I've had a lot of troubles. During the strikes, a real Jew lent me a van, and the strikers poured petrol on it and burnt it. And my son turned against me. You can't blame him. He had eleven children. Nine of them have survived. His eldest daughter is my best friend in the world. She's a woman, but a good soul all the same. Oy! A good day to you."

But this time, his "Oy!" contained a hidden note of joy.

Translated by Barry Smerin

4

THE SECOND WORLD WAR AND AFTER

The 1940s

The East End was heavily bombed during the Second World War, particularly during the Blitz, which began in September 1940. There was extensive damage to streets and buildings, and many Eastenders lost their lives, homes, and livelihoods. Despite the constant struggle for survival and maintaining a daily life, Yiddish cultural activity continued, and *Di tsayt* stopped its daily publication only for a few days at the start of the Blitz. Yiddish culture even continued to develop, and for the few days *Di tsayt* was unable to produce a newspaper, the Narodiczky Press published the first of Stencl's literary *heftlekh*. In the sketch "Celebrating the Fiftieth Yiddish Booklet," Stencl describes his single-minded passion to maintain Yiddish culture despite the war; indeed, the Friends of Yiddish literary circle continued meeting throughout the war, with lectures and readings by writers and actors.[1]

One highlight of wartime Yiddish culture was the 1943 play *The King of Lampedusa*, written by local writer Samuel Harendorf. It was based on a true story of a British Jewish pilot who ran out of fuel and made a forced landing on the island of Lampedusa. The island residents, fearing a British invasion, surrendered to him. The play is a comedy set in the East End and in a dream scene on Lampedusa, with amusing characters and an uplifting message. It was performed in the Grand Palais Theatre on Commercial Road

144   Chapter 4

in 1943 and ran for six months.[2] However, this moment of comic relief sat atop despair. Katie Brown's sketch "My Address Book" epitomizes the fear of losing everything: people murdered in Eastern Europe, a generation of Yiddish-speakers dying in the East End, and the fates of children fighting in the British army.

After the war London was fractured communally and politically. Many Jewish Eastenders who had lost their homes moved out of the East End to the North West and North East London suburbs, leading to a steep decline in the Jewish population of the area. There were political disagreements about the future of British Jewry and, notwithstanding the rise of Zionism, different views on the establishment of a Jewish state in Palestine. There was also a surge in antisemitism.[3] Oswald Moseley's British Union of Fascists, which had been clandestinely active during the war, now became more openly confrontational against Jews on London's streets. In 1946, "The 43 Group," made up of many Jewish former servicemen and servicewomen, took to the streets to disrupt the BUF meetings and to counter their attacks, leading to some fierce street battles.[4]

Within the immigrant community there was a feeling of heightened anxiety that Yiddish culture had disappeared across Europe and that Yiddish language culture was fast disappearing from Britain. But Yiddish did not disappear. In 1946 Stencl's *heftlekh* became the literary journal *Loshn un lebn*, a larger and more regularly appearing publication that would last for the next four decades. The journals were packed with stories, poetry, literary and theatre reviews, and an announcements section. It gave new opportunities for many more professional and nonprofessional Yiddish writers to publish their work. Stencl encouraged new local writing, and there was a greater representation of women writers in *Loshn un lebn* than in the mainstream Yiddish press.

In the mid-1940s there were successful productions of the New Yiddish Theatre Company in Adler House, and toward the end of the decade, there were lively theatre seasons at the Alexandra Theatre in Stoke Newington, bringing over famous Yiddish stars from America like Leo Fuchs.[5] Stencl's fighting resourcefulness, including his refusal to speak any language other than Yiddish, was impressive. However, although the Friends of Yiddish still drew a weekly crowd, it could attract its prewar numbers only when hosting a special guest from abroad. The majority of the membership was elderly and often the last generation for whom Yiddish was their first language.[6]

JUDAH BEACH (1882–1964)

"Judah Beach," detail from "Hon. Officers and Executive Council, Ben Uri Art Gallery," by Maurice Sochachewsky, *Di idishe shtime* (February 29, 1952). Courtesy of Dave Skye Sochachewsky. From the British Library collection.

Judah Beach was born in Rav'e (Rawa), Poland; he came to Britain in 1906 and worked as a tailor. Beach cofounded the Ben Uri Art and Literature Society in 1909, and throughout the 1920s, as its vice president, he housed the society's permanent collection in his home in Hampstead until the Ben Uri found a dedicated location. His home became a meeting place for Jewish cultural activists. Beach was involved in the Friends of Yiddish group and was its president for the last ten years of his life. During the Second World War, he wrote stories of Jewish London that were published in *Loshn un lebn* and later collected into the short story collection *Sheydvegn*.[7]

• •

The Wailing Wall on Archer Street

Stencl's *heftl,* 1944

Behind the prosperous thoroughfare of Shaftesbury Avenue, there's a narrow back street tucked away like the small print denoting the prayer for rain and dew in a large *siddur*.[*] The Apollo Theatre and a shoe shop stand apart from a few houses. The two very different buildings, one a temple of art and the other an ordinary shoe shop, converge in a large back wall. That wall is a meeting place for the many musicians who gather there every day to anguish over hard times. The wall absorbs the bitterness of people who are losing the hope of a better life.

---

   * Shaftesbury Avenue is part of the West End's theatre district. *Siddur*: prayer book. In the three-times daily *Amidah* prayer, the wording for the section praying for rain is different for summer and winter. Above the words, in small print, is an explanation of when it is read.

Chapter 4

You might think there's something special about Archer Street, since it attracts so many music-lovers. But it's just a small, dingy side street with a few Italian cafés, where young men and women sit and joke, their raucous laughter echoing from one café to the next. Among all the other good things you can buy there, the biggest draw is ice cream, apparently for Jewish youth to cool their hot, restless temperament.

At the entrance to the street, there's a short man standing with a basket next to him that is almost as tall as he is. The basket contains bags of nuts heaped up in a pyramid. The man casts a searching look at each passerby, screwing up his thin nose into a piteous expression suggesting that buying nuts from him is a religious good deed.

During the lunchtime hours, whole orchestras wander along Archer Street, as well as ordinary street musicians and conjurers, some of them singing songs, playing fiddles, or blowing on brass trumpets. The air is filled with a jumble of sounds that mingle with the noise of the passing motor cars. Heavy-laden carts cut through the street, drawn by large, powerful thoroughbreds. The horses' hoofbeats leave a despairing echo hanging in the fatigue of the day.

Years ago, Archer Street was a Garden of Eden for every musically talented individual, especially for Jewish youth who flocked enthusiastically and paid well to hear the jazz bands. Afterward they would congregate ostentatiously at the wall to do justice to the occasion and go home gaily humming one of the new tunes the modern world spits out every day. But times have changed, and the wall now stands as a silent witness to the ruin that new technology has made of the world of music.

The street is always lively, like an exhibition of modern paintings of different characters with varying temperaments and dispositions. Here, for example, stands a compact little Jew, round as a cylinder, with a modest double chin. In Archer Street they call him Yankel the Blower, because his cheeks are always puffed out from the habit ingrained by his profession. Yankel is blowing on a sousaphone, an instrument which, hoisted on his shoulders, looks like a goat with twisted horns.

Lame Michael slinks into the street unnoticed, lost in thought, hauling his cello. They call him Lame Michael because his legs are twisted outward from constantly holding his instrument between his knees. He's an angry man, with deep-set flaming eyes that are always searching. His face is pale, his forehead furrowed with lines of despair. He greatly resents his lowly status and can by no means reconcile himself to it and adopt the discordant

The Second World War and After   147

sounds of the latest musical fashion. He knows many of his colleagues don't like the jazz bands either, but they are the sort of people who can turn their hands to anything and don't differentiate between one genre and another, people who can't take a stand on principle. They think that if everyone's doing something, they must follow suit, or else that it's simply to their advantage to do so. For that reason, Lame Michael has always felt hatred for his colleagues on Archer Street.

In his youth Michael was bent on achieving fame, but time has reduced him almost to abject inferiority. Although he hasn't had any work for a long time, he is pleased to be standing here on Archer Street at the Wailing Wall. Deep in thought, he takes the most pleasure from how his wife, Milly, had snuggled up to his chest today as if she were hiding from something that frightened her. Then, despite himself, a nagging melancholic pain about his friend intrudes on his thoughts. He vainly attempts to brush it away like an irritating fly. "Why this sudden change?" he asks himself and feels like he is sinking into an unknown world. His soul is plagued by an unremitting cacophony. Different thoughts flash through his head. It seems only yesterday that he first met Milly on Archer Street and fell so heavily in love with her. His heart fills with misery, and he feels lost, and everything around him seems empty and desolate.

The crowd of musicians were fond of Michael. Aware of his poor situation, they offered him occasional gigs that they happened to obtain. But Michael, always the proud musician, rejected their offers with a wave of the hand and pressed closer to the wall, seeking an answer to his melancholy thoughts. There he would stand till nightfall, as if in a drunken stupor. It was always late when he left, taking his shadow with him, a silent witness to a world of music ruined by modern technology.

Translated by Barry Smerin

AVROM NOKHEM STENCL (1897–1983)

Avrom Nokhem Stencl was born in Tsheladzh (Czeladź), Poland, into a rabbinical Hasidic family, and had an Orthodox education in Bible and Talmud. In 1919, to escape military conscription, he fled to Holland, and from there to Berlin. Engaging with secular life for the first time, Stencl frequented the Romanische Café and began to write poetry in Yiddish. There he met the famous poet Else Lasker-Schüler, who took great interest in his

"The Poet A. N. Stencl," sketch by Maurice Sochachewsky, *Di idishe shtime* (January 9, 1953). Courtesy of Dave Skye Sochachewsky. From the British Library collection.

poetry, and they became close friends. It was in Berlin that Stencl became a published Yiddish poet.

Stencl arrived in London's East End in 1936 and lived there until his death. He was a passionate advocate for the Yiddish language in the Jewish immigrant community. From 1936 he began publishing pamphlets of his own poetry with the Narodiczky Press, and in 1938, he set up the weekly Literary Sabbath Afternoons, later called the Friends of Yiddish, which ran for decades. In 1940 Stencl produced the first of his literary *heftlekh*, which included poetry, prose, literary essays, and reviews, mainly his own work but also including that of a number of local Yiddish writers. Each *heftl* had a different name, but in 1946 they became the literary journal *Loshn un lebn*, which continued publication until 1981. Stencl was an extremely prolific poet; he became known as the Yiddish Bard of Whitechapel, which was the location and subject matter of many of his poems. Stencl, who as a general rule refused to speak the small amount of English he may have known, was a fierce advocate for Yiddish. The Yiddish playwright and journalist Samuel Harendorf, at a Yiddish poetry event in 1962, called Stencl an "institution," and claimed that Stencl's Christian neighbors would learn Yiddish before Stencl learned English. Nevertheless, Stencl's work appeared in English translation in Joseph Leftwich's anthology of Yiddish poets, *The Golden Peacock* (1939).

Stencl wrote feuilletons and opinion pieces alongside his poetry in *Di tsayt* and *Di idishe shtime*. He also wrote editorial essays in *Loshn un lebn* and, later, part of an autobiography.[8]

• •

Celebrating the Fiftieth Yiddish Booklet

Stencl's *heftl,* 1944

From the outset, the Yiddish booklet had two goals. The first was that it should carry on without any financial support or sponsors. The Talmud tells us that "a living thing carries itself," and that rule is the prime condition for viability.* The second goal was to ensure that every printed copy went to someone who can read Yiddish. Basically, the two come down to the same thing: If every copy is read, a publication pays for itself. Conversely, if you commit yourself not to take more than the cover price for each copy, you must have as many customers as the number of copies printed.

The first booklet had no issue number printed on it. It appeared in September 1940, during the first days of the Blitz, when there was not even a Yiddish newspaper being published. Who then thought of "founding," or continuing to publish, a Yiddish literary booklet here in Whitechapel? All we wanted from the first booklet was to maintain the continuity of the living Yiddish word. For those of us who believe in the physical and spiritual power of words in general, the Yiddish word is the magic charm that protects a Jewish community—and when were we ever more in need of shelter and protection than in those dangerous days?

The first issue, like the following ten, had only eight pages and cost only twopence. I'll always remember Rosh Hashanah Eve in 1940, when I took the whole first issue, almost five hundred copies, with me into the Tilbury Shelter.† The printed copies were ready just an hour before nightfall, so there was no time to take them somewhere for storage and then rush to the shelter before the shooting and bombing began. Anyway, if you are running for shelter, it's best to take your few possessions with you if you can.

To cut a long story short: In under an hour before nightfall, the whole issue—close on five hundred copies—was literally snapped up. On that Rosh Hashanah Eve in 1940, with the bombs raining down and the streets aflame for the umpteenth time, I knew in my heart that Jewish Whitechapel was safe.

Thousands of people under one protecting roof! Thousands of terrified hearts filled with prayer!

In one dark corner a small group of religious Jews stood reciting the Rosh Hashanah liturgy. How passionately they implored the Almighty to "remember us for life." When danger hangs over each person's head, how

---

* The phrase "the living carry themselves" comes from the Jerusalem Talmud, *Shabbat* 10:5:2–4.

† Rosh Hashanah: Jewish New Year. The Tilbury Shelter was a large goods depot partly beneath Commercial Road in the East End; it was used as an air raid shelter during the Second World War.

150   Chapter 4

close one is to God! And how close I felt in my heart to each Jew there. I grew fanciful, almost fanatical, in that terrible night. Had I had ten thousand copies of the booklet with me, wouldn't I have sold them all?! I stood there, a bundle of joy, in another dark corner and counted the takings. The whole issue was paid for. All the costs were covered, with even a little to spare.

Outside the bombs were falling, the streets were burning. And face to face with ten thousand terrified Jews, Yiddish-speaking Jews, I, who believe in the power of the word, made a solemn vow to do everything in my power to refute Sholem Aleichem's famous question: "London, why aren't you burning?"* And that's the question that everybody asks when they talk about the state of Yiddish culture here.

Do you believe in the power of the word, I asked myself, as devoutly as these pious Jews believe in their prayers? If so, then find the right words—words strong enough to protect the streets and shelter the people. If not—if Yiddish creativity, Yiddish culture, is not the innermost faith embedded in your heart, then join the throng of praying Jews and repeat their prayers word for word; perhaps we will all be saved, all of us together.

The second booklet, now proudly labeled "No. 2," came out when the little street where I lived had been almost wiped off the map by a landmine. And so it went on, till we reached No. 13—a lucky number! The "Soviet Russia" booklet cost threepence a copy, and the whole issue sold out in less than twenty minutes at a meeting in honor of Soviet Russia at the Whitechapel Art Gallery.

The booklets didn't make a rich man of me, but Whitechapel became a market for Yiddish: authors, sponsors, publishers, and not only booklets but whole books! And by the time No. 32 came out, I was no longer the only one selling Yiddish literature.

Nevertheless, even when the Yiddish booklet had increased from eight to sixteen pages and cost sixpence, the principle that "a living thing carries itself" remained in force. If Whitechapel can carry the cost of a Yiddish literary booklet every month, its existence is justified—both the existence of the booklet and the existence of Whitechapel itself.

Since September 1942 the booklet has appeared regularly on the fifteenth of every month. In the public battle against assimilation here in Whitechapel (and the hidden battle with scheming troublemakers!), it is now the monthly booklet of our Literary Sabbath Afternoons. As far as the

---

* This phrase is the title of a sketch in Sholem Aleichem's well-known memoir, *Motl Peysi dem khazns*.

The Second World War and After   151

Sabbath Afternoons are concerned, the battle against assimilation has been won 100 percent in favor of Yiddish, and personal and factional infighting among cultural activists has finally given way to constructive discussion—or so we hope!

In recent months, the "Friends of Yiddish" circle has contributed to the work on the Yiddish booklets. Its involvement is helping to boost sales, provide more opportunities to include photos of artworks, and increase the number of pages from time to time.

Today's issue is the fiftieth. We mention that only to draw attention to another current development. There has recently been a ruckus in the Jewish community over publishing and sponsorship issues, and there have even been literary petitions and letters to the press, and so on. We are not against them, God forbid. Absolutely not. Yiddish journals are no worse than the Hebrew collections that tell Yiddish authors and poets their writing is not "immortal" because, after the destruction of Jewish life in Eastern Europe, Yiddish is finished. "On the other hand," it is argued, "who here in London needs thick Hebrew journals? Hebrew cultural activists and literary sponsors speak only English! As soon as the war is over, all those books will be sent to our brothers in the east. Meanwhile, let them remain in storage."

Such ambiguity has its place, because if there was only one possible opinion, things would look very different. I'm not referring to our "distinguished" sponsors as much as to distinguished personalities among our "immortal" colleagues and fellow writers.

If only those "high-up" politicians who seek to rescue the survivors of our present troubled times had been as concerned to save the victims of the dreadful gas chambers.

The point we wish to make here is that we (although we quite see that Yiddish is no less entitled than Hebrew to have patrons and sponsors) have absolutely nothing to do with those "publishers," "appeals," etc. We have nothing whatsoever in common with them! Just as we do not wish to help our "tortured brothers in Eastern Europe" by sending them the immortal works of our London authors once the Red Army has liberated them.

We shall remain "fantasists"—"fanatics" of the living Yiddish language—never losing our faith in the compelling force of the Yiddish word! We shall maintain the continuity of the living Yiddish word here in our own community, studying it and immersing ourselves in it in all our deeds and thoughts, firm in our belief in the immortality of Yiddish literary creation. Thus will our own writers and poets be saved here in London.

Chapter 4

We are highlighting the fact that the present issue of the Yiddish booklet is already the fiftieth because we believe that the publication of fifty Yiddish booklets with such regularity *and* on an entirely self-supporting basis *is* an expression of a genuine cultural desire on the part of a Jewish community.

We hope to continue the regular publication of our literary booklets, especially now, when the hustle and bustle of the Yiddish book market is already an established fact of Jewish life here, and there is no need for proof of a living Yiddish language. We nourish the hope that our literary booklets will become not only a stimulus and a demand for the production of Yiddish literature but a genuine cultural expression of our cerebral and creative community.

Translated by Barry Smerin

KATIE BROWN

My Address Book

Arbeter ring, 1943

Of my numerous comrades, friends, people from the old country, and members of the Workers' Circle, my address book is a precious souvenir. It often happens, especially in hours of loneliness, that I open the book and browse through it slowly, stopping at each page, having a good look, and images from long ago arise before my eyes. Each address has a special value for me.

I find myself back again among my close friends in prewar times, in warm and cozy houses, discussing all sorts of interesting subjects. We debate and argue, and I am engulfed by a huge longing for those days and nights, and even for those times which, back then, I had thought were very boring.

Now, only ruins remain at each address: broken, destroyed houses and families torn apart. Everything is a memory of downfall and annihilation. The addresses are now no more than tombstones, cold, dead monuments to what once existed and will never return in the modern world. And I am overcome by a strong desire to destroy the address book with all its contents, which has, in any case, already outlived its life and is worthless.

However, recently my book was enriched with three new addresses—very important and necessary ones. And the three new addresses are more awkward, harder, blander, and nothing to compare with the simple, familiar addresses of my friends. They consist of large, difficult numbers and characters without words and without meaning. They stumble and dance like strange shadows in front of my eyes and make my head spin. In writing such addresses, I have to make a big effort, so that, God forbid, I don't make a mistake, don't switch one character for another, because it is these very addresses that have such value and significance for me now.

They are the addresses of my three sons in the army. Writing the addresses takes up almost the whole envelope. Although the three letters will be sent to different places in England and abroad, the addresses are all so similar, almost identical, with only a small difference. The address immediately makes it clear that the contents can't be entirely private. Inside an envelope with this sort of address, I also write differently, not always what I want to say and seldom what I feel, because the address is so cold and unwieldy and without any spirit of life in it.

And when I open my book and pause at these last three addresses, my three beautiful boys appear before me, young, fresh, with innocent faces, with sweet smiles that fill me with joy and hope—hope for a better world, a more beautiful future—a dream that all mothers dream about their children.

But reality is so strong and powerful, it destroys all fantasies and dreams. Cold, real life has taken my three sons away from me, and in their place I am left with nothing more than three large, difficult addresses that lend beauty to my address book and won't let me destroy it.

Translated by Vivi Lachs

DORA DIAMANT (1898–1952)

Dora Diamant was born into a Hasidic family in Pabyanits (Pabianice), Poland. In the 1920s, escaping her religious family, she moved to the vibrant secular Jewish scene in Berlin, working there as a teacher and agitprop actress. In the summer of 1923, she met Franz Kafka, who was already sick with tuberculosis. After an inseparable three weeks, Kafka decided to move to Berlin, and he and Diamant lived together until his death a year later.

While in Berlin, Diamant met Stencl in his Berlin Yiddish circle, and they became close friends. Stencl left for London in 1936 and was encouraged by Diamant to set up a secular Yiddish circle in London. In 1940 Diamant moved to England, and to London in 1942. She became an active member

Dora Diamant, circa 1950. Courtesy of the Lask Collection.

of the Friends of Yiddish Literary Sabbath Afternoons and, as an actress, frequently recited passages from Yiddish literature, especially that of Y. L. Perets. She became a popular performer at the Friends of Yiddish and an integral part of the Whitechapel literary scene.

Although not a regular writer, Diamant authored occasional pieces for *Loshn un lebn*, including tributes to the artist Yankl Adler, who lived in London from 1940, and the Yiddish actor and director Solomon Mikhoels, who visited London in 1943.[9]

Solomon Mikhoels, the Man

Loshn un lebn, 1948

It was the winter of 1936 in Moscow, the year in which the word *Jew* in Europe was synonymous with worthlessness, deprivation of rights, and—most deplorable of all—fraternal betrayal. And—with all due respect to other countries—not only in Germany. No, not only in Germany: The whole of Western Europe rolled up its sleeves and joined in. The orgy of persecution stopped only at the Soviet border, for lack of a visa. As a Jew, you were allowed through, but you could expect to be given a rough time by a Soviet border official and told to "go to hell, the whole bloody lot of you!" A curse which means, in plain Yiddish, "Give me a present or some money, and I'll turn a blind eye during the border search."

I arrived in Moscow in that very winter, the beginning of Western Europe's great moral and cultural bankruptcy. And since I came from Berlin, a city renowned for decades as a major theatrical center, my Moscow friends took me to the State Yiddish Theatre. It was showing Shakespeare's *King Lear*, produced and directed by Mikhoels, and with Mikhoels himself in the leading role.

Since then, volumes have been written about that production. It has been lauded and described in theatrical chronicles throughout the world, so I shall not endeavor to give an account of it here. On the other hand,

The Second World War and After   155

very little, indeed almost nothing, has been written about the reaction of the Moscow populace as a whole to the existence of the State Yiddish Theatre or to its founder and bedrock, Professor Solomon Mikhoels.

Try, if you can, to imagine the event I'm about to describe, happening as it did to a woman like me, a refugee from Germany and its Nuremberg Laws. How pale and innocent it seems now, but at that time it was impossible to imagine, even in your worst nightmares, what the future held in store. We emerged from the metro and walked toward the theatre. Standing opposite us on the other side of the road was a tall building. High up on it, in large, illuminated Yiddish letters, were the words "Yidish melukhe teater," and underneath, in slightly smaller Russian letters, "Yevreiski gosudarstvenni teatr." I stood staring at it, unable to take it in. Could this be the city, the country, whose best inhabitants went for decades on pilgrimages to Western Europe to study in its temples the laws of humanity and beauty? Those temples are now so utterly despised, and here there is a "State Yiddish Theatre!"

On the square in front of the theatre, a crowd of people were standing in a long queue, four deep. People of all origins, not only Jews, talking and exclaiming in all languages. Men, women, and children had been standing there for hours on that Moscow winter evening, shuffling from foot to foot, waiting patiently and hoping they might be lucky enough to buy a ticket to the Yiddish theatre for the Yiddish performance of the great Englishman's drama, *King Lear*.

If you can picture that scene, I can only admire your power of imagination. I haven't taken it completely on board to this day. It still seems to me that what happened that evening in Moscow was all just a dream.

And the soul of that awe-inspiring splendor was Solomon Mikhoels. He bore it all on his shoulders, supported by a community of faithful followers—the whole enchanted building whose blazing Yiddish letters illuminate and gladden whole areas of Moscow.

Seeing Mikhoels among his friends, pupils, and onlookers, you had the impression of a flock of doves fluttering round his head, basking in the warmth of the love, faith, and trust of the people around him. It was impossible not to love Mikhoels. It was impossible not to give him your wholehearted trust.

It is probably a very sad thing to say, but I really have never met another living soul of Mikhoels's generation who had such a strongly beating Jewish heart, a heart that bled with every drop of our blood that was spilt.

Anyone who attended the meeting in London at which Mikhoels told of the dreadful happenings in Russia will know what I mean. Who can forget the trembling voice with which he described how the Germans danced on Torah scrolls and trod them underfoot? All of it recounted by a man who grew up in the midst of the strife and battles of the Russian Revolution, when assimilation—the blending of bloodshed in a joint struggle—was almost a natural, self-evident phenomenon. For who else is as ready as a Jew to devote life and limb to those who sincerely combat the injustice under which he labors, on an equal footing with that suffered by everyone? And there stood before you just such a fighter for the whole of humankind, tugging with such trembling intimacy at the heartstrings of his own people. Such feeling, such connectedness, could belong only to one whose historical memory, whose instinctive humanity, remained young and fresh. Only to a man who still drew his spiritual nourishment from the roots of his race and was the organic outcome of generations of growth.

For years I have been plagued by the question: Assimilation, yes or no? If only it would leave me alone! And each time I'm confronted with it, two figures arise before my eyes, two persons depicted in the Book of Psalms: one in the verse "Blessed is the man" and the other in "The ungodly are not so." The first stands firmly on his two feet and looks you calmly in the eye. You know you can trust him—as a father, a husband, a friend, or a party comrade. You know he will not betray you, because he has never once betrayed himself. He is true to himself and to his world, bound to it in natural self-evidence, like a branch to its trunk. He warms himself and blossoms along with it in the springtime sun, shivers with it in the cold and storms, and goes up in smoke together with it when the forest burns. The other person, the one depicted in the verse "The ungodly are not so," appears before me standing on one foot, because with the other he has stepped outside his circle, searching in thin air for a foothold in a foreign milieu. And since the foreign milieu refuses to make room for him, he remains standing on one foot, with the other dangling in the air, shivering in every passing breeze, wobbling unsteadily on a shallow platform, tossed this way and that, from shame to fear. And always in his eyes the restless flutter of the guilty party, scared that at any moment he will be caught red-handed in a sin of which he himself has no conception—an object of pity to his own flesh and blood and a laughingstock to the world at large. Whenever I think of Mikhoels, I see before me the person depicted in "Blessed is the man."

The Second World War and After 157

And if in 1948, we in Europe, in this dreadful first half-century of our existence, have had to lose such a Jew as Solomon Mikhoels, there is perhaps still some consolation for us, however impoverished and orphaned we may be after such an irreplaceable loss. Yes, we can still hope that his pupils and colleagues, who adhered to him with such love and respect, will remain true to him and preserve his legacy—and not, God forbid, squander it! If we still have a glimmer of hope of building a continued existence in Europe, it is with our eyes turned toward Soviet Jewry, because right now there is no other Jewry in Europe to speak of.

So we ask with a beating heart: "What will come to pass? Will the State Yiddish Theatre abandon us? Will they have the courage and strength to keep going without their Mikhoels?"

Let us together summon all the remnants of our power of belief, and believe they will indeed realize their responsibility and prove worthy heirs to the majestic heritage Mikhoels has handed down to them. Then their names will always be bound up with the name of Mikhoels, and we shall speak of them with love and respect.

Translated by Barry Smerin

At Yankl Adler's Funeral

Loshn un lebn, 1949

A few of Yankl Adler's closest friends and acquaintances had gathered in the office of his lawyer friend Oikin, before setting out together to the cemetery. The incomprehensibility of the dreadful event, so sudden, so cruel, hung in the air like a nightmare, making it difficult to breathe. A lady dressed in gray and black, a neighbor of Yankl's, came in, sat down, and suddenly burst out laughing: "If only Yankl could see this!" she exclaimed. "All of us sitting here with such long faces, dressed for a funeral. How he would laugh!" She said it with such wonderful simplicity, in genuine amusement.

Her laughter brought a lump to our throats, and we were seized by dreadful foreboding. Will we ever be able to laugh like that again, in full, unbroken merriment, when Yankl's wholehearted laughter, cascading, as it seemed, from his bristling amber eyebrows, is no longer part of the chorus? What is happening here? What does it mean? Will all of this simply cease to exist for us? Will his joy in life, his delight in painting, all his plans, each more ambitious than the other, no longer exist? Will his ultimate contentment no longer exist, the final achievement of the repose brought by life here in this village, in the spacious studio he himself conceived and planned and helped to build with his own hands? The happiness, like that of a bridegroom, finally preparing, disturbed by no one and nothing, to begin working in earnest? His whole way of life, both everyday and festive, all his joys and worries, his interaction with people and friends—all of it was only a means to an end, a palette for painting. Harsh, ruthless, and merciless toward anything and anyone that proved to be the slightest hindrance to his work. And accepting as right and proper anything that facilitated his work and made it possible.

Where is it all now? What does it mean? Never to have prepared for anything in life or death apart from painting? What will happen now? What will become of his two magnificent studios and the wonderfully beautiful Egyptian goddess upstairs in Bedford Gardens? What will happen to the paintings he started on? Who will finish them? And what of the telephone number in your notebook? How to imagine that if you dial PAR 9627, the voice replying at the other end will never again be Yankl's—his deep, rich tones, sometimes with an undertone of impatience if you disturb him in his work. Where, where has it all gone? What do you mean, he doesn't live here anymore? It's enough to drive you crazy.

Opposite me in the ritual cleansing chamber at the funeral ceremony stands Yankl's exhibitor, Gimpel, bent over a thin prayerbook.

I can't bear it! I'm torn apart by despairing rage: What has this got to do with Yankl? He won't put up with it. Something has to happen. He'll push up the coffin lid, sit up, impatiently pull the black cloth aside, and look around with eyes blazing with anger: "What are you all doing here? Please just go away and leave me alone. I haven't got time for this. I've got work to do." Then he'll stalk past the coffin, out through the open door of the cleansing chamber, stride up to the open grave, and waving the gravediggers away, he'll leap nimbly into the grave, look around angrily again, and roar: "Please don't disturb me, I've got to work." Then he'll draw the cloth over the grave, just as he used to draw the curtain across the windows of his studio when the sun in Kensington was shining too brightly.

For the first time ever, I find myself wishing desperately that I could believe, if only for a moment, that life continues beyond the grave. For without that belief, it's impossible to leave the cemetery, go back out into the sunshine, and leave Yankl lying there.

Suddenly, with icy rigor, the full enormity of merciless existence penetrates the depths of my being.

Translated by Barry Smerin

SAMUEL J. GOLDSMITH (1910–94)

Samuel Goldsmith, 1926. Courtesy of Tessa Rajak.

Samuel Joseph (Shmuel-Yosef) Goldsmith was born in Yaneve (Jonava), Lithuania. He studied law in Kovno and wrote for the Kovno daily newspaper *Di idishe shtime* and edited its evening edition, *Hayntike nayes* (Today's News). He was sent to London as *Di idishe shtime*'s British correspondent in 1939. After the paper was forced to close in 1940, Goldsmith remained in London, working as a journalist in the Yiddish, Hebrew, and English press. He wrote in Yiddish for London's *Di tsayt* and New York's *Der tog* (The Day), among other publications, including a series of Yiddish feuilletons for *Di tsayt* in 1942 that explored London life during the Second World War. He edited *Joseph Leftwich at Eighty-Five* in 1978, which included a range of Anglo-Jewish personalities and Yiddish writers.

As a war correspondent Goldsmith entered the Bergen-Belsen concentration camp with the British forces after liberation. He reported on the Nuremberg trials, and from 1958 to 1970, he served as the editor of the Jewish Telegraphic Agency in Europe. He published books in English and Hebrew.[10]

• •

A Whitechapel Gallup Poll

Di tsayt, 1942

In a pub in Fleet Street, I got into a dispute with an English colleague about Jews in Palestine. After a whole series of arguments and whiskies, I finally convinced him that we need a Jewish state in Palestine.

"Yes," he said. "I'm afraid you're right. You do need a Jewish state in Palestine, but you don't want one. And who can force you to have a state if you don't want one?"

"What do you mean, we don't want one? We certainly do!"

"That's what you say, but I have Jewish friends, good people, who say you don't want one."

160   Chapter 4

"They are a small minority."

"So you say, but they say you and your friends are a small minority."

We took another gulp of whisky, and I had a good idea. "You know what," I said, "the current tendency is to determine public opinion by the Gallup method. Let's conduct a Gallup poll of Jews. We shall of course bear in mind that they're only English Jews, and we shall also make the other necessary correctives. Then we'll draw up a table of the results, and we'll find out whether Jews want a state or not."

"Agreed, but first we have to bet on the result."

I've always been a sportsman, so if someone asks me to bet, I bet. We bet a week's wages. I could already see myself doubling my week's wages and doing a good deed to boot by proving to an Englishman, in black and white, that we want and need a Jewish state in Palestine.

We sat down and worked out the technical details of our great wager, as follows:

We would hold the poll in Whitechapel. We would question both men and women, since we're both great democrats.

Only real Jews would be counted. We had another little argument about whether to include assimilationists, and I got him to agree that they wouldn't be included.

The question: "Do you want a Jewish state in Palestine?" Clear and simple.

The answer could be "yes," "no," or "I don't know." Any other answer would not be counted. I made that a specific condition, because I know our Jews better than he does.

The next morning there we both are, standing in Aldgate High Street, holding our notepads. Along comes a bearded Jew with a greasy hat on his head and a worn-out overcoat. He looks like someone I might see in Vilna, on Deutsche Street, not in the British empire's metropolis.* We stop him and put our question. He gets a bit confused and starts mumbling "er . . ." and "hmm . . ." and "what I mean is . . ." I tell him clear and simple, in plain Yiddish, that we want a straight answer, yes or no. He replies, also in Yiddish: "Since you speak Yiddish, you can understand what I'm saying. A Jewish state is a very important matter, and I don't decide important

---

* Deutsche (German) Street (today Vokiečių Street) is one of the main streets of Vilnius (Vilna in Yiddish). The street housed the Great Synagogue of Vilnius, and in the late nineteenth century, many Jews lived there.

matters without my wife, God bless her. That's been my custom for forty years. I have to consult her first. If you really want my answer, leave me your address, and I'll send you a note right after we discuss it this evening. Explain that to your partner, and goodbye to you."

My "partner" was about to put him down as a "no," but with difficulty I managed to convince him that, at most, he belonged in the "no comment" category, because I was sure he wanted a Jewish state in Palestine, but since he did nothing without his wife, he had been unable to state his opinion. My colleague, greatly moved by the "idyllic family feeling" of East End Jews, conceded the point.

After my initial rebuff, I proceeded with caution. I waited for someone I could be sure of. Then, thank God, along came a Zionist, a man I had seen applauding enthusiastically at every Zionist meeting, a member of the Federation. I seized upon him confidently: "Do you want a Jewish state in Palestine?"

"What do you mean by that? A national home?"

"My question was clear!"

"To tell the truth, I haven't got round to reading Weizmann's latest declaration, so I don't know what our position is."[†]

Only with great difficulty did I get my colleague to record him as "no comment." He had wanted to count him as one of his "noes."

The next to come along was an Orthodox Jew, a follower of Agudath Israel.[‡] I wanted to let him pass, but my colleague stopped him: His beard had given him away. In reply to our question, he said: "Provided they don't desecrate the Sabbath there." What can you make of such a Jew? I was forced to agree to put him down as a "no."

A Bundist, whom I also knew, explained that he would be able to give us a proper answer when the latest instructions arrived from the Bund headquarters in New York.[§] A member of Poale Zion asked us to wait a couple of

---

[†] Chaim Weizmann: president of the World Zionist Organization and later first president of the State of Israel.

[‡] Agudath Israel: ultra-Orthodox, non-Zionist movement formed in Poland in 1912 with branches in London and across the world. Their desire to settle in Palestine came from a religious motivation.

[§] The Jewish Labor Bund in Lithuania, Poland, and Russia was a secular Jewish socialist organization founded in Vilnius in 1897. It was not a Zionist organization and promoted the idea of fighting for rights in the countries where Jews lived.

minutes while he went into a phonebooth and rang the office.* He also asked us to change a sixpenny bit to coppers or give him tuppence. A German Jew replied: "Provided they don't speak Hebrew in the Jewish state."

We got one "yes" from an Englishman whom we mistook for a Jew, but his reply couldn't figure in our list. Just my luck!

I suggested we try somewhere else. Suggestion accepted. We moved our pitch to Commercial Road. With a heavy heart, I began putting the question to every Jew who passed by.† There I had some success. In ten minutes I got ten "yesses." In another five minutes I already had a good lead, and after half an hour, I was sure of winning the bet. My friend proposed that we move to Kensington, and I agreed.‡ "If you want to move to Kensington," I replied, "I propose that we set up pitch in Soho Square near No. 33, where all the Jewish relief organizations are based."§ Faced with the threat of a whole bunch of Jewish organizations, he withdrew his proposal and paid the bet.

Translated by Barry Smerin

---

* Poale Zion: The Jewish Labor Movement was a Marxist Zionist organization of workers. The first British branch was established in 1903.

† Commercial Road is one of the two main thoroughfares of the Jewish East End, the other being Whitechapel Road.

‡ Kensington in West London was not a Jewish area, although some of the wealthy Anglo-Jewish establishment resided there.

§ Soho in the West End had a significant Yiddish-speaking Jewish community. The Federation of Jewish Relief Organisations was based at 33 Soho Square.

"Playing Cards in the Union," sketch by Maurice Sochachewsky (date unknown). Courtesy of Dave Skye Sochachewsky. From the British Library collection.

"Ruins at the Corner of Whitechapel and Osborne Street," sketch by Maurice Sochachewsky, *Di idishe shtime* (June 15, 1951). Courtesy of Dave Skye Sochachewsky. From the British Library collection.

"Scene in Wentworth Street Market," sketch by Maurice Sochachewsky, *Di idishe shtime* (June 29, 1951). Courtesy of Dave Skye Sochachewsky. From the British Library collection.

"A Group of Unemployed Tailors and Machinists in Whitechapel," sketch by Maurice Sochachewsky, *Di idishe shtime* (July 13, 1951). Courtesy of Dave Skye Sochachewsky. From the British Library collection.

"A Scene in Aldgate," sketch by Maurice Sochachewsky, *Di idishe shtime* (July 20, 1951). Courtesy of Dave Skye Sochachewsky. From the British Library collection.

"Jewish Public House in Commercial Road, E1., known as the 'Latke House,'" sketch by Maurice Sochachewsky, *Di idishe shtime* (August 24, 1951). Courtesy of Dave Skye Sochachewsky. From the British Library collection.

"Baker's Shop in Wentworth Street, E1," sketch by Maurice Sochachewsky, *Di idishe shtime* (September 12, 1951). Courtesy of Dave Skye Sochachewsky. From the British Library collection.

"Old Montague Street, E1," sketch by Maurice Sochachewsky, *Di idishe shtime* (April 3, 1953). Courtesy of Dave Skye Sochachewsky. From the British Library collection.

5

NOSTALGIA AND THE DECLINE OF THE JEWISH EAST END

The 1950s

By the early 1950s, amid postwar reconstruction, industrial development, and the 1951 Festival of Britain, which exhibited British arts and culture and achievements in science and technology, there was a new feeling of optimism in the country. For Jews, the establishment of the State of Israel in 1948 left them with a feeling of pride and hope for the future, even though few of them immigrated there.[1] The Jewish East End, however, was declining, as Jewish institutions moved to other areas of London, young families moved out, synagogues, especially those damaged in the war, were relocated, and the population that remained in the East End was mainly elderly.[2] The East End synagogues that remained struggled to get a quorum of ten men for daily prayers, which is amusingly conjured up in L. Beyneshzon's feuilleton sketches translated in this section.

At the end of 1950, the newspaper *Di tsayt* ceased publication. Morris Myer, the paper's editor since 1914, had died just over five years earlier, but his son and successor, Harry Myer, did not have the same erudition, gravitas, or Yiddish expertise as his father. The place of *Di tsayt* was taken by the non-partisan weekly *Di idishe shtime*, edited by Ben-A Sochachewsky. *Di idishe shtime*'s feuilleton slot on page 2 continued to publish short local sketches and also serialized novels by local writers, such as *Unter zelbn dakh* (Under the Same Roof) by Katie Brown and a number of novellas by Sochachewsky himself.[3] Yet, as the longstanding Yiddish writers retired or died, there were no new Yiddish writers to take the place of the older, more accomplished feuilletonists.

There were still Yiddish plays performed at the last East End Yiddish theatre, the Grand Palais on Commercial Road, but not with the same regularity.[4] The lively Sunday markets of Hessel Street and Petticoat Lane and Bloom's restaurant in Whitechapel lured Jews back to the East End for visits. The Friends of Yiddish could still produce a crowd for a special guest, but the audience was elderly, and its regular numbers were much diminished. Although the Yiddish language was in decline, London's rich Jewish cultural activity had not disappeared but had moved out of the East End into areas where Jews now lived, in North East and North West London.

Loshn un lebn continued publication for another three decades and offered the few younger Yiddish writers a place for their work to be published, but the number of Yiddish readers had decreased. To capture some of the stories of the older generation, the British section of the Yiddish Scientific Institute (YIVO) held an autobiography competition, in parallel to a similar one in America. It was called "My First Year in England" and drew nine fascinating immigrant stories. YIVO also produced *Yidn in england*, a volume in Yiddish that had been worked on for some years prior to its publication in 1966; it contains essays on Jewish history and Yiddish culture in Britain.[5]

Two *Loshn un lebn* almanacs came out in 1951 and 1956, bringing together a range of previously published material. The thriving Jewish East End became a place that existed more often in memory than as an ongoing concern, and later Yiddish texts, such as Ella Zilberg's "Gefilte Fish" and Moshe Domb's "Petticoat Lane," look back to a past time with a nostalgic tone. The next generation of writers, brought up in the Jewish East End, were still able to understand the Yiddish of their parents and grandparents, and the English Jewish writer Emanuel Litvinoff even produced a feuilleton in Yiddish.[6] Yet the themes in the stories of Wolf Mankowitz, the plays of Arnold Wesker, and Litvinoff's biographical fiction, which continued to create an East End mythology, were written in English.[7]

L. BEYNESHZON

The identity of the writer L. Beyneshzon is unknown, and his name is possibly a pseudonym. The name "Beynish" is a version of the name "Borukh," meaning "blessed." The religious overtone of the name certainly connects to the theme of a series of humorous feuilletons that were published in *Di idishe shtime* in 1951.

• •

Chatting before the Afternoon Prayer

Di idishe shtime, 1951

A Jew hurries through Whitechapel. He's in a rush and a little distracted. He takes no notice of the red light telling him to stop and is about to cross the wide street.

"Mr. Moses, Mr. Moses," yells an acquaintance of his. "Careful how you cross the road, you could, God forbid, get run over."

Mr. Moses, the beadle, stays there waiting for the green light to signal "go." Meanwhile his acquaintance has caught up with him, and, as people do, he grabs him for a chat.

"I take it that you're running to the meeting where they've decided to establish a daily Yiddish newspaper. You needn't run, let me tell you. You can just walk slowly because banana trees will ripen before they raise the thirty thousand pounds they need. At the moment they only have five wealthy men who have each promised a thousand pounds."

"Really?" said Mr. Moses in surprise, clucking his tongue, tsk, tsk, tsk. "With five thousand pounds you can already make a start."

"Yes, you can certainly start with that, but, as you know, between what's said and what's done there's lots of time in between. They've promised but not delivered."

"I could do as much myself," Mr. Moses intoned triumphantly. "It doesn't cost anything to promise or love. It was the same with our blessed rabbi. Last Passover he promised us that next Passover the Messiah would come. Well, can you see him coming?"

"Since you know that," asked his acquaintance, "why are you in such a hurry?" In the meantime, the red light had turned to green several times, but the chat had only just begun.

"I'm hurrying," Mr. Moses continued, "to my synagogue for the afternoon prayer. It's my duty as beadle to gather together a prayer quorum of ten

170   Chapter 5

men. You have no idea what hard work that is, a real slog. I get a dry throat shouting and persuading people to come in for the afternoon prayer. And it's even harder when you're about to get your tenth man and the other nine are waiting impatiently, and the one who needs to say the memorial prayer for someone in his family is terrified that a tenth man won't be found, and he won't be able to say Kaddish.* It's good that you stopped me. You must come with me and be the tenth man."

His acquaintance couldn't refuse the request to help out, and the two of them hurried to the synagogue, where they found seven men there already, making enough noise for seventy. They were heatedly arguing about the same subject: a Yiddish newspaper for the ordinary Jews of England.

"Here's Mr. Moses," they all suddenly shouted. "He'll tell us what's happening. He knows what's going on in the newspaper business. He knows all the writers, and he's a regular visitor to the editorial offices.

"So, what do you say, Mr. Moses? Do we need a Yiddish newspaper? What will come out of the meetings?"

Mr. Moses felt very pleased that they knew him and knew that he wasn't a nobody. And as there wasn't a prayer quorum yet, he began pleasantly explaining the issue of a newspaper for Jews. Adopting a singsong intonation as if he was giving a sermon, he illuminated the debate from all angles:

"There's no doubt that we need a Yiddish newspaper because—just between you and me—what use are the English newspapers to us? We don't understand them well, and they don't understand us well. They scribble whole pages about oil in Iran. But how does that affect us Jews? Do we have to eat fried fish? What's wrong with a bit of boiled fish, or gefilte fish with pepper and onion?

"My wife, long may she live, also adds a carrot, which tastes like the heavenly Leviathan, as the saying goes.† Of course, the real Leviathan must taste even better, but it's only for the righteous, and we poor sinners will be lucky to lick the leftover bones. I mean, there are so many Jews in Whitechapel, God preserve them, yet we still can't manage to get ten men together for prayers. But where was I?

---

* Kaddish: the mourning prayer recited daily for a year by a son or relative after the death of a family member and annually on the anniversary of the death.

† Leviathan: legendary giant fish to be eaten by the righteous when the Messiah comes.

Nostalgia and the Decline of the Jewish East End 171

"Take, for example, what's going on with Gromyko.‡ The English papers report what the Soviet foreign minister said and how he was answered. Do I understand what they're on about? Or when they write that someone has stolen a mink coat and jewelry, does that concern us? No one will be stealing any jewelry of yours or mine. And now all the divorces! God in heaven, how many divorces they get through! And the Festival of Britain also doesn't concern us. A festival without a drop of liquor and a piece of sponge cake to go with it, how does that appeal to us?

"But a Yiddish newspaper is an inspiration. First, you understand what you read, and that is very useful. And we'd know when the new Hebrew month starts and the date of the independence day of our nation, which every Jew needs to know. What's more, a friend of mine recently lost his mother-in-law (may it not happen to you!). He made a beautiful funeral for her, but I didn't hear about it because there was nowhere to advertise it. Because of that I lost a good couple of pounds. I would have gone to see the mourner and offer my condolences. I'd have made sure that I let him know the date of the anniversary of the death every year, and I'd have made a few bob on it.§

"I also didn't know that childless Yankl had passed away, leaving no one to say Kaddish for him. That could have been my job. A Kaddish-sayer is well paid. Also I could have found a match for the rich widow and made a good sum there. Some other matchmaker will have nabbed it by now, or she's already remarried. I'm telling you, gentlemen, without a Yiddish paper, you won't even know when a firstborn son is born. I've had a room empty now for a few weeks because I've had no newspaper to advertise that it's to let. We are truly blind without a Yiddish newspaper. I could give you thousands of reasons for a Yiddish newspaper, but look, here comes another man, so we're quorate. Let's start the prayers." And he began chanting, "Happy are those who dwell in Thy house . . ."

Translated by Vivi Lachs

---

‡ Andrei Andreyevich Gromyko was the Soviet Union's deputy minister of foreign affairs in 1951. The following year he became the Soviet ambassador to Britain.

§ Bob: British slang for shilling.

172   Chapter 5

Between the Afternoon and Evening Prayers 1

Di idishe shtime, July 1951

Apart from the two or three old men who come regularly to the afternoon prayer, the rest are grabbed. That is: Mr. Moses, the beadle, drags them in off the street to make up the prayer quorum of ten men. They rattle off the prayers, grab a chat, and scarper pell mell.

Mr. Moses and the old men, who feel proud that they are the regulars, call these men "the grabbed."

When six or seven men have been gathered, and Mr. Moses is out on the street trying to grab the last two or three to make up the quorum, those inside grab the opportunity for a lively conversation. The grabbed and the regulars soon get acquainted and are friendly despite their bickering:

"How long have you been in this country?" one of the old men asks one of the grabbed.

"For donkey's years—since the destruction of the First Temple."

"What do you mean?"

"Since the First World War?"

"Talk normally! Does that mean that you're already getting your old age pension?"

"No, not yet, because on my identity card I made myself ten years younger."

"What was the point of doing that? A man shouldn't hide his age like women do."

"Well, it's like this. I was getting married to a young widow, so I had to make myself younger. I removed my beard, moustache, and a few years. In fact, I didn't have to do that, because the widow herself took those years off my life. But never mind that, may she rest in paradise."

"Oy, why are you harking on about paradise in here?" someone butted in.

"Why not?" yet another ploughed in. "You can talk about paradise in a holy place. Aren't you always talking about business in the middle of the silent prayer?"

"Don't make yourself out to be so pious," the former retorted. "I saw you chatting in the middle of the evening prayers when the Manchester cantor was praying in Great Garden Street synagogue."*

---

* Great Garden Street Synagogue was a large East End synagogue on what is now Greatorex Street.

Nostalgia and the Decline of the Jewish East End   173

"Ah!" the other one answered triumphantly. "I'm glad you reminded me of that, I was just giving my expert opinion. You, pardon me, are a bore who doesn't understand anything about vocal melody. The greatest ignoramus would know that the way the cantor interpreted the words 'And when thou liest down and when thou risest up' was an absolute masterpiece. As he sang 'And when thou liest down,' he decorated the deepest notes with a coloratura, going deeper and deeper in a real interpretation of the words. And at 'when thou risest up,' he soared to the very highest notes, as if to really awaken us and raise us to our feet."

"Mister, mister, if you're such a know-all about singing, why aren't you a cantor?"

"Mm, who isn't a connoisseur of cantors? Does that mean everyone should become a cantor? Is it such a wonderful livelihood?"

"Enough of your bickering," another man intervened. "Better see to it that we get a quorum. I'm worried that we won't be able to say Kaddish. We're still missing two."

"I've got one!" said a young man with a cynical smile. "I can call up Sholem Asch, who's in London at the moment.[†] He's certainly not recited the afternoon prayer for a while."

The company laughed heartily at this suggestion, and the two old men exclaimed:

"Good idea, he could give us a greeting from the Nazarene, the Apostles, and Holy Mary."

"Shush, shush!" Mr. Moses tumbled into the synagogue with another two men: "What kind of talk is that in a holy place? You haven't got anything else to say other than Holy Mary?"

"No!" the young man replied. "We're talking about Sholem Asch. If he's not leaving London soon, I'll grab him for the afternoon prayer."

"No need for that," said Mr. Moses, the beadle. "He's already been grabbed somewhere else, and if I could grab him, I'd give him a piece of my mind. All the same, if he did come here, he would still be counted as a Jew to make a prayer quorum. A Jew is a Jew. Incidentally, he has returned to Judaism. He's writing a book about Moses. So, Yankel, get up on the lectern and let's pray."

Translated by Vivi Lachs

[†] Sholem Asch was one of the most popular, but controversial, Yiddish writers, dealing with subjects in his novels and plays that were seen as taboo, such as Christianity and sexuality. He lived in New York but had a daughter in London and visited often.

174   Chapter 5

● ●

Between the Afternoon and Evening Prayers 2

Di idishe shtime, August 1951

"Thank goodness we've got through the three sad weeks and the Fast of the Ninth of Av and we can talk of happier things," said Mr. Moses, the beadle, to his congregation. "As you know, in the last few days both young and old have suffered enough. Young people haven't been able to play tennis, football, cricket, go swimming, running, jumping, or do any other kind of sport.

"Older people couldn't play solo, bridge, pontoon, okey, and not even sixty-six. Do you think it's so easy to do without all that? But so what, if you can't. A Jew is a Jew and stays a Jew. People don't get married during the three weeks, they wait until the *shabbes* after the fast day. Now, thank God, we can do everything, everything except commit sins.

"This bloke told me . . . hush up, you should listen to this. This bloke got married fifty years ago, straight after the fast day and before the following *shabbes.* And fifty years ago, he said, when they had a wedding in Shnipshok, in the suburbs of Vilna, the dowry wasn't as big as it is here.* Here today a doctor would rather get old and gray than take fewer than five thousand pounds. But in Shnipshok the promised two hundred rubles was a large sum: one hundred was handed over at the engagement, and the other hundred was squabbled over until the wedding. The in-laws got involved, and the remaining sum was guaranteed for after the wedding, anything to get the groom somehow or other under the wedding canopy.

"'But I'm no fool,' the man told me. 'For me it had to be cash on the table, so from my two hundred rubles I didn't lose a kopek. The wedding was meant to be on Lag B'Omer, but because I hadn't received all of the cash, I postponed it for three months until after the Ninth of Av.† Then, on the day of the wedding, I stood there in my wedding clothes and refused to go under the wedding canopy until I'd received the outstanding fifty rubles. The father of the bride swore blind he'd give it to me with interest after the wedding, but I knew that was a hollow promise, and I refused to go to the wedding canopy. Suddenly I

---

* Shnipshok (Šnipiškės in Latvian), the Vilnius suburb where the town's oldest Jewish cemetery is located. The name Shnipshok is used in Yiddish texts to denote provincialism.

† Lag B'Omer: A festival, thirty-three days into the fifty-day counting period from Passover to the Feast of Weeks. The period is a time of mourning, but on Lag B'Omer mourning restrictions are relaxed and couples plan their weddings for that day.

heard a racket. I looked through the window and saw Esther, my bride, going past in a carriage with Haim, the ladies' dressmaker, on the way to the train station, where they jumped on a train to Riga.'

"'Do you think,' the man continued, 'that I gave back the hundred and fifty rubles? No bloody way, I'm no one's fool. But that girl did me wrong. She was pretty and clever, but if I had known she was going to play that dirty trick on me, I wouldn't have cared about the extra fifty rubles. It's fifty years since it happened, and every year when the *shabbes* after the Ninth of Av comes round, I remember it and get upset.'"

"Mr. Moses, Mr. Moses, excuse me interrupting you, but you're talking about something that happened fifty years ago in Shnipshok. Let me tell you what happened a year ago in London."

"Don't interrupt, don't interrupt," the others cried. "Let Mr. Moses finish the story he's telling."

"It's all right, let him speak!" Mr. Moses replied. "Let's hear it. We've still got enough time before the afternoon prayer." And so the other man began to tell his tale:

"This was a year ago, like today, the Thursday after the Ninth of Av."

"Stop going on about the date," others interrupted. "Just get on with the story."

"Let him speak, let him," Mr. Moses almost pleaded with them, "What's the matter? Are you in a hurry? Are you short of time? Is there a marriage contract waiting for your signature?"

The man began again:

"It was exactly a year ago, the Thursday after the Ninth of Av. The bridegroom was a qualified solicitor with an office in the City.‡ Invitations with the initials of the bride and groom were already sent out, and it had been advertised in the *Jewish Chronicle*. A lovely hall was booked. The caterers had already ordered the fish, meat, chicken, *lokshen*, salmon, peaches, grapes, even flowers as well.§ Suddenly, on the Thursday, the guests received phone calls and telegrams that the wedding was postponed for a while, but in truth it was postponed until the Messiah comes. And what do you think the reason was? Also the dowry. The promised five thousand had become four; the four thousand had become three, three thousand in cash. And the missing thousand put paid to the wedding.

---

‡ The City refers to the area of the City of London.

§ *Lokshen*: noodles.

176   Chapter 5

"True, the groom wasn't entirely to blame. It was his mother, a Cossack of a woman, who argued, haggled, and shouted, 'I won't let my son the solicitor sell himself so cheap. No, no, no!'"

"Oy, oy, the fashion for these damn dowries," Mr. Moses, the beadle groaned. "That's why my three daughters are sitting around unable to find a boy to marry, that damn dowry! It's already time for them to get married. And yes, it's already time for us to say the evening prayer." And he began chanting, "He is merciful and forgiveth sin . . ."

Translated by Vivi Lachs

• •

Between the Afternoon and Evening Prayers 3

Di idishe shtime, October 1951

I, the insignificant Mr. Moses, the beadle, known by that name across the whole of England, hereby announce to the world that I have given notice to the board of my synagogue and the whole holy community that after the Day of Atonement I will resign as beadle for evermore, amen. And so anyone, according to the rules, can take over my seat without having to pay key money and without committing an encroachment, God forbid.[*] The United Synagogue and Sir Robert Waley Cohen should bear this in mind.[†]

I also hereby proclaim and announce, and the whole world should know, that my leaving this important position is not, God forbid, anything to do with making a living or higher wages because, as everyone knows, I have never lacked for sustenance. I have had more than enough to eat and drink at one Kiddush or another: here a bar mitzvah, there a wedding, a party at the end of a Psalm Society recitation cycle, or a Ladies Guild dinner.[‡] I could always get a drop of liquor and sponge cake, and sometimes even a bit of cheesecake.

---

[*] Key money was paid by renters to secure a home.

[†] Robert Waley Cohen (1877–1952) was a British industrialist and president of the United Synagogue. The London Ashkenazi synagogues were brought together in the United Synagogue, which, together with the Chief Rabbinate, controlled synagogue issues including burial and charitable relief.

[‡] Kiddush reception: reception in synagogue after Sabbath prayers or special events.

Nostalgia and the Decline of the Jewish East End   177

I've been given so many clothes, I could open a secondhand shop. One synagogue officer used to give me all his old worn-out suits. Another officer would send me his old shoes, because we're the same size. And if they didn't fit me, I had the right to pass them on to the dustman.

And so, as you see, I wasn't short of anything and didn't have to leave this job. As God is my witness, I'm not doing this for money.

So, you will ask, why am I doing this?

Let me tell you: When a man gets lucky, it can come from any direction. I received a letter written in traditional biblical Hebrew, not that modern Hebrew they use in the Israeli newspapers. It was a letter from the Neturei Karta, and I will translate it for you here word for word:§

> To the honorable and distinguished gentleman, Mr. Moses, the beadle,
>
> As you know, the heretical, Zionist antisemites have held a congress here in the holy city of Jerusalem, and as we haven't managed to burn down the Knesset parliament building, we have thought of another way to clear them out of the Holy Land. We pious and righteous *hasidim* know that the Messiah will come this year, because if you rearrange the letters *t*, *sh*, *y*, *b*, whose numerical equivalents denote the year 5712, they spell out 't-sh-b-y,' which is the name of the Messiah, Eliyahu Hatishbi.¶ So we are going to put a watchman on Mount Sinai to look out for him, and as soon as he comes, the watchman will rush down from the mountain and alert us to the coming of the Messiah. Then we'll get the whole of the Orthodox enclave of Mea She'arim to come and greet him, and on the way we'll seize power from the heretics and bring the Messiah into the Knesset.** The Zionists will be left looking pathetic, and they'll know what it's like to be what they call us. Your pay will be the same as what you get as a beadle, but you will have a secure job forever, and you can even leave it to be inherited by your children and grandchildren.
>
> Awaiting your answer, we wish you well over the Yom Kippur fast.

---

§ Neturei Karta: anti-Zionist, Haredi messianic group opposed to a secular Jewish state in Israel.

¶ Each Hebrew letter has a numerical value. One type of Orthodox interpretation of texts makes connections between words with the same numerical value.

** Mea She'arim is an ultra-Orthodox Haredi district in Jerusalem.

Chapter 5

So, gentlemen, what do you think, God preserve me, of such a stroke of luck? This must have been ordained for me by God last Yom Kippur, because when I was reciting the closing prayer at the open gates of heaven, I saw there that there would be a miracle for me this year, a miracle from God. Is it a trifle to have the honor of becoming the watchman for the Messiah?! To be the first to greet him, the first to charge down Mount Sinai, from which our great leader Moses, not just Mr. Moses, the beadle, once descended. And, above all, to be the first to tell the Neturei Karta the news that the Messiah is coming!

But as you know, Satan interferes in such things, and it may have been he who put the thought in my head: Yes, running down the mountain is simple, but what about clambering up the mountain? Remember, I'm no longer such a young man!

But I soon exclaimed, in the words of the liturgy: "Prevent Satan from meddling in our prayers!" I understood that the thought was caused by my doubts, and the truth is that it's much harder to drag a Jew to the afternoon prayer than it is to clamber up a mountain.

So in summary, I will tell you that I answered immediately by letter, in a cable and on the wireless, that I am coming with God's help to take on this job with great joy. Only, may God help me get through this Yom Kippur fast and all the five afflictions, and not let it spoil my fast-breaking meal.* Meanwhile, until the Messiah gets here, may the Creator of the Universe inscribe us in the Book of Life for a good, healthy year, a year of life and peace for us and all the Children of Israel, amen and amen.

Translated by Vivi Lachs

ELLA ZILBERG

Ella Zilberg was primarily a poet. She wrote poetry regularly for *Loshn un lebn* from the 1950s and throughout the 1970s. She was a weekly attendee at the Friends of Yiddish, where she gave literary readings and sang.[8]

---

* The Yom Kippur five afflictions are fasting, not washing, not wearing perfume or lotions, not wearing leather shoes, and not having sexual relations (Mishna, *Yoma* 73b).

Nostalgia and the Decline of the Jewish East End 179

Gefilte Fish

Loshn un lebn, 1951

Why, when I smell the aroma of gefilte fish, do my eyes well up with tears and my heart beats with painful longing? Oh, the sweet, spicy smell awakens so many dormant memories, reveals images of old times, brings back the faces of dearly beloved forever wiped off the face of the earth.

As if on invisible wings, the smell carries me back over mountain and sea to the little Lithuanian shtetl Gorzhd, on the banks of the river Minija.[†] I find myself back again in the wooden two-story house, the jewel and pedigree of the town. I see the long stone high street leading to the marketplace, the center of Jewish business and pleasure. I see the old scattered houses with shingle and thatched roofs, and the gray edifice of the study house, the hallowed place for every Jew to come in the evening and pour out his heart to his creator and friend. I see the images of the five hundred beloved inhabitants of the shtetl: the rabbi with the pale face and the pious black eyes; the synagogue beadle with his long, shiny black kaftan; and the teacher, the shtetl's aristocrat. I see the cobbler with his communistic thoughts and the seamstress with her red, washed-out eyes, and of course, more than anyone, my dear blood relations: my sisters, their husbands and children, my uncles and aunts and their children. Every single one of these five hundred living, striving, and feeling Jewish bodies were devoured in one short afternoon. Not one of these precious martyrs remained alive, and there is not even a stone to mark their last resting place. Bloodthirsty, like wild beasts, the Germans arrived in Gorzhd in the first days of the war (the town lying so unfortunately close to the German border), and my little shtetl was destroyed together with its inhabitants.

Gone, nothing, no one there to relate this terrible act. No one to accuse the angry murderers of their brutal, inhuman massacre. And only a few surviving orphans, scattered to the Land of Israel, America, Africa, and also here in England, weep and wail the terrible fate of our families and the downfall of the shtetl of Gorzhd.

Gefilte fish, the symbol of Jewish Friday nights, when mother lit the *shabbes* candles and a holy grace radiated in her pale face, and hot, bleak tears rolled down her cheeks like dew as she sent her prayers up to the creator with such trust, love, and belief, of which I have never since seen the

---

† Gorzhd (Yiddish) is Gargždai in present-day Lithuania.

180   Chapter 5

like. Who can forget it; who can understand it, except for we who lived through it and heard the weeping? Father, his silver beard freshly combed, covered to his knees in his black kaftan, laid his bony hands on our childish heads and blessed us with a voice gripped with worry.

All of these images are suddenly alive and fresh again. They dance before my eyes and torture my soul with agonizing memories. But however great the pain, however much these sad images affect my health, I come back to them every time with joy and love. I walk in the back streets of the East End and stand hidden near a Jewish house where I can see the beauty of the Friday night candles and, with a thirsty soul, take in the smell that creeps through the crevices of a wooden door, the smell of Friday night and gefilte fish.

Translated by Vivi Lachs

RACHEL MIRSKY (?–1973)

Rachel (Rukhl) Mirsky was the honorary secretary for the women's committee of *Di idishe shtime*. She wrote sketches about urban London life that were published in *Loshn un lebn*. She was an active member of the Friends of Yiddish during the 1950s, reciting both her own work and that of others. She wrote a moving obituary of Katie Brown in 1955.[9]

• •

A Sketch

Loshn un lebn, 1953

On a warm day in May, three children sat opposite me on an underground train that was going in the direction of Battersea Park.* One was a little boy of five with his nose pressed up against the window, peering into the darkness. His small body was huddled up to the fourteen-year-old girl sitting next to him. On her other side sat a little girl of seven or eight. All three children looked like they came from a poor home. You could tell it from the way they were dressed, half in summer and half in winter clothing. The little boy wore thin short trousers, a thick woolen jacket, and a pair of heavy black shoes that must have made a loud noise when he walked. The other

---

* Battersea Park is a large Victorian park in London, just south of the River Thames.

Nostalgia and the Decline of the Jewish East End   181

small child, the girl, was similarly dressed, in a thin light-green dress and a pink woolen jacket. She too wore heavy winter shoes. Her hair was bound up in a pink ribbon tied in a large bow. She was also huddled up tight against the older girl and held her arm in arm, craning her neck to look through the window with great curiosity.

The older girl, who was only concentrating on the two younger children, wore a thick coat buttoned up to her neck. Pinned to the left breast of her coat was a brooch with a multitude of green and white stones. She too wore a pair of heavy black leather shoes. Her hair was a nondescript sandy color and hung down to her shoulders in thick strands. The strands stuck together—a sure sign that she didn't wash her hair very often. She too wore a green ribbon in her hair, with a lot of hairpins. She was holding a handkerchief squeezed tightly in her left hand, with which she kept wiping her nose. She rubbed her nose hard, each time leaving it red and her upper lip dripping. You could see she was doing it unconsciously. I sensed that her thoughts were entirely taken up by the two young children. Her every movement showed it.

It must have been getting a little too hot for her in the train, because the girl began unbuttoning her coat. It was then that I noticed her hands, and I couldn't take my eyes off them. Her hands were too big for a child like her. They were very red, with short, thick fingers and nails that ended very near where they began. What surprised me most were the thick, protruding veins. Her hands were dreadful to look at.

I suddenly realized that the child I saw before me was a child-mother, a poor mother who cooked and washed clothes and was burdened with all the household and family chores. The sight of that girl with the terribly worn hands made me think about the poor home in which she took the place of the mother she had lost. I saw a home that was run not by a mother who knew what she was doing, but by a child. And next to the little mother I imagined her big father, looking forlorn when he was alone in the house, sitting by himself at the window. He's a big man with a pair of heavy, work-worn hands hanging helplessly at his sides. His shirt is open at the neck, exposing a strong red throat full of narrow wrinkles. His face is also covered with wrinkles—a face such as you see only on men who work outdoors in all weather. He too has nondescript sandy-colored hair.

The children are out, and he is at home alone. He feels his loneliness. Sadness cries out from his blue childlike eyes. He's in a bad way, orphaned along with his children. His beloved eldest child is the mother. He feels a wave of pity for her and for himself. The girl has a huge burden to bear, and he cannot help her. The house is empty. He longs for a kind word, a warm look. He is thinking it would be nice if his fourteen-year-old daughter was as thoughtful to him as she was to the younger children. He sits down and stares out of the open window, just as his children are at this moment staring out of the window in the underground train. He sits there for a long time, lost in thought, until his head sinks slowly onto his chest.

Translated by Barry Smerin

OK

Loshn un lebn, 1953

I made her acquaintance in a boardinghouse at the seaside. We sat at the same table during meals.

She is a woman in her sixties, of middling height, with a fine, intelligent face, a head of thick gray hair, and eyes that are greenish gray or deep gray, depending on her mood. When she's excited, her eyes are greenish gray. Her whole appearance is attractive. You get the impression, from the first look, that she is more than an average woman. She is one of those people who, when you see her for the first time, you ask, "Who is that woman?"

She never talked much. She was not one of those people who want to show they are cleverer than others. When it came to an exchange of views, she was always very logical and thoughtful, and everyone who took part in the conversation listened to her with great interest. She always spoke tactfully, so that no one felt belittled.

All of the many guests in the boarding house were so convinced of her superior intelligence that, whenever there was an argument, someone always said: "Come on. Let's ask Mrs. L." I myself was convinced that the woman had absorbed a great deal of life's wisdom.

One thing surprised me, however. She didn't know how to read or write.

One morning we were both sitting by the sea. The water was splendid. I was feeling good, completely captivated by the beautiful surroundings. I was sure Mrs. L. felt the same, because we had both remarked on the beauty of God's world. Quite unexpectedly, Mrs. L. opened her handbag, turned her face to me with a quick movement, and, with an even quicker movement, took out a bunch of envelopes. "See this, my dear," she said, holding out the envelopes to me. "It embitters my life!"

Nostalgia and the Decline of the Jewish East End   183

The moment she said that, I saw her eyes had turned green. They shone with anger and a deep melancholy. I could see she was controlling herself, trying to stay calm.

"I'm not ashamed to tell you that it often makes me feel humiliated and bitter. I could explain why I never learned to read or write, but it's all so long ago. I'd have to begin with the shtetl I was born in, and it would take too long.

"I have five children, three daughters and two sons. All of them were given a good education. They're doing well. They treat me with love and respect. When my husband died, I remained alone. I didn't want to leave the home where we had brought up our children together. Each of the children wanted me to go and live with them, so as not to be alone. But my reason told me: 'Children, you are married. Go live with your families in good health. You have your own lives to lead. I shall stay where I am.' I lack nothing. I have pleasure from my children and from my grandchildren, who give me great joy. I live quietly and modestly.

"Only, when I travel away from home, there's this!" And she points once again to the envelopes. "It makes me ashamed and bitter. You see why?" She shows me all the envelopes. Each has an address written on it, and each contains a slip of paper with only two letters written on it: "OK."

She looks at me for moment and says: "You don't mind me telling you this? I consider you to be a very thoughtful person. And there are times when we all feel the need to unburden ourselves. You understand, of course, that a person can't tell just anyone about the weaknesses she suffers from. With you it's different. I feel a closeness between us.

"The thing is," she continued, "I don't know which child's name is on the envelope when I send the 'OK.' My children have arranged with me that I should send off three envelopes every week, and when any one of them receives an 'OK,' all of them will know that I'm well and everything is fine.

"But in my head," she went on, pointing to her temple, "there are so many nice things I'd like to tell them about. I would like to tell my children how good I feel here, how beautiful everything is, and about all the people I've met. How pleasant it is here in the boardinghouse, and how nice all the people are to each other. I would like to tell them about you. Certainly about you! Please don't laugh if I say I would like to tell them a lot about you. You have no idea how happy I am that we met.

"Of course, I'll have a lot to tell my children when I get home, but meanwhile so much of what is in here," she said, pointing to her head once

184   Chapter 5

again, "is getting lost. It would be different if I knew how to write. Believe me, I feel ashamed when I drop an envelope in the letter box with 'OK' written in advance."

She remained sitting in silence, her clever eyes lost in distant thought. And I understood that it was best for me to keep silent, too. The two of us listened to the sound of the sea and said nothing more till we got back to the boardinghouse for lunch.

Translated by Barry Smerin

The Glass Hill

Loshn un lebn almanac, 1956

My neighbor, Shloyme Mannes, is a respectable, good-natured man, with a good reputation and a good head on his shoulders. Everyone has great trust in him. If someone needs a bit of advice, they turn to him. Even if he can't help, the person feels better after Mannes has listened to him. Mannes always finds the right words of reassurance.

I'm always happy when my neighbor comes to see me. He always has something interesting and beautiful to relate. He never talks about business. If he does mention his work, it's only about the first years after his arrival in London. He loves to talk about the years of his youth.

He enjoys coming in to see me. I know he does, because he often says: "It's nice in your home. It's warm and cheerful. It's easy to talk to you and tell you things. You're a good, attentive listener." It's true. I listen with interest to my neighbor's tales of the long-gone years of his childhood and youth.

When he talks about the shtetl where he was born and raised, his face shines. But sometimes it makes him a little sad: "I was a mere youth when I came to the great London metropolis, one of many who came here in those years. I worked hard and lived in poverty. Here I met a girl who also came from a shtetl in Poland. The same circumstances that brought me here also brought her to a foreign land.

"Both of us longed for the home we had left behind, and that longing united us. We got married. We both continued working, to make something of ourselves. My wife worked on preparations for Jewish weddings. In those days it wasn't the fashion to hire large halls with everything already prepared. Her work was a great help in earning us a living.

Nostalgia and the Decline of the Jewish East End   185

"So, what was my work, you ask? Well, I used to buy and sell second-hand goods, anything I could get hold of. When we'd saved up some money, we rented a small kiosk. My wife stayed at home, and I went on selling secondhand articles door-to-door.

"When our first child was born, I had to stay home, too. I'm not religiously observant, but I'm a Jew with faith. I believe that if you do all you can to help yourself, then God will help you, too! And indeed, we were helped. Things got better and better. We succeeded. Since I used to buy anything I could lay hands on—string, bags, paper, old boxes, and so on—I got to thinking that those oddments could bring in money. Our kiosk became a small shop, and over the years it grew much bigger. And that's the business we have to this day.

"We gave our two sons and our daughter a good education. We wanted our children to have a better, easier life than we had had. We always remembered how hard life had been for us. Our children are all married now, and they work in the store. In fact, they have already taken it over. Let them be the bosses now. They are young, with new ideas, and times are different now. When I want to, I go into the store for a few hours a day. If I don't feel like it, it doesn't matter, I can leave it to the children. The thing is, though, I have a lot of time on my hands. And the more free time I have, the more I think about the old days, especially when a Jewish holiday comes round. I see the old days most clearly of all in the period between Purim and Pesach. It was then we used to feel that the shtetl, which was our whole world, would come back to life after the winter, and with its revival, everything would get better. Life would be easier."

Mannes looked up at me and said: "You come from those parts, too. You also have things to tell. So I'm sure you know that everything I tell you is not made up." I look back at him, answering only with a smile. I know that my neighbor Mannes is something of a dreamer. He has a beautiful, poetic soul, and everything he tells me is always connected with nature. And, indeed, I soon see his face take on a mild expression. A smile takes shape around his eyes, and they mist over, as if with dew. Slowly, in a deeper voice, he says:

"Oh, if you had known my shtetl, with the two hills overlooking the little houses and the old synagogue, which was the town's tallest building—two hills, like a big and a little brother holding hands, the smaller green 'chapel hill' and the tall white 'glass hill.' (I don't know why it was called by that name.) At the top of the small green hill stood a little chapel with

186   Chapter 5

tiny windows. Candles burned in the chapel on festivals and Sundays, and on dark nights their light could be seen all over the shtetl. Children coming home from *cheder* on such nights were afraid to raise their eyes. They were sure that if they looked up, they would see ghosts and demons.

"The glass hill, on the other hand, was ours—the Jewish hill. It was much higher than the green hill and was on the side facing the shtetl. It was white, and Jews said that people had dug into it and hacked pieces out of it for so long that it was left with open wounds. The white hill was visible all around, and you could see what was done in its innards. Women took chalk from the hill to clean the Sabbath candlesticks and whiten the thresholds of their houses. At the top of the hill stood a wide-spreading tree, and behind it some rosebushes. When you looked up at it, the tree seemed like a human head. In winter the snow lay there longer than on the other hill. It often lay on the tree, which, seen from afar, looked like a tall Jew in a white robe—a head with a dark beard wearing a white yarmulke.

"Even before Purim, Jewish men and women would begin joking about the glass hill: 'Our hill is already getting ready for the Passover seder.' The Jews in our shtetl were proud of their Jewish glass hill. As the days grew longer and warmer, the narrow streets were filled by black, muddy streams from the water that dripped from all sides. Oh, how I loved the white hill at that time of year. Deep in thought, it looked down on our shtetl, freeing itself from the melting ice. And I loved the days before Pesach, when matzah-baking time came round and the world was mine! Why, you ask?

"I think I already told you that my father died when I was very young. It wasn't easy for my mother to provide for us children. She was still quite young herself, and she suffered greatly from the fact that she was unable to give her children everything that children desire and need. And so, when matzah-baking time came round, I felt like a grownup. I knew what I would do. I would go and earn some money to help my mother make Pesach. Today, when I recall that time, I'm filled with a warm feeling. On the other hand, I think to myself, I was still almost a child, and I already needed to earn money to help my mother. Now all those memories make me pity myself for having grown up so soon."

My neighbor fell silent. He sat for a few moments without speaking. When I looked at him, it seemed to me that something was weeping inside

Nostalgia and the Decline of the Jewish East End   187

him. "So what had I thought of doing? You'll be wanting to know what my work was in the matzah-baking business. It wasn't very nice," my neighbor said with a smile, "but I have a lot to tell about that time. I was what they call a matzah-sweeper, a job for which small children are needed. You don't know what a matzah-sweeper is, I suppose? Let me explain. The kneader passed the dough to the roller, the roller sent it on to the hole-maker, and from him it went to the baker. The whole thing had to be done very quickly, and the matzah had to be taken out of the oven very quickly, too. That's what the rabbinical law says. A straw mat was spread out round the oven, and the baked matzah was thrown onto it. My job was to grab the hot matzah and brush it clean with a feather duster. But that's not all," Shloyme Mannes laughed. "The matzah-sweeper had to be barefoot, and, as luck would have it, a burning-hot matzah always fell on his foot. And since I had to work fourteen to sixteen hours a day, my feet were covered in burns. If I wasn't embarrassed, I'd show you the scars, which I bear to this day. When I look at my feet, I remember my childhood with sadness. That's how I feel about it now, but at the time I just suffered in silence. I was too proud to complain. And I was also proud of earning money to help my poor mother bring Pesach into our home.

"There was one more thought I consoled myself with. After Pesach I would climb up our white glass hill and rest, and cool my wounded feet in the fresh young grass. I would lie under the tall wide-spreading tree, looking up at its branches with their newly opening buds and bright green leaves, which reached up to the sky to thank the sun for the warmth it was giving them for their new young life."

He fell silent once again. The gentle smile took shape again around his clever eyes. "What fun we had on the last day of Pesach, when we paraded the festival out of town! Men, women and children, everyone, big and small, walked together in the festival parade. The weather was usually fine and warm. We walked slowly up the hill. Children pointed out their houses, which they could recognize in the distance. The grownups looked over to the other side of the shtetl, to the wide river, which was now free of ice, and the sun was reflected in its clear water. We children—among them I had forgotten that I was now a grownup—leaped about like young deer. We weren't afraid of the chapel on the small green hill, because the sun was shining, and the adults were with us."

Translated by Barry Smerin

188   Chapter 5

AVROM NOKHEM STENCL

••

At the Seaside

Di idishe shtime, 1954

I could include Westcliff, our Whitechapel Galilee, in my "portrait miniatures" with a good conscience.* Don't its days of sun and rain, its bright and gloomy aspects, really belong entirely to the streets and alleyways of our Jewish East End?

The sun rises, with great effort, in proletarian Southend, and sets, in sentimental mood, in aristocratic Chalkwell. But the intervening hundred meters are a separate country, a stretch of land filled with a hubbub of Jewish voices—a veritable koshering pot bubbling away. Here you don't hear drunken singing from pubs, nor smell the odor of nonkosher cockles.

Groups of Jews from various congregations stroll around, perfectly at home, having lengthy discussions on major political issues—the election of new synagogue presidents and "honorary officers." Others settle down, though I shouldn't mention it, to a game of cards.

And our kosher womenfolk, God bless them, all have a Friday-night look about them, red in the face as if rushing to light the *shabbes* candles.

These are honest, hard-working people enjoying a good rest after a year's toil, gathering fresh strength for the labor in store for them.

I would gladly paint portrait miniatures of them all, not only because they are part of our Whitechapel community but because their beautiful faces call out to me: "Record us, paint us in Whitechapel colors, immortalize us!"

After all, I'm already something of a Whitechapel Jew myself, a long-standing resident with various ailments who wants to have a bit of a rest and take some fresh air home in his pockets to last him through the winter fogs. But I'm not a butcher, a machinist, or a presser. I'm not a cantor, hardly a choirboy, and I'm not entitled to—and certainly have no right to

---

* Stencl wrote a column of "portrait miniatures"—short portraits of Jewish Whitechapel and its people as if they were pictures in frames. Westcliff-on-Sea is a suburb of Southend. Southend-on-Sea is the closest seaside resort to the East End, and Chalkwell is the adjacent town to Westcliff.

Nostalgia and the Decline of the Jewish East End   189

demand—any paid holidays. I'm a Yiddish writer, and a Yiddish writer must be able to hold the quill in his hand until the day they hold the feather under his nose.

But what am I to do when I'm so "fed up" that I can't write? What I mean is that I've eaten so much here that my hand no longer moves. I've settled in, it seems, and have myself become a Whitechapel portrait miniature.

My dear Sochachewsky, send your son Maurice here for a few days with his sketchbook. This place is a veritable goldmine for a Jewish artist. Whole galleries of pictures walk about here quite openly, for all to see. I myself am an overweight, walking Madame Tussaud's waxwork.

Over there a young Hungarian is sitting, reclining in a deck chair, as if in the rabbinical chair in Mukachevo, a silk yarmulke on his head, his blond sidelocks flapping in the breeze.†

If only I had your son's pencil in my hand. This is driving me crazy.

> Petitionary notes in a skullcap,
> My thoughts in my head.
> When I pass by the youngster
> He lowers his head,
> Thinking I'm a *goy*.
> And don't I indeed look
> Like a peasant from the old country?
> A hot tear falls from my eye,
> A mere drop in the sea.
> Oy, he thinks I'm a *goy*.

You see, Sochachewsky, they're already about to hold the feather under my nose, and only then do immortal rhymes unfold. (Don't worry, I'm only talking about my own rhymes.)

> I did not come here
> To sing an ode to the sea.
> A poet can write
> A whole book of sea poems
> About a single tear.

---

† Mukachevo: town in Ukraine. Before World War II, Jews made up half of the population.

Chapter 5

His heart a little boat
Tossed this way and that
By the waves!
If a poet travels to the sea,
There's already something wrong with him.

So let me just rest here for a while, and I'll return to our basement café a new man, a nicer and more decent human being. It's only here, at a little remove from our literary circle, that you really feel how dear a colleague is to you. I wouldn't exchange one of our number for ten master tailors and fifteen synagogue presidents. All their checkbooks cannot make up for the absence of a creative Yiddish word, nor even for the lack of a bit of Yiddish gossip or a silly Yiddish joke.

How I long for a friend with whom to share a witty remark. This lack of companionship will be the end of me!

By a miracle I run into a traditional rabbi on holiday here, taking a break from his London graveside duties—not some modern, narrowminded bigot but a familiar, homey rabbi who has swum deeply in the sea—the sea of the Talmud—and I enjoy a pleasant chat with a Talmud scholar. I also chance to meet a Yiddish actor who has discarded his theatrical costume, and we stroll together through the former Yiddish theatre, right here on the open seashore.

Such chance conversations do me more good than the finest sea air.

Translated by Barry Smerin

The *Idishe Shtime*

Di idishe shtime, 1955

Sochachewsky, ill and exhausted, had come to see me in Westcliff and stayed the night. We sat gazing at the gentle movement of the sea, thinking more than speaking. He had brought bad news from our London world: deaths in our family of writers, several deaths in our small, narrow circle. And I had absolutely no wish to mount my "portrait miniatures" in black mourning frames. So we sat there sadly, facing the gently moving sea, and said nothing.

Suddenly, Sochachewsky broke the silence. "Oh, Stencl," he mused, "who will write *our* obituaries?" It was said very seriously, but in the midst of our silence and in the presence of the sea, it sounded almost comical. I felt

Nostalgia and the Decline of the Jewish East End   191

a painful stab in the depths of my heart. I looked at Sochachewsky's face. How greatly it had changed in the last few months since his illness. And Joseph Hillel Levy, too, was no longer among the living.*

We didn't talk much more that day; both of us found speech difficult. We just stared at the gently moving face of the sea, so communicative, understanding, and immortal. And so today, two weeks later, reading the announcement on the front page of the *Idishe shtime* that the paper is celebrating an anniversary, I take the opportunity to join in the celebration and pay tribute to the editor, Ben-A Sochachewsky. I shall mount my portrait of him, if not in a golden frame, then at least in a silver one. Do you have to die first? If you're battling with death, isn't that enough? And if at the same time you're a Yiddish editor, struggling to keep a Yiddish newspaper going in Whitechapel?

Recently, reading a chapter of Sochachewsky's "Impressions from a Sickbed" about his clothing, I understood for the first time how a Yiddish newspaper—and only a weekly one at that—is still able to come out here in our dying Yiddish world.† It's one of the ten marvels created at sunset on the eve of the first Sabbath! It isn't the Jewish institutions, parties, and associations that we have to thank for the fact that a Yiddish newspaper still appears—if only once a week on Friday. That would be giving them too much credit. As for the advertisements, reports, and other announcements the party hacks place in a Yiddish newspaper, they would be better off peddling their wares to the English press, despite all Sochachewsky's expertise as a tried and tested reporter and a journalist with fifty years' experience. It would cost them less, and they'd get pictures into the bargain. And that's all they care about.

If a Yiddish newspaper still appears in England, and we can hope that its existence is assured, it is thanks to Ben-A Sochachewsky's talent as a writer, his poetic approach, and his determination to maintain his own creative identity. The continued existence of a Yiddish press organ in this country is entirely due to Sochachewsky's literary energy and persistence. For where will a Yiddish poet be able to publish his works if he does not put every effort into maintaining the existence of his newspaper? And others also

---

   * Joseph Hillel Levy (Lowy) was a Yiddish poet who lived in London from 1939. He died a month before this feuilleton was published.

   † Ben-A Sochachewsky wrote many novels, stories, and memoirs that were serialized in *Di idishe shtime*—what Stencl calls "impressions."

192   Chapter 5

benefit from his selfless devotion. Despite all the arrogance and humiliation inflicted on him, he persists with the greatest heroism, to give his works life and save them from extinction. I am by no means sure that Sochachewsky would have risen from his sickbed had it not been for the newspaper, and I rejoice that I was able to read his lyrical psychological "impressions" that led me to that conclusion.

It is indeed thanks to the poet's creative drive, expressed every year with renewed energy and courage, that London's Jewish institutions, parties, and synagogues have a Yiddish press organ in which they can announce their meetings and events and place reports of their proceedings, and in which their "honorable officers" can receive some praise in exchange for the few coppers they throw into the till.*

My dear Sochachewsky, your creative drive and output are prolonged with every page of the newspaper that appears. What greater reward can there be? And what greater satisfaction can a poet have?

And, of course, your coeditor Leyb Sholem Creditor also knows the secret. Would he have embarked on his important Maimonides monograph without a press organ? He knows the secret well, and it accounts for his strength of will and creative energy. And would Ben-A Sochachewsky have begun to write the novel *The Righteous Convert*, in which he sets out to portray a piece of Jewish history in England, if the newspaper he edits had not existed? It is my fervent hope and wish that those two works will not remain only as old newsprint but will take their place as books in the showcase of Yiddish literature.

Translated by Barry Smerin

RAHEL DONIACH (1884–1976)

Rahel (Rokhl) Doniach was born in Riga, Latvia, and trained as a teacher of Russian. She arrived in London with her husband in 1904. There, she helped found a conversational Hebrew language circle that included Yosef Haim Brenner; she served as a translator at the London office of the World Zionist Organization; and she published plays and poetry in Hebrew. In 1920 she took on the position of librarian at the Jewish Free Reading Room in the

---

* "Honorable officers" is a sarcastic reference to the members of the synagogue board.

East End, and she continued in that role for thirty-three years.

Although her main focus was on Hebrew-language writing and events, in 1937 she encouraged Stencl to set up the Literary Sabbath Afternoons, which later became the Friends of Yiddish. She wrote occasional pieces for *Loshn un lebn* and authored the play *Der ofshtand in geto* (The Ghetto Revolt), which was produced in 1945 at the Grand Palais Theatre.[10]

Rahel Doniach, 1926. Courtesy of Ruth and Iona Doniach.

• •

Corrections

Loshn un lebn almanac, 1956
(first published in *Heftl*, 1943)

At the beginning of the twentieth century, when a group of Hebrew scholars, writers, thinkers, and poets suddenly came to London from Eastern Europe, Narodiczky was already a resident here, with a home and a print shop in Mile End next door to Isaac's Fried Fish Shop.† He had a young man as a typesetter, and a Mr. Cohen who stood at his foot-press printer as if welded to it, pressing his foot down and printing advertisements, cards, and leaflets on all sorts of Jewish topics. But more than everything, Narodiczky's press printed work about Hebrew in Hebrew.

Narodiczky didn't hold with billing his customers. If and when they paid, they just paid. And if they didn't pay, they didn't. So what? Was he supposed to stop printing these important things?

When you went there to make an order, you'd always find Narodiczky with oil-smeared hands in his threadbare cardigan, with rolled-up sleeves, deeply absorbed with love and dedication in the work in hand. Here he corrected a plate, there he added a strip of print, and here he inserted a Star of David. "If this material was printed without a Star of David," he said, "it would look, as the saying goes, like a Jew before the giving of the Torah." And over there he looked for better quality paper, and so on.

---

† John (Johnny) Isaacs Fish shop on Mile End Road, opposite Whitechapel underground station, was a popular haunt for Jewish youth.

194   Chapter 5

You called on him with your order. Momentarily, he threw everything else aside and, with his black, deeply penetrating eyes, he devoured your text with great enjoyment. At each poetic and artistic expression, his face lit up in delight. But he didn't say anything. When he found a poorly constructed expression, he would cross it out with his black lead pencil and, pointing at the sentence, look at you questioningly; his sharp gaze more pointed than the pencil itself. Sometimes he would play a practical joke on us and have a really good laugh at our expense, laughing in his silent way.

Our group's ideology aimed at reviving and spreading Hebrew language and literature, and awakening love for the Land of Israel. To achieve this we had to first revive the system of Hebrew education and study in London. And who could not be impressed when we succeeded in establishing an *Agudat Hamorim* [Association of Hebrew Teachers] here in London. We felt strongly that we had to be not only teachers but also students. So we brought together all the Hebrew scholars from East to West London and arranged a course of six lectures in Toynbee Hall during Passover.* The lectures were on highly academic topics. For example, Dr. Lionel Barnett of the British Museum gave a lecture on Torah and the Vedas (the Hindu Torah), and other pedagogical, psychological, and philological themes, the academic study of Judaism, and so on. At that time we already all knew some English, and the lectures were held either in Hebrew or English, but the large posters that we ordered were naturally only in Hebrew.

Suddenly, the telephone rang. Not, God forbid, in our home—who were we to own a telephone, Rothschild? It rang in the house of our neighbor, the wealthy "traveler's" wife.† I got a message that I must go to Narodiczky's print shop right away to read the corrections on the posters. I flew there like an arrow from a bow. Passover eve or not—the festival was insignificant for such an important matter. I arrived there gasping for breath, and saw our large poster with all the big names of the speakers, Jews and gentiles, and the subjects of their lectures. And absolutely all of it was in Hebrew, not, God forbid, one English word. But suddenly I saw at the top, instead of an *H* for *Agudat Hamorim*, the Association of Teachers, a large letter *CH*: as large and long as the Jewish exile: *Agudat CHamorim*—the Association of Asses.

---

* Toynbee Hall was founded in 1884 to foster young leadership. The venue was used for meetings and events, and many Jewish activities took place there.

† Traveler: Traveling salesman. The narrator is implying that it is a posh term for door-to-door peddler.

That mistake, for which I alone was to blame, was followed by a practical joke at my expense. Here's what happened. I was all of a sudden elevated to a premier job in the well-heeled West End. I taught a number of students there and charged them ten shillings and sixpence an hour, instead of the ninepence an hour I got in Whitechapel from Cohen the milkman, who had a cow and sold kosher milk, and whose only child, Yankel, was a nightmare to teach.

And as soon as I had risen to teaching in the lofty heights of the West End, Whitechapel, naturally, didn't suit me anymore. I had to have a respectable address. We quickly moved to Clissold Park Road, the "Mayfair" of Whitechapel; so, in need of business cards, I ran over to Narodiczky and enthusiastically told him my story and ordered cards.‡ "Nu," he said, "now you'll get three square meals a day."

He knew what he was talking about, because up to then even getting one meal a day was a miracle. You see, Yosef Brenner was then a typesetter for Narodiczky, and Narodiczky's print shop was next door to Isaac's fish shop, and here lies the miracle. Brenner had no more than tuppence a day to spend, so he would come home with a big bag of "chips" (fried potatoes), and the *Agudat Hamorim* would sit down at the table. No one suffered from lack of an appetite, and, if God gave a helping hand, then Gutman brought in a large loaf of rye bread, and the one they called "the Litvak" was lucky enough to get a salted herring on credit. He would come in drinking the herring juice and guzzling the herring, and give the order to cook potatoes, because herring with hot potato is, ay ay ay! Mrs. Creditor knew that the famous Hebrew poet Gnessin had a nasty cough. She would take the last glass of milk from her little children and would bring it to Gnessin.§ I myself, the mistress of the house, had learned how to cook a large pot of pea soup without meat. And so we used to prepare our meal every evening with a skip and a song. The only thing that was missing was the sound of the shofar. "Now," Narodiczky said, "we can have three meals a day every day. When I've printed your cards, we'll soon be able to afford the flesh of the Leviathan

---

‡ Clissold Park is in Stoke Newington, N16, a more affluent area north of the East End. As the immigrant generation became upwardly mobile, it was one of the areas they moved into. Mayfair is a wealthy area of Central London.

§ Uri Nisan Gnessin was a Hebrew and Yiddish writer and translator. He spent some time in London in the early 1900s helping Yosef Haim Brenner to publish the Hebrew periodical *Ha-Me'orer* (The Awakener).

itself." The most important thing was that the address was printed correctly. "For God's sake, remember," I told him, "Clissold has two 'esses.'"

He took full account of my enthusiasm and, as usual, said nothing. I returned to my work at a run. In the evening, I went back for the cards. He handed them over to me, and I read "Clisssold." "Narodiczky, you ass, why have you printed *Clissold* with three 'esses'?" Narodiczky was silent.

Then the penny dropped: The printing mistake on the poster was because of me and only me. He had honored me with the three "esses" in the Association of "Asses."

Translated by Vivi Lachs

MOSHE DOMB (1910–?)

"Moshe Domb," sketch by Maurice Sochachewsky, *Di idishe shtime* (September 25, 1953). Courtesy of Dave Skye Sochachewsky. From the British Library collection.

Moshe Domb was born in Chmielnik, Poland, and was the sole survivor of his family, all of whom were murdered in Treblinka. Saved by the Russian invasion of Poland, he was sent to Siberia. From there he joined the Free Polish Army ("Anders' Army") and fought in the Middle East. He arrived in London in 1950, where he married and had two daughters.

Domb published a novel about his wartime partisan life and wrote occasionally for Stencl's journal, *Loshn un lebn*. He was active in Stencl's Literary Sabbath Afternoons, where he read from his work.[11]

Petticoat Lane

Loshn un lebn almanac, 1956

Petticoat Lane. Most people who come to the Sunday market, including visitors from all over the world, don't only come to buy; they also come for entertainment, like going to a film. So let's try and capture it as if with a camera.

Nostalgia and the Decline of the Jewish East End   197

Here stands bespectacled Zelig at a market table selling various bits and pieces, his pitch-black hair hanging in shreds over his haggard sweaty face. His dark eyes are intense. Words spill from his big toothless mouth as he draws in the passersby with a story about partisans in the Polish forests fighting with wolves and brutal Germans with long whips. A miscellaneous crowd of curious listeners gather round. When the space in front of his table is quite full, Zelig whips out one of his items for sale and asks who will give most for it. Captivated by Zelig's stories, the onlookers forget everything, and all of them bid for the item. Zelig knows well that people are like children, and with a story you can get them to do anything. He's so good at it that students and doctors come to see how he captures customers with his psychological tricks.

But Zelig himself forgets what he's doing when two characters, one with a leg missing and the other with only one arm, come leading a white goat hitched to a cart in which a grayish brown monkey, attached by a thin chain, is leaping up and down a ladder and grabbing pennies from the crowd with its small, clawlike feet. Quick as a flash, the monkey grabs some peanuts from the table and nibbles away at them, glaring angrily at the onlookers. Zelig's face lights up in a smile, and he forgets all about selling his wares. The grayish-brown monkey is craftier than all the bystanders. It keeps glaring at the people with angry eyes and trembling lips, as if to say: "Oh, you stupid humans, if I wasn't tied by this chain, I'd leap across all the tables and grab the grapes and peanuts, and you wouldn't be able to catch me, but just stand there shouting like idiots."

People look on sheepishly, with curiosity, as the monkey grabs peanuts along with the money. The owners smile and stroke its neck affectionately, as if to say: "You've learned cunning ways at the market, you crafty animal."

It's noisy at Petticoat Lane market. Women and men shout to attract customers. A band plays, all disabled in some way. The madman from Aldgate is dancing and singing. A Polish fiddler plays soulful melodies that remind you of Polish fields and forests. And here comes Jock the Scot, a drum and bells hanging round his neck, playing his trumpet and dancing—a veritable one-man band. When he has finished dancing and playing, and collected the pennies, he spots rotten tomatoes, apples, berries, and bananas lying in the gutter, and immediately starts picking them up. He is quickly joined by the Polish fiddler, who also grabs a rotten apple. The tramps hanging around in the market shuffle as well. They are old down-and-outs from the nearby Salvation Army hostel. Dressed in rags, their faces unshaven, eyes swollen from sleepless nights, with sagging cheeks, twisted noses, and parched lips, they are always wandering about in the market with heads bent down, constantly on the lookout for a tasty morsel.

"Petticoat" is the English word for a woman's underskirt, and there are indeed a lot of women in Petticoat Lane market: lots of Jewish women carrying slaughtered chickens, ducks, and geese from the nearby ritual slaughterhouse. You can hear the poultry squawking in the slaughterhouse, like a crowd of women arguing and shrieking at each other. And from time to time, you hear the chant of the ritual slaughterer checking that his knife has no flaws.

Then everything is drowned out by the sound of a nearby gramophone. Young women stand gaping at it, listening to the sickly sentimental melodies and proudly displaying their slender legs in their tiny slip-on shoes, their black-spotted, calf-length silk stockings underlining their shapely thighs. Their steps are dainty too. Their hair is cropped short, like a brood hen, and their breasts, raised in the current fashion, resemble the puffed-up chest of a male pigeon. They come here to listen to the gramophone music and inhale the exotic odor of bananas, grapefruit, apples, and oranges, but above all to chat with the boys in drainpipe trousers and wide-shouldered jackets, with hair freshly slicked back into a shining ducktail, like the purplish backside of a drake. That's how men dressed in King Edward's time, which is why these youths are called "Teddy boys." Proud of their royal nickname, they hold their duck-tailed heads high, nodding haughtily and chewing gum, like young Americans at a dance. They approach the young women, whose laughter is now interspersed with girlish shrieks. One of the gang must have stolen a kiss from a pretty girl. Now and then, when one of the boys spots a Jewish girl with a modest expression on her face, he runs quickly to the gypsy woman selling multicolored roses, buys a white rose, and presents it to the bashful young lady. Then all the girls burst out laughing.

Gramophone music and girlish laughter mingle with the cries of the market men and women and tradesmen, and the squawking of the hens, geese, and ducks in the slaughterhouse echoes far and wide across the market.

The lanes of market stalls empty out one by one, as if swept by a receding tide, leaving behind scraps of paper, rotten fruit, string, rags, and shoes with holes in them. Here and there, ragged down-and-outs with unshaven faces can be seen searching the ground for coins, scraps of food, and tasty fruit, like in the old country after the pilgrimage markets.*

---

* Pilgrimage market: The most important pilgrimage market in the old country (Poland) was the fair known as "Fat Thursday," held on the last Thursday before Lent and associated with the carnival celebrations.

Nostalgia and the Decline of the Jewish East End   199

But old Reb Yoshke from Vilna, the greengrocer, is still sitting at the edge of the market. From him you can buy garlic, horseradish, dill, and black, red, or white radish. He's an old man with a tired face and a grayish-white beard, wearing a hard hat that looks like a beaker. His ritual sidelocks are combed back behind his ears. His eyes have an angry look, his nose is slightly twisted, and his lips are swollen and dry from too much talking. He holds a prayerbook, open at the Hymn of Unity for the First Day of the Week.[†] When a policeman comes and tells him the Sunday market is over, he raises his pale face and replies in Yiddish: "In a minute, my righteous counselor, I just want to finish a verse." Not understanding a word Yoshke says, the policeman goes off with a thin smile on his stern face, like a chastised child. And Reb Yoshke ends the Sunday market with the verse from the Hymn of Unity, reciting the Hebrew words in a respectful whisper: "To this day hast Thou held fast my hand; life and loving-kindness hast Thou given me."

The marketplace empties. There are bits of yellow orange peel and dark green cabbage leaves lying around here and there. You can hear quiet echoes from distant streets and the clinking of silver coins. Feathers fly around like tiny summer birds. And the last to leave the marketplace is Reb Yoshke from Vilna. He's barely able to push the two-wheeled cart squeaking in front of his feet. He shoves it forward a little way, then stops and groans. When the market folk tell him a wealthy Jew like him shouldn't have to push his cart by himself, he raises his eyes to heaven and whispers a prayer, as if to thank the Master of the Universe for sustaining the Jews of Whitechapel and the good Sunday market. And to all the passersby he says, pointing to the sky: "There, there things will be different." And keeping his eyes raised aloft, as if the heavens are opening to receive his words, Reb Yoshke mutters: "To this day hast Thou held fast my hand—Oy, oy, Master of the Universe."

Translated by Barry Smerin

---

† Hymn of Unity: a lengthy medieval liturgical poem divided into seven parts, one for each day of the week, praising God, extolling His uniqueness, and emphasizing the smallness of His creatures.

AFTERWORD

Yiddish popular culture, written in the vernacular by the people for the people, is fertile ground. The urban feuilleton sketches in this volume give us glimpses of small details of the daily lives of the immigrant generations on the streets, in the shops, and in restaurants, markets, and motorcars. They deal with the division of labor in sweatshops and in homes. They tell of the poorest and of the upwardly mobile. They engage with civilians in time of war, religious celebration, and ideological debate. They tell of deep sorrow, furious indignation, and the daily struggles for maintaining and improving lives. And they do it with side-splitting humor, curt satire, and careful narrative, giving us curious, meaningful, trivial, and thought-provoking views of London's Jewish immigrant past.

And what do we get to see? A vibrant world, changing over the generations. It is a Yiddish East End in decline, and yet paves the way for an exciting, developing, and continuing London Jewish culture.

This volume is tiny. Morris Winchevsky wrote scores of "Crazy Philosopher" columns, but you only get three. Katie Brown wrote her column "In the Women's Kingdom" for more than three years, yet you get one month. Avrom Nokhem Stencl wrote introductions to his *Loshn un lebn* journal and prose pieces for the Yiddish press for twenty years, yet you simply get three of his crafted memories. Every writer in this volume contributed significantly to London Yiddish culture, not only in their time, but for us today.

Yiddish popular culture, written in the vernacular by the people for the people, still holds secrets. Not only in its urban sketches in the Yiddish press, but also in its plays, poems, novellas, novels, creative essays, songs, memoirs, jokes, riddles, cartoons, and comic verse. Sidestepping any news and journalism, even ignoring reviews, the creative Yiddish popular culture of London still waits to be read.

If, in the small output offered in this volume, we are given so much food for thought, I hope that we can challenge ourselves and each other and continue to mine the riches of the old East End and its Jews.

APPENDIX 1

Index of Feuilleton Sketches and Translators

Writer	Title	Publication	Translator
An'eygener; see Beilin, Asher			
Avreml; see Margolin, Avrom			
Bal Rekide	*A sefer toyre protsesye in vaytshepl* A Torah Scroll Procession in Whitechapel	*Tsayt*, April 10, 1924, 2	Lachs
Batlen, Leybele; see Creditor, Leon			
Beach, Judah	*Di trern vant in artsher strit* The Wailing Wall on Archer Street	*Vilne yerushalayim d'lite* (Stencl's *heftl*), no. 55, August 1944, 12–14	Smerin
Beilin, Asher (An'eygener)	*Mayn shokhen* My Neighbor	*Tsayt*, June 10, 1927, 3	Lachs
Beilin, Asher	*Id for oyf "plezher"* A Jew Takes a Pleasure Trip	*Tsayt*, August 26, 1927, 3	Lachs

Writer	Title	Publication	Translator
Beilin, Asher	*Teater genus* Fun at the Theatre	*Tsayt*, June 10, 1927, 3	Lachs
Beyneshzon, L.	*Shmuezn far minkhe* Chatting before the Afternoon Prayer	*Idishe shtime*, May 25, 1951, 2	Lachs
Beyneshzon, L.	*Beyn minkhe lemayrev* Between the Afternoon and Evening Prayers 1	*Idishe shtime*, July 13, 1951, 2	Lachs
Beyneshzon, L.	*Beyn minkhe lemayrev* Between the Afternoon and Evening Prayers 2	*Idishe shtime*, August 17, 1951, 2	Lachs
Beyneshzon, L.	*Beyn minkhe lemayrev* Between the Afternoon and Evening Prayers 3	*Idishe shtime*, October 19, 1951, 2	Lachs
Brenner, Yosef Haim	*A mayse mit a gilgul* A Tale of Reincarnation	*Naye tsayt*, November 4, 1904, 5	Lachs
Brown, Katie	*In froyen kenigraykh* In the Women's Kingdom	*Familyen fraynd*, November 1922– January 1923, 3	Lachs
Brown, Katie	*A khazn, a preser* The Cantor's a Presser!	*Post*, September 6, 1932, 3 (version from *Loshn un lebn*, September 1947, 8–11)	Smerin
Brown, Katie	*Mayn adresn bikhl* My Address Book	*Arbeter ring*, April 1943, 6	Lachs
Capitanchik, Yankev Yitzkhok	*Der umfargeslekher donershtik* That Unforgettable Thursday	*Ovent nayes*, July 4, 1919, 2	Lachs
Creditor, Leon (Leybele Batlen)	*In volyitsh arsenal* In Woolwich Arsenal	*Velt*, June 24, 1915, 2	Lachs
Creditor, Leon	*A luft minister* An Air Minister	*Velt*, July 13, 1915, 2	Lachs

Appendix 1   205

Writer	Title	Publication	Translator
Creditor, Leon	*Kh'ob gesetlt dem koyln-strayk* I Settled the Coal Strike	*Velt*, July 22, 1915, 2	Lachs
Diamant, Dora	*Shloyme mikhoels der yid* Solomon Mikhoels, the Man	*Loshn un lebn*, February 1948, 5–8	Smerin
Diamant, Dora	*Oyf der levaye fun yankl adler* At Yankl Adler's Funeral	*Loshn un lebn*, June 1949, 45–46	Smerin
Domb, Moshe	*Petikot leyn* Petticoat Lane	*Loshn un lebn* almanac, 1956, 71	Smerin
Doniach, Rahel	*Korekturn* Corrections	*Loshn un lebn* almanac, 1956, 94 (first published in *Heftl*, 1943)	Lachs
Finkelstein, Y.	*In groseri shop* In the Grocery Shop	*Tsayt*, November 27, 1913, 2	Smerin
Finkelstein, Y.	*Der natsionalist* The Nationalist	*Tsayt*, December 25, 1913, 2	Smerin
Finkelstein, Y.	*An "erlekher" meshores* An "Honest" Servant	*Tsayt*, December 25, 1913, 2	Smerin
Finkelstein, Y.	*Antisemitizm in kar* Antisemitism on the Tram	*Tsayt*, May 28, 1914, 2	Smerin
Finkelstein, Y.	[no Yiddish title] Flower Day	*Tsayt*, May 28, 1914, 2	Smerin
Goldsmith, Samuel. J.	*A galup-referendumin vaytshepl* A Whitechapel Gallup Poll	*Tsayt*, February 26, 1942, 2	Smerin
Izraeli, L.; see Kussman, Leon			
Kaizer, A. M.	*A frayer hand* A Free Hand!	*Tsayt*, October 18, 1931, 2	Smerin

206   Appendix 1

Writer	Title	Publication	Translator
Kaizer, A. M.	*Der nes-khanike fun london bridzh* The Hanukkah Miracle on London Bridge	*Tsayt*, December 9 and 10, 1936, 2	Smerin
Kreitman, Esther	*Di shayle* The Question	*Post*, January 6, 1928, 3	Lachs
Kreitman, Esther	*Der nadn* The Dowry	*Idishe shtime*, August 24, 1951 (written c. 1930), 2	Lachs
Kussman, Leon (L. Izraeli)	*Der politiker fun vaytshepl* The Whitechapel Politician	London: Progress, 1912	Lachs
Lisky, I. A.	*Der sod fun a londoner meydl* A London Girl's Secret	*Tsayt*, June 7, 1931, 2	Smerin
Lisky, I. A.	*Mendl un di sefer toyre* Mendl and the Torah Scroll	*Tsayt*, November 23, 1933, 2	Smerin
Margolin, Avrom (Avreml)	*A monolog fun a vaytshepler "rekrut"* A Monologue of a Whitechapel Recruit	*Velt*, March 1, 1916, 2	Lachs
Margolin, Avrom	*Bal shtimungen* At the Ball	*Velt*, January 14, 1916, 2	Smerin
Mirsky, Rachel	*A skits* A Sketch	*Loshn un lebn*, May 1953, 23–24	Smerin
Mirsky, Rachel	*O.K.* OK	*Loshn un lebn*, July 1953, 13–15	Smerin
Mirsky, Rachel	*Der glezener barg* The Glass Hill	*Loshn un lebn* almanac, 1956, 123	Smerin
Oved, Moshe	*Ben-eli* Ben-Eli	*Vizyonen un eydlshteyner*, (London: Narod Press, 1950), 190–97 (first published 1931)	Smerin

Writer	Title	Publication	Translator
Sochachewsky, Ben-A	*Dos letste mitl* The Last Resort	*Tsayt*, October 29, 1919, 2	Smerin
Stencl, Avrom Nokhem	*Lekoved dem fuftsikn heftl* Celebrating the Fiftieth Yiddish Booklet	*Fuftsik yidish heftlekh* (Stencl's *heftl*), no. 50, March 1944, 1–4	Smerin
Stencl, Avrom Nokhem	*Yam shpritsn* At the Seaside	*Idishe shtime*, August 27, 1954, 2	Smerin
Stencl, Avrom Nokhem	*Di idishe shtime* The *Idishe Shtime*	*Idishe shtime*, May 13, 1955, 2	Smerin
Stone, Isaac	*Bizi un slek in london* Busy and Slack in London	*Poylisher yidl*, September 19 and 26, October 3, 1884	Smerin
Winchevsky, Morris	*Vert a dikhter* How Do You Become a Poet?	*Arbayter fraynd*, 6 September 1889	Lachs
Winchevsky, Morris	*Reformirte nezer* Reformed Noses	*Arbayter fraynd*, October 31, 1890	Lachs
Winchevsky, Morris	*Gelt* Money	*Arbayter fraynd*, October 27, 1890	Lachs
Yankele	*A gzeyre oyf blumen farkoyfers* An Evil Decree against Flower Sellers	*Velt*, April 29, 1915, 2	Lachs
Yankele	*Der tremvey strayk* The Tramway Strike	*Velt*, May 25, 1915, 2	Smerin
Yankele	*Vaytshepler "vor ofis"* The Whitechapel War Office	*Velt*, May 27, 1915, 2	Smerin
Yankele	*Milkhome parnoses* Wartime Livelihoods	*Velt*, June 18, 1915, 2	Smerin
Zilberg, Ella	*Gefilte fish* Gefilte Fish	*Loshn un lebn*, July 1951, 14–15	Lachs

APPENDIX 2

Newspaper Titles and Dates

This appendix is a list of the London Yiddish newspapers and journals that published the feuilletons and drawings in this volume.

Name of Newspaper	English Name or Translation	Type	Frequency	Dates
Der arbayter fraynd	The Worker's Friend	Socialist newspaper, anarchist after 1892	Monthly and weekly	1885–1932
Arbeter ring	The Workers' Circle	Newspaper of the Workers' Circle	Quarterly	1934–46
Der bloffer	The Bluffer	Satirical journal	Weekly to monthly	1911–13
Der familyen fraynd	The Family Friend	Newspaper	Weekly	1922–26
Heftlekh or *Stencls heftlekh* (singular *heftl*; informal name—each separately titled)	Stencl's pamphlets	Literary journal	Periodic	1941–45

Name of Newspaper	English Name or Translation	Type	Frequency	Dates
Di idishe shtime	The Jewish Voice	Newspaper	Weekly	1951–67
Loshn un lebn	Language and Life	Literary journal	Monthly, bimonthly	1946–81
Di naye tsayt	The New Times	Newspaper of the Social Democratic Federation	Weekly	1904–7
Ovent nayes	Evening News	Newspaper	Daily	1914–40
Di post	The Post	Newspaper	Daily	1926–35
Der poylisher yidl	The Polish Jew	Socialist newspaper	Weekly	1884
Di tsayt	The Times	Newspaper	Daily	1913–50
Di velt	The World	Newspaper	Daily	1915–16

APPENDIX 3

Artist Biographies

PEARL BINDER (1904–90) was born in Staffordshire and schooled in Manchester. She moved to London to study art at Central School of Art and Design after the First World War. She settled in Whitechapel and produced lithographs of the life around her. She was also a writer, and she illustrated and wrote more than a dozen books, including providing the illustrations for Thomas Burke's *The Real East End* in 1932.

MAURICE SOCHACHEWSKY (1918–69) was born in Hackney, the son of the Yiddish writer Ben-A Sochachewsky. He received a scholarship to the St. Martin's School of Art at the age of fourteen. In the 1930s he spent some months in Wales painting miners and their families. In the 1950s he sketched a series called *Londoner idish lebn in bild* (London Jewish Life in Pictures) for the newspaper edited by his father, *Di idishe shtime* (The Jewish Voice).

MIN TABOR (1919–2010) grew up in Hackney, East London, and received a scholarship to art school at the age of thirteen, but was taken out after eighteen months to work in her father's tailoring workshop. Her artistic career was put on hold until the age of forty-five, when she retrained and began to paint scenes of life in the Jewish East End from the memories of her childhood.

NOTES

INTRODUCTION

1 For examples of Jewish feuilletons in a range of Jewish languages, see "Below the Line," https://www.feuilletonproject.org/s/below-the-line/page/introduction, accessed April 20, 2023. The Yiddish scholars editing the site include Shachar Pinsker, Naomi Brenner, and Mathew Handleman.

2 The Shund website is a database of Yiddish popular fiction, including serialized novels from the Yiddish press and many other published popular works. Saul Zaritt, "Shund," https://shund.org/home/about, accessed March 11, 2024. The word *shund* is a contested concept. Literally meaning "trash," the word was used as a derogatory term by the critics of popular fiction and popular theatre. Yet it was Yiddish popular culture that drew large working-class audiences and readers, partly because the fiction, drama, and songs were entertaining, and partly because popular texts engaged with important issues of the day. Lachs, *Whitechapel Noise: Jewish Immigrant Life in Yiddish Song and Verse, London 1884–1914* (Detroit, MI: Wayne State University Press, 2018), 41–42.

3 Saul Zaritt, "A *Taytsh* Manifesto: Yiddish, Translation, and the Making of Modern Jewish Culture," *Jewish Social Studies* 26, no. 3 (Fall 2021): 206–28.

4 The situation in the Jewish East End during the First World War concentrated on the issues around conscription of Jewish men and its effects. See Anne Lloyd, "Jews under Fire: The Jewish Community and Military Service in World War 1 Britain" (PhD diss., University of Southampton, 2009); David Feldman, "War, Patriotism and Nationality," unpublished paper, 2019.

5 There was clearly Jewish interest in the Channel Tunnel, judging by the *Jewish Chronicle* listings. There was a debate on the Channel Tunnel by the Debating Society of the Young Men's Institute (*Jewish Chronicle*, March 20, 1907, 34), and a debate by the Sheffield Literary Circle (*Jewish Chronicle*, December 5, 1913, 35).

6 A number of local feuilletonists are not included here: those who did not write about local issues, and those whose writing did not achieve the quality

desired for translation. These missing writers include Hannah Berman, Yankef Abramtses, Shaul Albert, Yankl Freylekh, Yankef Leibush Fayn, Isaac Goldberg, and Dovid Shtiber, among others. It is important to note that the feuilletonists included in this volume wrote in other genres. Winchevsky, Stencl, and Sochachewsky were better known as Yiddish poets. Margolin was a comedic satirist in verse, Kussman was a critical essayist, and Leon Creditor wrote a monograph on the twelfth-century commentator Maimonides. Doniach and Brown wrote plays performed on the London Yiddish stage, and around ten of the writers in this volume also edited Yiddish newspapers and journals.

7 Liliane Weissberg, "Newspaper Feuilletons: Reflections on the Possibilities of German-Jewish Authorship and Literature," in *The Future of the German-Jewish Past: Memory and the Question of Antisemitism*, ed. Gideon Reuveni and Diana Franklin (West Lafayette, IN: Purdue University Press, 2020), 147–49; Karen L. Ryan-Hayes, *Russian Publicistic Satire under Glasnost: The Journalistic Feuilleton* (Lewiston, NY: Edwin Mellen Press, 1993), 1–2.

8 Ryan-Hayes, *Russian Publicistic Satire*, 2; Katia Dianina, "The Feuilleton: An Everyday Guide to Public Culture in the Age of the Great Reforms," *Slavic and East European Journal* 47, no. 2 (Summer 2003): 192.

9 Dianina, "The Feuilleton," 188.

10 Shachar Pinsker, "Coffeehouses, Journalism, and the Rise of Modern Jewish Literary Culture," *Prooftexts* 38, no. 2 (2000): 384–85.

11 Weissberg, "Newspaper Feuilletons," 156.

12 Weissberg, "Newspaper Feuilletons," 153.

13 Paul Reitter, *The Anti-Journalist: Karl Kraus and Jewish Self-Fashioning in Fin-de-Siècle* (Chicago: Chicago University Press, 2008), 6–7; Pinsker, "Coffeehouses," 392; Weissberg, "Newspaper Feuilletons," 150–51.

14 Reitter, *The Anti-Journalist*, 4–5.

15 Ryan-Hayes, *Russian Publicistic Satire*, 4–9.

16 "Sketches by 'Boz,'" https://www.britannica.com/topic/Sketches-by-Boz, accessed April 1, 2024.

17 *The Sketch* was published by the *Illustrated London News* newsgroup. British Newspaper Archive, "The Sketch," https://britishnewspaperarchive.co.uk/titles/the-sketch, accessed April 1, 2024.

18 Nathan Cohen, "The Yiddish Press and Yiddish Literature: A Fertile but Complex Relationship," *Modern Judaism* 28, no. 2 (May 2008): 149–50; Pinsker, "Coffeehouses," 395–96. Eddy Portnoy, *Bad Rabbi and Other Strange but True Stories from the Yiddish Press* (Stanford, CA: Stanford University Press, 2018), 7–9.

19 William Pimlott, "Yiddish in Britain: Immigration, Culture and Politics, 1896–1910" (PhD diss., University College London, 2022), 260–62.

20 Dianina, "The Feuilleton," 194.

Notes   215

21 Jacob Hodes, "Tsu der geshikhte fun der english-yidishe prese," in *Yidn in england: Shtudyes un materialn 1880–1940* (New York: YIVO, 1966), 56–57.

22 Leonard Prager, "A Bibliography of Yiddish Periodicals in Great Britain (1867–1967)," *Studies in Bibliography and Booklore* (Spring 1969), 10–28; Leonard Prager, *Yiddish Culture in Britain: A Guide* (Frankfurt am Main: Peter Lang, 1990), 530–32. Prager lists more than two hundred Yiddish newspapers and journals published in England.

23 For the relationship between the London Yiddish press and that abroad, see Avrom Vevyorke, *Di idishe prese un dos idishe teater in london* (London: M. Susman, n.d.), 4–8. The writers named wrote from Eastern Europe, America, and Palestine. Anna Margolin was published under the pseudonym Clara Levin.

24 Katie Brown, A. M. Kaizer, I. A. Lisky, *London Yiddishtown: East End Jewish Life in Yiddish Sketch and Story, 1930–1950*, ed. and trans. Vivi Lachs (Detroit, MI: Wayne State University Press, 2021), 171–212.

25 Israel Zangwill, *Di kinder fun der geto*, trans. Leon Kobrin, *Der idisher zhurnal* (July–December 1905). On Zangwill's relationship to London's Yiddish literary scene, see William Pimlott, "Yiddish in Britain," 231–35, 248–49, 264–65.

26 Y. H. Brenner, *Londoner felyetonen*, *Di idishe velt*, supplement to the English-language Jewish weekly the *Jewish World*, January 31, 1908, 30.

27 The storyline of Brenner's feuilleton "A Tale of Reincarnation" in this volume is described in Ezra Spicehandler, "Yosef Haim Brenner: A Biography," in Yosef Haim Brenner, *Out of the Depths and Other Stories*, trans. with introductions by David Patterson and Ezra Spicehandler (London: Toby Press, 2008), 55. Spicehandler does not mention that Brenner used the pseudonym *A farblondzheter*. Leonard Prager, however, does note that Brenner used the pseudonym—in his spelling, "*A ferblondzhenten*" ("Brener, Yoysef-Khayim," in *Yiddish Culture*, 171). An explicit connection to Avrom Margolin's pseudonym *Avreml* is in a full-page poster for a concert held in honor of Margolin's arrival in London in the satirical journal *Der bloffer* 8 (December 1911), 17–18. The poster reads: "Avreml (Dr. Margolin)." The pseudonyms *An'eygener* and *Der eygener* seem to be interchangeable. Although Prager attributes the name to Leon Creditor, my discovery of a program in the YIVO archives proved this to be incorrect. The program for a Living Newspaper listed the speakers, including "A Beilin (der eygener)": *Redevdike tsaytung* (Whitechapel: Yiddish Journalists and Writers Union of England, 1930), 2. Finally, a scrap of memoir in English by Arnold Harris cites a conversation with L. [Leyb] Creditor, where Creditor confirms his use of the pseudonym Leybele Batlen. Writers used a range of spellings in transliteration, and Harris misreads two similar-looking letters in the Hebrew alphabet, *beys* [*b*] and *kof* [*k*], so his spelling appears as "Laikalle Butlan." Harris explains: "Mr Creditor is a scholarly Hebraist, a good Talmudist, he is still a butlan, and he admits it." Ansel Z. Harris, "Extracts from the Memoirs of Arnold Harris," in

The Jewish East End 1840–1939: Proceedings of the Conference Held on 22 October 1980 Jointly by the Jewish Historical Society of England and the Jewish East End Project of the Association for Jewish Youth (London: Jewish Historical Society, 1981), 346.

28 Cohen, "Yiddish Press," 150, 160. See also Ayelet Brinn, "Beyond the Women's Section: Rosa Lebensboym, Female Journalists, and the American Yiddish Press," *American Jewish History* 104, nos. 2–3 (April–July 2020): 349, 355–56.

29 The poet Avrom Nokhem Stencl called Brown "Whitechapel's best seller." Stencl, "Keyti Braun," *Loshn un lebn* (May 1955): 3.

30 Brinn, "Women's Section," 356.

31 Most of the women who were published in *Loshn un lebn* were poets, and although they were fairly frequently published, they are less represented in this volume.

32 Historian Yosef Clausner called Winchevsky the pioneer of the form in Hebrew. By the time Winchevsky came to London, Yiddish had become his language as a writer. Quoted in Prager, *Yiddish Culture*, 237.

33 For details about the socialist and anarchist debate in Winchevsky's time in London, see William J. Fishman, *East End Jewish Radicals, 1875–1914* (London: Duckworth, 1975), 138–214.

34 Vivi Lachs, *Whitechapel Noise*, 91–132.

35 Jeffrey Veidlinger, *In the Midst of Civilized Europe: The 1918–1921 Pogroms in Ukraine and the Onset of the Holocaust* (London: Picador, 2021), 93–155.

36 Advertisements for the protest march had appeared daily in *Di tsayt* since June 17, 1919.

CHAPTER 1

1 Avrom Nokhem Stencl, "Yidish shafn in london: Ershter peyod," *Heftl: Yidish shafn in london* (November 1942); republished as "Undzer yidish shafn in England," *Yoyvl almanak* (London: Loshn un lebn, 1956), v–vi. For London's Yiddish theatre and music halls, see Vivi Lachs, *Whitechapel Noise: Jewish Immigrant Life in Yiddish Song and Verse, London 1884–1914* (Detroit, MI: Wayne State University Press, 2018), 40–63.

2 The population of Jews in Britain was around 300,000, with substantial communities in Manchester and Leeds, and smaller ones in Liverpool, Glasgow, and Birmingham. Todd M. Endelman, *The Jews of Britain 1656 to 2000* (Berkeley: University of California Press, 2002), 198–201. Vivian Lipman, *A History of the Jews in Britain since 1858* (Leicester: Leicester University Press, 1990), 12, 45–46.

3 For scholarship on the Jewish East End work and unions, see David Feldman, *Englishmen and Jews: Social Relations and Political Culture, 1840–1914* (New Haven, CT: Yale University Press, 1994), 215–31.

Notes   217

4 Vivian Lipman, *A Century of Social Service, 1859–1959: The Jewish Board of Guardians* (London: Routledge & Kegan Paul, 1959), 89, 78–79.

5 The immigrants' push to keep a Yiddish culture in Britain is one of the main arguments throughout William Pimlott, "Yiddish in Britain: Immigration, Culture and Politics, 1896–1910" (PhD diss., University College London, 2022).

6 Susan Tananbaum, *Jewish Immigrants in London, 1880–1939* (Abingdon, Routledge, 2016), 1–14.

7 For socialist campaigns around work and the conflict between the socialists and anarchists, see William Fishman, *East End Jewish Radicals, 1875–1914* (London: Duckworth, 1975), 163–215.

8 Feldman, *Englishmen and Jews*, 185–257; Bernard Gainer, *The Alien Invasion: The Origins of the Aliens Act of 1905* (London: Heinemann, 1972), 3–6.

9 Lachs, *Whitechapel Noise*, 41–42, 57–58, 60–63.

10 In response to the popular theatre and music halls, the proponents of a more literary theatre attempted to build a new literary theatre; however, the new Feinman Yiddish People's Theatre, built in 1912, failed, because regular Eastenders could not afford to attend, and in any case, popular theatre was what the public demanded. David Mazower, "Whitechapel's Yiddish Opera House: The Rise and Fall of the Feinman Yiddish People's Theatre," in *An East End Legacy: Essays in Memory of William J. Fishman*, ed. Colin Holmes and Anne J. Kershen (Abingdon: Routledge, 2018), 155–87; Lachs, *Whitechapel Noise*, 60–63.

11 L. Izraeli, "Repertuar fun idishn teater," *Der idisher ekspres*, February 21, 1912, 2; "Di pavilyen: Ir repertuar un personel," *Der idisher ekspres*, February 28, 1912, 2; Leon Kussman, "Faynman–yidish folks teater (batrakhtungn vegn 'templ')," *Der idisher ekspres*, June 26, 1912, 2.

12 The satirical magazine *Der bloffer* was published monthly between 1911 and 1913. In standard transliteration the title would be *blofer*. However, the cover of each edition includes the English spelling as *bloffer*.

13 Isaac Stone, *Di yerushe*, 17 serialized chapters in *Der arbayter fraynd*, July 1–November 12, 1886.

14 Leonard Prager, "The Beginnings of Yiddish Fiction in England," in *Studies in the Cultural Life of the Jews in England*, ed. Dov Noy and Issachar Ben-Ami (Jerusalem: Magnes Press, Hebrew University, 1975), 245–50; Leonard Prager, "Ston, Ayzik," in *Yiddish Culture in Britain: A Guide* (Frankfurt am Main: Peter Lang, 1990), 626–27; Yiddish Leksikon, "Isaac Stone," http://yleksikon.blogspot.com/2018/03/isaac-stone.html, accessed August 6, 2023.

15 Melekh Epstein, *Profiles of Eleven: Profiles of Eleven Men Who Guided the Destiny of an Immigrant Society and Stimulated Social Consciousness among the American People* (Detroit, MI: Wayne State University Press, 1965), 13–35; Rudolph Rocker and Colin Ward, *The London Years* (Nottingham: Five Leaves Press, 2005),

57–59; Fishman, *East End Jewish Radicals*, 138–44. For Winchevsky in London, see Lachs, *Whitechapel Noise*, 91–132, 179–84.

16 Anita Shapira, *Yosef Haim Brenner: A Life* (Stanford, CA: Stanford University Press, 2014), 55–123; Ezra Spicehandler, "Yosef Haim Brenner: A Biography," in Yosef Haim Brenner, *Out of the Depths and Other Stories*, trans. with introductions by David Patterson and Ezra Spicehandler (London: Toby Press, 2008), 15–79; Prager, "Brener, Yoysef-Khayim," in *Yiddish Culture*, 171–72. See also William Pimlott, "Yiddish in Britain: Immigration, Culture and Politics, 1896–1910" (PhD diss., University College London, 2022), 309–17.

17 Prager, "Kusman, Leon," in *Yiddish Culture*, 388–89; Yiddish Leksikon, "Leon Kussman," http://yleksikon.blogspot.com/2019/03/leon-kusman-l-kussman.html, accessed August 6, 2023.

18 Prager, "Finklshteyn, Y.," in *Yiddish Culture*, 239; Lachs, *Whitechapel Noise*, 148.

CHAPTER 2

1 For example, notice of an address in the Whitechapel Synagogue, *Jewish Chronicle*, November 13, 1914, 29. A motivation for encouraging patriotism was to avert antisemitism and counter accusations of Jewish German loyalty. Marsha L. Rozenblit, "The European Jewish World 1914–1919: What Changed?" in *World War I and the Jews: Conflict and Transformation in Europe, the Middle East, and America*, ed. Marsha L. Rozenblit and Jonathan Karp (New York: Berghahn Books, 2017), 35–36.

2 David Feldman, "War, Patriotism and Nationality," unpublished paper, 2019, 5–6.

3 See, for example, Maurice Myers, "This Cringing Mealy-Mouthed Attitude," in "Letters to the Editor," *Jewish Chronicle* November 13, 1914, 11.

4 Feldman, "War, Patriotism and Nationality," 6–9.

5 The sense of cocky Jews trying to defeat the system was portrayed in the *East London Observer* in the opposite context, as their lack of patriotism. They described Jews having considerable "swank" and behaving in an offensive manner toward members of the military tribunal hearing their reasons for being released from army service. Feldman, "War, Patriotism and Nationality," 6. For my analysis of this sketch, see Lachs, "Good *Goy*, Bad *Goy*: Representations of Non-Jews in the London Yiddish Press, 1915–1930," *Prooftexts* (forthcoming).

6 Leonard Prager, "Kreditor, Leyb-Sholem," in *Yiddish Culture in Britain: A Guide* (Frankfurt am Main: Peter Lang, 1990), 383; Ansel Z. Harris, "Extracts from the Memoirs of Arnold Harris," in *The Jewish East End 1840–1939: Proceedings of the Conference Held on 22 October 1980 Jointly by the Jewish Historical Society of England and the Jewish East End Project of the Association for Jewish Youth*

(London: Jewish Historical Society, 1981), 346. For the use of the pseudonym, see Introduction, note 27.

7 Prager, "Margolin, Avrom," in *Yiddish Culture*, 437; Harold B. Segel, *Egon Erwin Kisch, the Raging Reporter: A Bio-Anthology* (West Lafayette, IN: Purdue University Press, 1997), 224–29; Leksikon, "Avrom Margolin," https://congress forjewishculture.org/people/3047/Margolin-Avrom-1884-January-12-1961, accessed July 28, 2024.

8 Prager, "Kapitantshik, Yankev-Yitschok," in *Yiddish Culture*, 352; Y. Kapitantshik, *Slek: a bild fun arbeter lebn in london* (London: Arbayter fraynd drukeray, 1922). This is a different play from the one Prager claims was based on a tragic event in Whitechapel.

9 For an analysis of this feuilleton, see Vivi Lachs, "Good *Goy*, Bad *Goy*: Representations of Non-Jews in the London Yiddish Press, 1915–1930," *Prooftexts* (forthcoming).

10 Prager, "Sokhatshevski, Ben-A," in *Yiddish Culture*, 611–12; "Mr. Ben-A. Sochachewsky," *Jewish Chronicle*, April 18, 1958, 11; Rabbi Dr. J. Litvin, "The End of an Epoch" *Jewish Chronicle*, April 25, 1958, 19.

CHAPTER 3

1 David Dee, *The "Estranged" Generation? Social and Generational Change in Interwar British Jewry* (London: Palgrave Macmillan, 2017), 27–33; Susan Tananbaum, *Jewish Immigrants in London, 1880–1939* (Abingdon: Routledge, 2016), 71–90, 109–30. The headmaster of the Jews' Free School (JFS), Moses Angel, campaigned to ban the Yiddish language from his school. Gerry Black, *JFS: The History of the Jews' Free School, London, since 1732* (London: Tymsder Publishing, 1998), 125–29.

2 See David Cesarani, "The Transformation of Communal Authority in Anglo-Jewry, 1914–1940," in *The Making of Modern Anglo-Jewry*, ed. David Cesarani (Oxford: Basil Blackwell, 1990), 115–40; Vivian Lipman, *A History of the Jews in Britain since 1858* (Leicester: Leicester University Press, 1990), 203–23.

3 David Cesarani, "A Funny Thing Happened on the Way to the Suburbs: Social Change in Anglo-Jewry between the Wars, 1914–1945," *Jewish Culture and History* 1, no. 1 (1998): 6–8, 13.

4 Henry Felix Srebrnik, *London Jews and British Communism* (London: Vallentine Mitchell, 1995), 28–29.

5 Todd M. Endelman, *The Jews of Britain 1656 to 2000* (Berkeley: University of California Press, 2002), 198–201.

6 Daniel Tilles, *British Fascist Antisemitism and Jewish Responses, 1932–40* (London: Bloomsbury, 2014), 101–14, 123–34; Srebrnik, *London Jews*, 14–15, 24; David Rosenberg, *Battle for the East End* (Nottingham, Five Leaves, 2011), 140–66.

220   Notes

7 Katie Brown, A. M. Kaizer, I. A. Lisky, *London Yiddishtown: East End Jewish Life in Yiddish Sketch and Story, 1930–1950*, ed. and trans. Vivi Lachs (Detroit, MI: Wayne State University Press, 2021), 186–87.

8 Actress Anna Tselniker claimed that audiences felt they didn't get their money's worth without "*a zing, a lach un a trer* [a song, a laugh and a tear]." Anna Tselniker, *Three for the Price of One* (London: Spiro Institute, 1991), 9.

9 See Vivi Lachs, "Change and Decline in London's Jewish East End: The Yiddish Sketches of Katie Brown," *Shofar* 42, no. 1 (2024): 73–99.

10 Katie Brown, *Lakht oyb ir vilt* (London: N. Zilberg, 1947); *Alts in eynem!* (London: N. Zilberg, 1951). Katie Brown, *Life Is a Dance—You Should Only Know the Steps*, trans. Sydney Bacon, with Rose Kashtan; illus. Gail Geltner (Toronto: Bacon Publishing, 1987); Lachs, *London Yiddishtown*, 122–70. Rokhl Mirski, "Oyfn frishn kever fun keyti bron," *Loshn un lebn* (May 1955): 13; Stencl, "Keyti Bron," *Loshn un lebn* (May 1955): 3.

11 Leonard Prager, "Beylin Osher," in *Yiddish Culture in Britain: A Guide* (Frankfurt am Main: Peter Lang, 1990), 155; Yiddish Leksikon, Joshua Fogel, "Asher Beylin (Beilin)," http://yleksikon.blogspot.com/2015/01/asher-beylin-beilin.html, accessed August 8, 2023; Stencl, "A. M. Kaizer," *Loshn un lebn* (September–October 1967): 70.

12 Esther Kreitman's *Der sheydim tants* was translated by her son, Maurice Carr: *Deborah* (London: W. and G. Foyle Ltd., 1964). It has been republished several times. *Diamonds*, trans. Heather Valencia (London: David Paul, 2010); *Blitz and Other Stories*, trans. Dorothea van Tendeloo (London: David Paul, 2004). Scholarship on Kreitman includes Anita Norich, "The Family Singer and the Autobiographical Imagination" *Prooftexts* 10, no. 1 (1990): 91–107; Michael Boyden, "The Other 'Other Singer': Linguistic Alterity in Esther Kreitman's Transit Fiction," *Prooftexts* 31, nos. 1–2 (2011): 95–117; Dafna Clifford, "From Diamond Cutters to Dog Races: Antwerp and London in the Work of Esther Kreitman," *Prooftexts* 23, no. 3 (2003): 320–37; David Stromberg, "'I'm Doing Much Better': The Letters of Esther Kreitman to Isaac Bashevis Singer," *Jewish Renaissance* (Winter 2024): 17–23. See also Maurice Carr, *The Forgotten Singer: The Exiled Sister of I.J. and Isaac Bashevis Singer* (Amherst, MA: White Goat Press, 2023).

13 Y. H. Levi (Lewy), "Iber i a liskis tetikeyt un zayn shafn," *Di tsayt*, February 3, 1943, 2; Dovid Katz, "I. A. Lisky, 1899–1990," in *Oksforder Yidish*, vol. 2, ed. Dovid Katz (Oxford: Taylor and Francis, 1991), 277–85; Lachs, *London Yiddishtown*, 21–27. Translations include I. A. Lisky, *The Cockerel in the Basket*, trans. Hannah Berman (London: J. S. Bergson, 1955); Lisky, "Geese," trans. Hannah Berman, *Jewish Literary Gazette*, March 15, 1951, 2. *The New Left Review* (November 1935): 57–62; Lachs, *London Yiddishtown*, 29–67.

14 Lachs, *London Yiddishtown*, 71–76; A. M. Kaizer, *Mir zenen hungerik* (London: Federation of Jewish Relief Organizations, 1930); A. M. Kaizer, *Bay undz in*

vaytshepl (London: Narodiczky, 1944). See translations in Lachs, *London Yiddishtown*, 77–120.

15 Prager, "Oyved, Moyshe," in *Yiddish Culture*, 502. For Oved's connection to the Ben Uri, see David Mazower, "Ben Uri and Yiddish Culture," in *Ben Uri: 100 Years in London—Art, Identity, Migration* (London: Ben Uri, 2015), 43.

CHAPTER 4

1 Katie Brown, A. M. Kaizer, I. A. Lisky, *London Yiddishtown: East End Jewish Life in Yiddish Sketch and Story, 1930–1950*, ed. and trans. Vivi Lachs (Detroit, MI: Wayne State University Press, 2021), 200–203.

2 S. J. Harendorf, *Der kenig fun lampeduse / The King of Lampedusa*, ed. and trans. Heather Valencia (London: Jewish Music Institute / International Forum for Yiddish Culture, 2003); Katie Power, "'Sacred Is the Duty': London's Naye Yidishe Teater Company (New Yiddish Theatre Company), 1943–1949" (PhD diss., University of Southampton, 2023), 97–99; Katie Power, "Rediscovering *The King of Lampedusa*," http://katie-power.co.uk/rediscovering-the-king-of -lampedusa, accessed March 12, 2024; David Mazower, *Yiddish Theatre in London* (London: Museum of the Jewish East End, 1987), 24–25, 52–53.

3 Geoffrey Alderman, *Modern British Jewry* (Oxford: Clarendon Press, 1998), 318–20.

4 See Morris Beckman, *The 43 Group: The Untold Story of Their Fights against Fascism* (London: Centerprise, 1992).

5 Mazower, *Yiddish Theatre*, 25–26.

6 H. Leyvik, *Mit der sheyres hapleyte* (New York: Tsentrale yidishe kultur organizatsye, 1947), 42–44.

7 Leonard Prager, "Bietsh, Yude-Y," in *Yiddish Culture in Britain: A Guide* (Frankfurt am Main: Peter Lang, 1990), 157.

8 Dovid Katz, "Stencl of Whitechapel," *Mendele Review: Yiddish Literature and Language* 7 (March 30, 2003), http://yiddish.haifa.ac.il/tmr/tmr07/tmr07003 .htm, accessed November 26, 2020; "Story of Three Poets," *Jewish Chronicle* 9 (March 1962): 10; Heather Valencia, "A. N. Stencl," in *All My Young Years: Yiddish Poetry from Weimar Germany*, trans. Haike Beruriah Wiegand and Stephen Watts (Nottingham: Five Leaves Publications, 2007), 11–12.

9 Kathi Diamant, *Kafka's Last Love: The Mystery of Dora Diamant* (London: Secker & Warburg, 2003), 240–45; Prager, "Dimant, Dore," in *Yiddish Culture*, 202.

10 Prager, "Goldshmidt, Shmuel-Yoysef," in *Yiddish Culture*, 286–87; Yiddish leksikon, "Shloyme-Yoysef Goldshmidt (S. J. Goldsmith)," http://yleksikon.blogspot.com/ 2016/01/shloyme-yoysef-goldshmidt-s-j-goldsmith.html, accessed August 1, 2022. S. J. Goldsmith, ed., *Joseph Leftwich at Eighty-Five: A Collective Evaluation* (London: Federation of Jewish Relief Organisations / Association of Jewish Journalists and Writers / World Jewish Congress Yiddish Committee, 1978).

CHAPTER 5

1 Todd M. Endelman, *The Jews of Britain 1656 to 2000* (Berkeley: University of California Press, 2002), 235.

2 Aubrey Newman, *The United Synagogue 1870–1970* (London: Routledge and Kegan Paul, 1977), 161–73.

3 Katie Brown, *Unter zelbn dakh*, *Di idishe shtime*, November 6, 1953–June 25, 1954.

4 David Mazower, *Yiddish Theatre in London* (London: Museum of the Jewish East End, 1987), 26.

5 Historian William Pimlott explores YIVO and its attention to maintaining a Yiddish culture in Britain. He argues that the concept of the decline of Yiddish needs to be extended, because although the prevalence of Yiddish language as a spoken vernacular among secular immigrants might have declined, its use was encouraged in written and scholarly form. The YIVO competition is one example, and another is the book of essays about Jewish life and Yiddish culture in Britain, edited over several years: *Yidn in england: Shtudyes un materialn 1880–1940* (New York: YIVO, 1966). William Pimlott, "British Yiddish and Decline," paper presented at the British and Irish Association of Jewish Studies (BIAJS) Annual Conference, King's College London, July 12, 2022.

6 Emanuel Litvinoff, "In kheshbn fun yorn," *Di idishe shtime*, June 5, 1953.

7 Simon Blumenfeld's novel *Jew Boy* had been published in 1932, and Willy Goldman's *East End My Cradle* in 1940. During the 1950s, Wolf Mankowitz wrote *A Kid for Two Farthings* (1953), and the playwright Arnold Wesker produced the first two works in his trilogy, *Chicken Soup with Barley* (1958) and *Roots* (1959). Later writers on East End themes included Ralph Finn, Emanuel Litvinoff, and Bernard Kops. Many self-published memoirs included childhoods in the East End of the 1950s.

8 Leonard Prager, "Zilberg, Ele," in *Yiddish Culture in Britain: A Guide* (Frankfurt am Main: Peter Lang, 1990), 726.

9 Prager, "Mirski, Rokhl," in *Yiddish Culture*, 466; *Jewish Chronicle* articles mentioning her name as contributing to the Friends of Yiddish were published on November 2, 1951, April 30, and July 9, 1954, and December 15, 1956.

10 Prager, "Doniach, Mara R.," in *Yiddish Culture*, 205; "Rachel Doniach," *Jewish Chronicle*, October 29, 1975.

11 Prager, *Yiddish Culture*, 205; Ruth Rothenberg, "UK Property Claims," *Jewish Chronicle*, December 7, 1990, 10.

ABOUT THE TRANSLATORS

DR. VIVI LACHS is a social and cultural historian and a Yiddish performer and translator. Her books include *Whitechapel Noise* and *London Yiddishtown* (both Wayne State University Press). This volume is the result of a research fellowship at Queen Mary University of London on the project Making and Remaking the Jewish East End. Lachs records with the bands Klezmer Klub and Katsha'nes, leads tours of the Jewish East End, and runs London's Great Yiddish Parade.

BARRY SMERIN holds a first-class degree in Hebrew Literature and Jewish History from University College London. He is a translator of historiography and original historical source documents from Yiddish, Polish, German, and French, and has taught Yiddish language and literature at universities and cultural institutions in Poland, France, and England for over thirty years.